Refugee Poems

VOLUME 1

Refugee Poems

VOLUME 1

Life in Exile

SURYARAJU MATTIMALLA

RESOURCE *Publications* · Eugene, Oregon

REFUGEE POEMS
Life in Exile

Copyright © 2025 Suryaraju Mattimalla. All rights reserved. Except for brief quotations in critical publications or reviews, no part of this book may be reproduced in any manner without prior written permission from the publisher. Write: Permissions, Wipf and Stock Publishers, 199 W. 8th Ave., Suite 3, Eugene, OR 97401.

Resource Publications
An Imprint of Wipf and Stock Publishers
199 W. 8th Ave., Suite 3
Eugene, OR 97401

www.wipfandstock.com

PAPERBACK ISBN: 979-8-3852-4764-6
HARDCOVER ISBN: 979-8-3852-4765-3
EBOOK ISBN: 979-8-3852-4766-0
VERSION NUMBER 05/19/25

To my beloved son Saviour Suryaraju Mattimalla, my wife Selamawit Hailu Bezabih and our unborn child.

Contents

Section I: Europe Poems
1. Rest in Peace, My Baby, Stanford | 3
2. The Four Seasons of Exile: Song of Stanford | 5
3. A Father's Grief, A Mother's Love, A Son's Rest | 7
4. The Agony of a Black Untouchable Father | 9
5. Friendly Father | 11
6. Cherish Life, Reject Death | 13
7. Saviour Questions | 15
8. My Son's Question | 17
9. The Color of Hate | 18
10. Tears of Mother Earth | 20
11. Crossing the Waters of Fate | 23
12. Exile Among Beasts | 25
13. The Rejected Asylum | 27
14. An African Journey Through Shadows | 29
15. White Is Beautiful | 31
16. The October 7 | 33
17. The Agony of a Jewish Star | 35
18. The Unmasked Truth | 37
19. O Janus faced Europe | 38
20. Persecution of the German Greeting in the German Asylum Camp | 40
21. White Western Christian Land in Islamic Transition | 42
22. Masks of Freedom, Chains of Hate | 44
23. Thorns of German Refugee Camps | 46
24. Echoes of Islamic Terrorism | 49

25. The Black Christian's Bread | 51
26. The Smell of Black Exile | 53
27. Souls of Division | 55
28. Names and Chains | 57
29. Hypocrisy and Theft | 59
30. March for Black Jesus | 61
31. The Hypocrite's Theft | 63
32. Dodgy Black | 65
33. Judgment Day Awaits | 67
34. Unmasking Global Human Rights Hypocrisy | 69
35. Nazis of Global Human Rights | 71
36. The Ukrainian Refugee's Racism | 73
37. Abortion Is Genocide | 75
38. Abortion Is Terrorism | 76
39. A Tribute to the Unborn | 78
40. A Tribute to the Precious Life | 79
41. Ode to Life and Loss in a Foreign Land | 81
42. Royal Blood and Colonial Chains | 83
43. Echoes of Deceit and Resilience | 85
44. Shadows of the Refugee Convention | 87
45. Islamic Nails in the European Refugee Camps | 89
46. European Complicity in Antisemitic Shadows | 91
47. Nazis in the Free Palestine Tent | 93
48. The Crescent Shadows the Cross | 95
49. October 7—The Modern Holocaust | 97
50. Greedy Jew: A Song of Defiance | 99
51. Sound of Liberation | 101
52. The Muddy Piece of Hindu, Islamic, Antisemitic, UN Spaces… | 103
53. The Unfreedom of the Untouchable | 105
54. The Agony of the Black | 107
55. O Hyenas, We Are Not Your Prey | 109
56. Stolen Identities, Stolen Souls | 111
57. O Hyenas of Asylum, Rise Above | 113
58. Africa's Hypocrisy Unveiled | 115
59. Song of Gratitude to the German Social Worker | 117
60. To Charlie Hebdo: A Dedication | 119
61. Ode to Zineb El Rhazoui | 121
62. Ode to Samuel Paty | 123

63. The Wounds of Untouchability & Racism: A Tale of Identity and Struggle | 125
64. The Weight of German Shadows | 128
65. White Western Christian Streets of Silence | 131
66. Silent Screams in the White Western Christian Streets | 133
67. Forbidden Voices in the White Western Liberal Spaces | 135
68. Islamic Nails in the European UNHCR Camp | 137
69. O Kunta Kinte, Chained in Time | 139
70. O Kizzy, Daughter of Chains | 141
71. Gratitude Song for Elder Henry and Elder Connor | 143
72. The Shadows of Saree and Scarf | 145
73. Redefining Home and Belonging | 147
74. Whispers in the White Western Christian Spaces | 149
75. A Song of Gratitude for Oscar Schmid | 151
76. Ode to the Boots on the Ground | 153

Section II: Philosophy Poems
77. The Wounded Philosophy | 157
78. Ode to Philosopher John Rawls | 159
79. To Philosopher Bertrand Russell, the Mind Unchained | 161
80. Ode to Father of Modern Archaeology Gordon Childe | 163
81. Ode to Philosopher Stephen Hawking | 165
82. Philosopher Paulo Freire's Pedagogy of the Oppressed | 167
83. O Maurice Halbwachs, Keeper of Memory | 169
84. Ode to Indian Philosopher Gnana Aloysius | 171
85. To Philosopher Slavoj Žižek, the Provocateur of Thought | 174
86. Aimé Césaire's Thingification | 176
87. Thingification of My Skin | 178
88. Cornel West's Philosophy Against Race | 179
89. Franz Fanon's Brown Skins, White Masks | 181
90. Ode to Alex Haley | 183

Section III: Words Against the Blood and Iron Policy of Hindus
91. Burn the Karma Theory | 187
92. Consuming Cow Dung, Urine | 189
93. Jewish and Untouchable Carcasses | 191
94. The Weight of Hindu Scriptures | 194
95. Thus the Untouchable Speaks | 196
96. Thus the Madiga Speaks | 198
97. Thus Spoke 'Untouchable' Kanchikacherla Kotesu Madiga | 200

98. Thus Speaks the Untouchable | 202
99. O Shudra, the Loyal Slave | 204
100. Hindu Cruelty | 206
101. The Vedas, the Creator of the Genocide | 208
102. O Shudra, Servant of Servants | 210
103. O Shudra Reddy, Kamma, Kapu, Velama Caste, Learn to Rise | 212
104. My Aryan Christian Mother, Patnala Suguna Yadav alias Mattimalla Suguna Madiga | 214
105. My Christian Mother: Patnala Suguna Yadav alias Mattimalla Suguna Madiga, Mother of Grace | 215
106. The Child I'll Never Know | 217
107. My Silent Grief | 219
108. Venomous Hindu Roots | 221
109. Gatekeepers of Untouchable Genocide | 223
110. Boundaries of Untouchability Genocide | 225
111. Hindus: The Inventors of Atrocity Crimes on Earth | 227
112. A Hindu World Without Love | 229
113. The Core Ideology of a Sanātana Hindu Dharma | 231
114. Arranged Marriage Is Prostitution; Prostitution Is Not Freedom | 233
115. Genocide Against My Skin | 234
116. My Birth Is Primed for Death | 236
117. Scars of the Incredible India | 238
118. India: The Hyenas Democracy | 240
119. Primed for Death | 242
120. Jewish Allies in the Indian Democracy of Mosquitoes | 244
121. Hindu Religion: The Blackwater | 246
122. Your Body, My Choice | 247
123. Jewish Badge, Broom, and Pot: The Burdens We Bear | 249
124. The Illusion of Namaste | 251
125. Hindu Matrimonial: A Mirror of Fascist Purity | 253
126. O Brahmin, The Venom Runs Deep | 255
127. Vegetarian Only: The Mask of Genocider in Hindu Religion, Ideology, and Society | 257
128. Brahmin, Bhagavad Gita, Bharat, Briton, Britanica, Bible | 259
129. Water | 262
130. The Mask of the Civilian | 264
131. Brahmin Agraharam: Settlements of Genocider | 266
132. Gandhi's Mask: The Face of Genocide | 268

133. Calling Mahatma or Great Soul or Call Him Genocider, Racist, Casteist, Paedophilic, Dehumanizer, Subjugator, Gay, Untouchability Practitioner? | 271
134. Of Saints and Sinners | 273
135. The Saint's Shadow | 275
136. Glorifying "Mahatma" with Gandhi? | 276
137. The Madness of African-American Leaders Adoring Gandhi | 279
138. The Western Educated Indian Gold-Diggers | 282
139. The 1948 Refugee Convention: Globally Accepted Antisemitic Law | 283
140. Indian Drama | 285
141. Hindu Swaraj (Hindu Self-Rule) Atrocities | 287
142. Western Educated Hindu Mother: Partner in Crime Against my Skin | 289
143. An Untouchable Anthem Against The Indian Ideology | 291
144. The Journey of an Untouchable | 293
145. Against the Madness of Cremation | 295
146. Against the Madness of Hindu Culture | 297
147. Why I Am Not Indian: The Untouchable Rejecting India's Citizenship | 299
148. A Son's Apology | 301
149. The Fathers of a Nation | 304
150. The Theater of Violence | 307
151. The Skin of History | 309
152. In the Shadows of Hindu, Muslim, Buddhist, Sikh, Jain, Parsee, Antisemitic, Liberal, Left, Feminist, Queer, African, BLM... | 311
153. Corruption on Earth | 313
154. The Masks of Xenophobia | 315
155. Ode to the Jewish Community | 317
156. Untouchable Words | 319
157. Forever There Was a Caste | 321
158. Worshipping a Brahmin Cow | 323
159. An English Madiga Nation: A Dream Unchained | 325
160. O Untouchable Girl | 327
161. O Fascist Bharata Mata, How Long? | 329
162. Justice and Creativity: A Tale of Titanic and Caste | 331
163. The Day of Chains | 334
164. I Am a Walking Relic of Ruin | 336
165. I Am a Walking Corpse | 338

166. Blood of the Untouchable | 340
167. O Hindu, I Can't Breath | 342
168. O Hindu Genociders | 344
169. Broken Daughters of Christian Kuki-Zomi Community in the Land of Hindu Meiteis | 346
170. Bayyavaram: The Hindu Space of Hyenas, Vultures, Wolves... | 348
171. The Silence We Carve | 350
172. The Burden of Hindu Religion | 352
173. The Weight of Hindu Words | 354
174. A Hindu Temple of Hyenas, Vultures, Wolves, Snakes... | 356
175. A Call for Justice, Against the Hindu Chains | 358
176. Ironical Idol Krishna the Prostitute | 360
177. Hindu Riddles in Stone and Fire | 362
178. In the Shadows of Hindu Caste | 364
179. In the Shadows of Hindu Vultures | 366
180. August 15: A Nation's Independence, Untouchable's Chains | 368
181. Ode to Indian Christian Philosopher Gurram Jashuva Madiga | 370
182. Manda Krishna Madiga: The Voice of John Rawls's "A Theory of Justice" | 372
183. Jotibha Phule, A Masked Icon | 374
184. B. R. Ambedkar: A Dual Legacy | 376
185. The Burden of Everyday Social | 378
186. Tribute to Simon Robert Charsley: Champion of the Untouchables | 380
187. O Kanshi Ram, The Cyclist of Revolt | 382
188. Mayavati: Untouchable Icon of a Silent Revolution | 384
189. No Gods, No Icons, No Chains | 386
190. Kanakarathnam Nukapangu, a Shield of Grace | 389
191. I Am Nagalim | 390
192. The Nagalim Wound and the War | 392
193. Scato Swu: A Name in Ashes | 394
194. Unshaken Love, Unforgotten Wounds | 396
195. Love and Betrayal Under Bruised Skies | 398

Section IV: Words Against the Blood and Iron Policy of Muslims
196. Salman Rushdie: The Pen That Would Not Break | 403
197. The Man Who Spoke *Satanic Verses* | 405

198. Ibn Warraq: The Pen That Dared | 407
199. Taslima Nasrin: The Unyielding Flame | 409
200. Taslima Nasrina's Exile | 411
201. Ode to Salwan Momika | 413
202. The Silent Cry of a 12-Year-Old Muslim Girl | 415
203. The Agony of Silenced Innocence of a
12-Year-Old Muslim Girl | 417
204. The Agony of a Four-Year-Old Muslim Girl Child Forgotten | 419
205. The Lost Four-Year-Old Muslim Girl Childhood | 421
206. The Weight of the Muslim | 423
207. Bound by the Muslim Way of Life | 425
208. Islamic Cycles Unbroken | 427
209. The Scarf of Slavery | 429
210. The Agony of Homosexual | 431
211. Muslim Immigrant Invaders | 433
212. Shadows of the Crescent | 435
213. The Shroud of Jamia Milia Islamia | 437
214. The Blood of a Gay *Professor Srinivas Ramchandra Siras* | 439
215. Ode to Mosab Hassan Yousef | 441

Section V: Words Against the Blood and Iron Policy of Africans
216. Ode to My Great-Grandfather, His Royal
Highness Emperor Yohannes IV | 445
217. Father of Ethiopia, His Excellency Bezabih Negusse Haftu | 447
218. The 1943 Woyane Rebellion Leader, His
Excellency Bezabih Negusse Haftu | 449
219. Her Royal Highness Mamit Sebhat Weldegebriel | 451
220. Her Royal Decree | 453
221. The Madness of African-American Leaders Adoring Gandhi | 455
222. O Barak Obama, Where Is Your Western Knowledge? | 458
223. O African Mother, Teach Me | 461
224. Chicken Tenderloin | 463
225. We the Pathological Liars | 465
226. African Drama | 466
227. River of Lost Hyenas | 468
228. Hyenas of Mai Kadra | 470
229. Ashes of the Hyenas | 472
230. Hyenas of Silence | 474
231. Can the Ethiopian Change his Skin? | 476

232. The Myth of White and Black Cloths | 477
233. Paedophilic Africa | 479
234. A Dark Glorification | 481
235. Impurity of Impurity | 483
236. Against the Madness of African & Islamic *Female Genital Mutilation* | 485
237. Daughter's of Hyena Lament | 487
238. Ode to the Rainbow Community | 490
239. In the Animal Kingdom of Africa | 492
240. The Taboo of Breath | 494
241. In the Forest Culture of Africa | 496
242. Blood on Our Hands | 498
243. We Love Blood and Immorality | 499
244. Twelve Wounds of Animal Kingdom | 501
245. Lifeline of African Animal Kingdom | 502
246. Shadows of the Hyenas War | 504
247. War of Hyenas, Wolves, Vultures, Mosquitoes | 505
248. Escape from Hyenas Cage to Wolves Cage | 507
249. In the Shadows of Hyenas, Wolves, Vultures. . . | 509
250. Echoes of the Hyenas and Wolves War | 511

Section I

Europe Poems

1. Rest in Peace, My Baby, Stanford

Rest in peace, my baby boy Stanford,
A name which is like an echo in the spaces you never got to see,
Born into the world of war, exodus, and hope,
But taken too early by hands that should cure, not harm.

When the civil war ripped Ethiopia apart,
Two merciless forces—Tigray and Amhara—perpetually at war with each other,
I fled so desperate to save you and your brother Saviour,
From a land no longer homely.
Imagining Canada as our haven, our haven of safety.

But deviousness took another turn,
Into the Czech Republic, where hope staggered.
In those asylum walls, we were not just refugees,
We were targets of prejudice, of unseen hate.

Racism everywhere, at every look and ungiven touch,
Teachers pampered others, not my black Christian child.
You, Stanford, never got to see those teachers' smiles,
Never got to feel their gentle hands,
For they did not see you; they did not want to.

When we sought solace in Germany,
Racism followed, draped in white coats and sterile halls.
A neo-Nazi gynecologist became the face of terror,
Her injection, her weapon, your innocent body, her field.
You died like so many, silenced, without justice, without care.

If only Ethiopia could heal,
If only my homeland knew peace, prosperity, and truth,

Then maybe, my sweet child, you would be alive.
But corrupt leadership, war, and treason
Forced us into an exodus that led to your death.

They termed it natural, but well, I know the truth,
It's not nature, but prejudice, that sting of the needle.
They said your black skin was good enough for experiments,
Just like Josef Mengele's victims, just like many others.

And your brother Saviour he waits,
Carries in his memory, fragile yet strong,
Traumatized, he asks why they took you,
Why such a brutal world had to take my little brother.
From Tigray into Germany you deserved better,
From the Czech camps into the asylum wards,
Every step taken, pleading for safety, yet the world shut its doors.
They called us monkeys, criminals, names deeper than any blade cuts,
But greater than their words, my child, you are.
Stanford, my love, I was supposed to see you grow,
To see you play, learn, laugh, know joy.
You should have been the poet, dreamer,
Like your mama and daddy, like your brother,
But now your poems are unsaid, your dreams unravelled.

They killed you because of racism, my son,
They stole your breath with a jab,
A vaccination that was to save but was laced with cruelty.
Yet even now, in my grief, I hold your name high,
For you are more than a memory, you are my strength.

Rest, my baby, in a peace that this world could not give,
Rest, knowing we will carry your story, your truth,
And let the world know that your life, though short,
Was precious, was powerful, was loved.

2. The Four Seasons of Exile: Song of Stanford

Spring
We ran from the cold fists of Prague,
through the April bloom, our hearts light,
holding hands with hope, whispering prayers,
dreaming of a place where our son would cry, then laugh.
Stanford, our flowermoon, nestled in the warmth
of a promise not yet broken.

Summer
The sun rose red, not in glory, but in grief.
A doctor's hands, a system's will—
No vaccine, no heartbeat, no justice, no name.
July 4th, a wound carved in time,
and by July 11th, the earth swallowed our dreams.
You lie beneath German soil, son,
as the State calls us strangers, calls us ghosts.

Autumn
The leaves fell like verdicts, like orders, like chains.
"Leave," they say, "or we will make you."
The law that shelters wolves denies a grieving mother.
Where does justice live if not here?
Does it drift with the autumn winds,
lost in the echoes of forgotten cries?

Winter
Now the cold speaks in threats, in hunger, in fear.
No shelter but trembling hands, no country but exile.
We walk on snow-covered streets, unseen, unheard,
while the State's pen signs away our fate.

To flee, to stay, to fight, to break—
where does a father's love belong
when even the Church locks its doors?

Stanford, our light, our loss,
your name will not be buried.
Your father still breathes, still speaks, still stands.
For you, for Saviour, for a place that is home.

3. A Father's Grief, A Mother's Love, A Son's Rest

Every day, we board Bus 11 from Weinweg,
To Hauptbahnhof, where journeys diverge,
Taking routes 13, 14, 15 or 17, 117
To the Friedhof am Dreifaltigkeitsberg[1],
Where Stanford lies unseen.

In the quiet of Bergfriedhof, green carpets stretch wide,
A sanctuary where death meets dignity's stride.
Trees whisper secrets, flowers bloom in grace,
Here, every soul finds its respectful place.

Unlike our homeland, where caste stains even the dead,
Here, no untouchable grave is left unsaid.
Stanford rests among German children, pure and free,
Untouched by the caste, unburdened by cruelty.

We walk past Jewish stones, crosses standing tall,
Christian and Muslim side by side, equal to all.
This is civilization, this is profound,
A place where humanity and love abound.

But my heart breaks, my spirit torn,
For my son Stanford, from my arms was shorn.
Killed by a vaccine, unnecessary and cruel,
A Nazi remnant in a modern tool.

Your mother bore you with strength, my son,
Her love unmatched, but her battle undone.

---

1. "Cemetery on Trinity Hill", Regensburg, Bavaria, Germany

I failed to protect you, trusted too much,
In a system that masked venom with a healer's touch.

We buried you with prayers, with tears so vast,
A German Father blessed you, though racism cast
Its shadow on rituals meant to console,
Yet your peace shines brighter than any role.

Saviour, your brother, misses your smile,
Your memory walks with him each lonely mile.
We will not abandon you, though threats persist,
Our love for you is a flame that will always exist.

Stanford, my angel, you are never alone,
Daddy will join you, to call your name home.
For you, my child, are the star in my sky,
Guiding my path, though the world may deny.

Never again, July 4 or October 7,
Justice for Stanford, the call to heaven.
Love, truth, and justice light our way,
For my son, my star, in eternity's sway.

4. The Agony of a Black Untouchable Father

I did not know pain so raw and deep
Until my first child was laid to sleep.
In India, 2010, my bloodline slain,
Honor became a dagger, my family's bane.

The Vishnu Smriti whispers cruel decree,
"An Untouchable shall not touch the three."
A law of death, etched in ancient script,
Tore my baby from me, a life unjustly ripped.

I read Jeremiah's somber verse,
"A leopard cannot change its spots," a curse.
Black as sin, as shadow, as night,
The Bible too robbed me of light.

Germany, July 4th, 2023,
Stanford, my son, lost to tyranny.
Not by blade but a racism vile,
That masked its hate behind a clinical smile.

Brazil, Australia, Ethiopia's lands,
The Czech Republic, Belgium, where injustice stands.
Wherever I turned, my black skin bore,
A mark unseen, a silent war.

In every nation, the tale's the same,
Canonized cruelty, another name.
Be it Hindu, Christian, or Quran's verse,
The ostracized bear the universe's curse.

Jews and Untouchables, souls intertwined,
Victims of hatred, malice designed.
The world claims progress, yet we remain,
Bound by texts that perpetuate pain.

But I, a father, broken yet whole,
Carry the weight, the stories untold.
Through tears and loss, my spirit burns,
For justice, for truth, a tide that turns.

My children are gone, their laughter stilled,
Yet their memory fuels my unyielding will.
To break these chains of caste and race,
To reclaim our world, our rightful place.

For every life the canons betray,
A father's love will light the way.
Through the ashes of grief, I rise anew,
A voice for the silenced, the forgotten, the true.

5. Friendly Father

O Father in Heaven, my friend, my guide,
You who never bend to hate or pride.
You do not weigh by caste or skin,
Nor shun the souls the world calls sin.

Yet, why did You turn Your face away,
When my children bled into the clay?
One unborn, stolen by hands of caste,
A shadow lost, too small, too fast.

The other, my Stanford, fragile, bright,
Snatched by hands cloaked in white.
A needle pierced, a silent breath,
No law could guard against this death.

You bore the cross, endured the stake,
Yet let six million burn and break.
On October's dawn, under desert sun,
Fourteen hundred fell—yet You saved none.

Tell me, Father, must I still believe,
When justice folds, when mothers grieve?
When untouchable blood floods each shore,
And silence reigns forevermore?

They worship gods of war and chains,
They carve their idols out of pain.
But You, O Father, bore the curse,
Yet never turned the world to worse.

If You are love, then teach me how,
To lift my head, to trust You now.
For though the earth is cruel and blind,
You are the friend I fail to find.

6. Cherish Life, Reject Death

O killers of innocence, murderers of truth,
How can you take away a child's first breath, their youth?
You speak of love, compassion, and rights,
But you deny a child the chance to see light.

How do you abort a life you've yet to know,
A tiny heart with so much to show?
You claim it's freedom, your body, your voice,
But what about the baby who has no choice?

O Satan's child, you worship death, not life,
Your heart is a blade, sharper than any knife.
"My body, my choice," you scream with pride,
But innocent souls are left to die.

You are a curse to love, light, and good,
A poison spreading where life once stood.
More dangerous than hate-filled creeds,
You kill your own child, neglect their needs.

When I carried my baby, Stanford, I rejoiced,
I was ready to sing with my heart, my voice.
But your neo-Nazi gynecologist took him away,
My heart shattered, my world turned gray.

I cherished my son, his smiles and touch,
I was ready to die for him, loved him so much.
Yet you, moron, you take what is pure,
Killing the innocent, who could have endured.

Let children be born, let their laughter ring,
Let them grow, let them sing.
Protect life, don't hide behind lies,
Let a child's smile reach the skies.

O Satan, stop this cruel deceit,
Let the unborn child's heart beat.
Have care, have sense, learn to be wise,
Don't live in shadows where life dies.

Life is a gift, a chance to be,
A soul with the right to breathe freely.
To be human is to cherish life's breath,
Not to bring about silent death.

7. Saviour Questions

"Mommy, can I be white like them?"
His small voice asks, again and again.
In German halls, his color's a mark,
My son's black skin, called ugly and dark.

They see him and mock, they call him names,
They push and shove, igniting flames.
His innocence, once pure and bright,
Now tainted by their words, by their spite.

Each day, he returns, confused and alone,
Asking me why his skin feels like stone.
Wishing for a world where he can be free,
Without judgment, without cruelty, just to simply be.

In classrooms and playgrounds, he's left aside,
A silent plea, a heart full of pride.
The teachers smile, but they turn their heads,
Not seeing the pain, the tears he sheds.

They say it's just play, nothing to fear,
But when he cries, who will hear?
When his heart breaks, when his spirit falls,
Who will answer his desperate calls?

My son, I see the hurt in your eyes,
But you are more than their foolish lies.
You are my hero, my joy, my song,
In a world so cruel, where you don't belong.

Prince Saviour, so brave and small,
Know that you are more than the names they call.
In a world of shadows, you are the light,
Your skin is strength, your soul is bright.

Let the world see the beauty you hold,
In every shade, in every fold.
For you are worthy, strong, and free,
And I will fight to help you see—

That their hate is their burden, not yours to bear,
And with every tear, I'll be right there.
Together, my son, we'll rise above,
For you are wrapped in your mother's love.

8. My Son's Question

"Mommy, can I be white like them?"
His small voice asks, again and again.
In German halls, his color's a mark,
My son's black skin, called ugly and dark.

They say he's "poop," they laugh and shove,
His innocence crushed in a world void of love.
Each day he returns, confused and alone,
Wishing his skin wasn't his own.

In classrooms and playgrounds, they turn away,
As teachers smile and say, "It's play."
But when he cries, when he hurts inside,
Who will stand with him, who'll turn the tide?

To my son, Prince Saviour, brave and small,
Know you are more than the names they call.
In a world of shadows, let your heart shine bright,
For your skin is strength, your soul is light.

9. The Color of Hate

My son Saviour, just six,
Comes home with his heart in pieces,
Not from scraped knees,
But from words that break him like brittle glass.
"Mommy, Daddy, can you change me?"
He pleads, a whisper against a storm,
"I don't want to be black. I don't want to be poop."

His skin, the color of midnight skies,
Is painted with the cruelty of a thousand insults.
He's told his darkness is the stain
On a world too pure to see him.
A child—whose only crime is his hue—
Is pushed away,
Like a shadow too heavy for the sun.

They say it's not racism.
They call it "normal"
When the biting words fall like stones,
And fists, soft as clouds,
Leave marks that last longer than the scars they claim don't exist.
One child, teeth bared like a wolf,

Bites him deeply,
His skin a canvas of their hate.
The teachers, blind as statues, say,
"It's just kids being kids."
But these children, so young in years,
Already carry the weight of centuries in their eyes.

The playground, once a sanctuary of play,
Becomes a cage of glass walls,
Where my son is the bird whose wings are clipped.
His name is a whisper,
Drowned by laughter that sounds like thunder in his ears.
He's not allowed to sit at their tables,

Not called by name,
As if the sin were his presence.
His face, the shape of a starless night,
Is the mirror they do not wish to view.

But the crime is far deeper than that crime,
Is this:
They children of the cross
Are taught to blot him out.
To bleach him from their life
With every utterance,
Every silence,
As though he is a stain that wouldst infect their world.

And still, every day,
He asks,
"Why am I not like them?"
As if the color of his skin
Is a question no child should ever have to ask.

10. Tears of Mother Earth

When I lost my babies in the Holocaust,
I cried and cried, my pain too vast to bear,
Unstoppable tears that flooded the earth.
My tears became a mass of water,
The mass of water became a river of water,
The river of water became seawater,
Seawater became ocean water.
The ocean water is my blood and my tears.

Again, when I lost my babies on October 7,
I cried and cried, unable to stop the storm within me.
My tears, a flood of loss and despair.
They became a mass of water,
The mass of water became a river of water,
The river of water became seawater,
Seawater became ocean water.
The ocean water is my blood and my tears.

When I saw my babies running for life,
In the Holocaust and in the modern-day Holocaust
That is October 7,
I cried and cried, the pain suffocating me,
My tears became a mass of water,
The mass of water became a river of water,
The river of water became seawater,
Seawater became ocean water.
The ocean water is my blood and my tears.

When I saw my babies burned alive,
In the Holocaust and again on October 7,

I cried and cried, my heart breaking for them.
My tears became a mass of water,
The mass of water became a river of water,
The river of water became seawater,
Seawater became ocean water.
The ocean water is my blood and my tears.

When I see my babies haunted by anti-Semitic lynching gangs,
Even across so-called safe havens,
I cried and cried, the grief never ceasing.
My tears became a mass of water,
The mass of water became a river of water,
The river of water became seawater,
Seawater became ocean water.
The ocean water is my blood and my tears.

When I see my babies battling against 3 billion Jihadists,
It is not just a conflict—it is a fight for life,
Between civilization and savagery, decency and depravity,
Good versus evil, life versus death.
I cried and cried in unbearable pain,
My tears became a mass of water,
The mass of water became a river of water,
The river of water became seawater,
Seawater became ocean water.
The ocean water is my blood and my tears.

When I see the contrast between a Jewish soul that cherishes life
And a Jihadi religion that worships death,
I cried and cried, my heart torn in two.
My tears became a mass of water,
The mass of water became a river of water,
The river of water became seawater,
Seawater became ocean water.
The ocean water is my blood and my tears.

When I lost my two babies, Stanford and his sibling,
To the hands of casteists and racists,
I cried and cried, their absence too much to bear.

My tears became a mass of water,
The mass of water became a river of water,
The river of water became seawater,
Seawater became ocean water.
The ocean water is my blood and my tears.

Never again, July 4^2, or October 7^3.
The ocean water is my blood and my tears.
Never again.

---

2. On June 28, Wednesday, 2023, in the asylum camp of Bajuwarenstr., 1A, my African wife Selamawit Hailu Bezabih became a vessel for their cruelty, injected with Repevax, a vaccine she never needed, a shot that was never mandatory, a decision disguised as care but woven with malice. They spoke of protection, of winter's looming chill, but instead, they froze my son, Stanford Suryaraju Mattimalla, in death's embrace. My baby was a victim of a neo-Nazi gynecologist. As usual, the German state and its institutions covered up the murder in the name of natural death, as they did to six million Jews during the Holocaust period.

3. Muslims murdered thousands of Jews on this darkest day in the human history of 2023. Muslims started gang raping, beheading, and killing tiny minority but knowledge-producing Jewish people across the globe. Antisemitism and hatred of Jews in Europe and the West are deep-rooted. The UN, legacy media, global human rights bodies, and European and Western states and societies are complicit in the crimes against the Jewish community.

11. Crossing the Waters of Fate

How do I cross this ruthless sea,
Where waves claim lives so endlessly?
A father's fear, a child in tow,
Yet where to run? Where to go?

The traffickers whisper with hollow lies,
Their boats are graves beneath the skies.
Sixty-five souls packed tight in doom,
Bound for the Channel, a watery tomb.

Germany turns, its heart of stone,
No refuge here, I stand alone.
They count no dead, they feel no pain,
They cast me out, they call my name
Not as a man, not as a mind,
But a shadow cast, a fate unkind.

I am no terrorist, no beast of crime,
No war-born fugitive, fleeing time.
I was born in chains, yet walked with grace,
Now seeking shelter, a safer place.

Two children lost to hands of hate,
One to caste, one to fate.
Now Saviour walks this path with me,
Through cold and dark, through storm and sea.

The Czech lands stripped me of my name,
Branded me thief, marked me with shame.

Monkey, criminal, lesser being
Their words still echo, raw, unseeing.

Yet here I stand, the shore in sight,
A father grasping for the light.
Should I step onto this fragile boat?
Will it carry hope, or steal my throat?

Winter howls, the waters rise,
The trafficker's greed burns in his eyes.
He does not ask if I will live,
Only what I have to give.

Europe stands with open hands,
Yet cradles those who stain its lands.
Murderers, rapists, veiled in lies,
Walk free beneath their careless skies.

But I am marked, a man apart,
A scholar with a shattered heart.
My crime was truth, my sin was skin,
The weight of history etched within.

O Saviour[4], child, my blood, my breath,
How do I shield you from this death?
I dream of shores, of light, of peace,
Yet all I see are walls that cease.

To cross, to stay, to fight, to flee
What fate remains for you and me?

---

4. My six years old son Saviour Suryaraju Mattimalla

12. Exile Among Beasts

I fled the land[5] where my name was a stain,
Where my ancestors walked in shackles of pain.
Six thousand years beneath their chains,
Marked as filth, erased from names.

They took my child, his breath erased[6],
For love they deemed a vile disgrace.
Her mother wept, her sister stood,
Yet blood was spilled where love once stood.

I ran to lands where crosses shine,
Where prayers are sung in holy rhyme.
But Africa held a mirror bright—
A jungle masked in sacred light.

A land of ghosts, of dreams betrayed,
Where trust is lost, where love decays.
Where hands that bless can also strike,
And truth dissolves in webs of lies.

I married to save, to shield, to keep,
Yet found my fate in shadows deep.

---

5. I am untouchable, unseeable, unshadowable, unapproachable, unspeakable, a walking carrion, a walking carcass, a walking corpse, a Negro, dirty, impure, a Madiga, ugly, a slave, in the muddy piece of India, Nepal, Pakistan, Bangladesh, Japan, Sri Lanka, and other caste-based and untouchability-based societies in our times.

6. My unnamed baby was torn from his/her Kapu-Hindu (Mamidi Richa) mother's arms and lost to the unrelenting jaws of a Hindu honor killing. My unnamed child was killed by his or her own maternal parents and maternal aunt in India. I do not know whether my baby was a daughter or son. They kidnapped my wife and killed my child for being an untouchable.

A woman's eyes, a hunter's snare,
A love that moved through empty air.

They chase the pale, the distant gleam,
A passport stamped, a golden dream.
Yet hearts are cold, like shifting sand,
No roots, no vows, no promised land.

We reached a shore where names dissolve,
Where "monkey," "thief,"[7] become resolve.
Where masks are worn and lives erased,
Unless your skin reveals your place.

I bore their scorn, their whispered jeers,
For shadows cast by ancient fears.
For crimes not mine, for sins unknown,
Yet guilt is carved into my bones.

And now my son walks haunted ground,
Where silence screams, where hate resounds.
Where every face, each glance, each hand,
Reminds him he is foreign land.

I must protect, I must defend,
From wolves who grin, from foes who bend.
Yet walls are high, and chains are tight,
And justice fades in endless night.

O world of beasts in polished skin,
Where does the exile's road begin?
Where does it end, and who will stand,
To forge a home from borrowed land?

---

7. My names are monkey, chimpanzee, thief, negro, dirty, and criminal in the Czech Republic. European spaces are no different from the Czech Republic. Racism and antisemitism are deep-rooted in Europe and the West. European states and societies, churches, kindergartens, schools, and educational institutions are examples of deep-rooted racism against Asian Blacks. Make no mistake: Muslims and Africans enjoy significant freedom to commit crimes against humanity in Europe and the West.

13. The Rejected Asylum

Germany, you turned me away,
For I am not what you love today.
Not wrapped in lies, nor steeped in crime,
Not veiled in terror, nor masked in time.

You open your gates for the ones who deceive,
For hands that plunder, for hearts that deceive.
Millions arrive with tales spun tight,
While truth is exiled, cast from sight.

Your streets embrace the bearded hymn,
The whispered plots, the shadows dim.
You kneel to those who mock your grace,
Yet turn from me, I have no place.

A scholar's hands, an honest tongue,
But truth is drowned where lies are sung.
The flags of woke, they fly so high,
Yet beneath them, only virtues die.

To speak, to question, to stand alone,
Is to be marked, to be disowned.
For where they bare their flesh with pride,
The clothed are scorned, cast aside.

You call it freedom, you call it choice,
Yet silence falls on reason's voice.
A home for those who slay and steal,
Yet none for those who think and feel.

Ten million warriors march unseen,
Not with swords, but war machine.
And still, you cheer, and still, you bow,
To hands that strike, to creeds that vow.

I walk alone, through lands gone blind,
Where truth is treason, and thought a crime.
I search for those who stand upright,
Who hold to ethics, who speak with light.

Yet, like a speck within the sand,
They vanish swift, a dying strand.
Jews, you freeze within your walls,
While ancient foes still make the calls.

So where shall one like me belong?
Between the lost, between the wronged.
I seek a home where truth may grow,
But find none left, I do not know.

For nations fall, for minds decay,
For virtues fade in slow decay.
Yet still, I walk, and still, I dream,
To find a land where truth still gleams.

14. An African Journey Through Shadows

I was born in a land where the warmth of the sun felt distant,
A land bound by chains invisible,
Where my people walk in the shadows of their ancestors' tears.
The weight of history weighs heavy,
The air thick with the silence of unheard cries.

In the heart of Ethiopia, where violence and lies embraced,
Where every footstep speaks of brutality and bloody days,
I was to succumb to my fate,
That the value of me was measured by my skin,
By where my home was.

I abandoned the broken ground of my native soil,
In search of refuge, searching for peace—
Only to meet with a new prison,
Where the world still whispers the same hate.

They called me a criminal in the Czech Republic,
A monkey, a thief—
Labels painted across my heart,
And my child's innocent eyes reflected the same judgment.
Even in the spaces where I sought shelter,
I was not free.

They gave us rooms of filth and shadow,
Where even the air appeared to deny its right to breathe.
I cleaned the dirt, but it clung like the scars of my past-
Sticky, defiant, and just a reminder
Of how the world looked at me.
I grumbled, but the voices of right turned silent;

The ombudsman, an icon of indifference;
A helping hand to their cruelty, their systematic denial of dignity.
Racism, draped in garbs of legality,
Denied us what rightfully was due to us.

We ran to Germany for safety,
But even there, the shackles were unseen—
And my son's[8] life taken,
In the garb of a death by medication,
A fact so bitter; lies by the state, so serene.

The weight of bureaucracy crushed our cries,
As our family became fodder for a broken system.
But in the darkness, there were glimmers—
A few who saw us, who heard us,
And for them, we will forever be grateful.

The journey continues, but the scars are deep,
Deeper than the oceans we crossed,
Deeper than the borders that divided us.
We are not just survivors—we are witnesses,
To a world that still has not learned
The true meaning of humanity.

---

8. Stanford Suryaraju Mattimalla

15. White Is Beautiful

Founders of civilization,
Wheels that turned the world,
Modern knowledge, technology, and factories,
Factories of ideas, homes, roads, and buildings,
Institutions, spaces, machines,
Knowledge, sports, games, laws, and order,
The rule of law, one man, one value,
Parks, public and private spheres,
Love, life, peace, and freedom,
Liberty, light, cheerfulness, and democracy,
Liberalism, individualism, rights,
Coexistence, tolerance, and fraternity,
Human values, humanity, comedy,
Arts, aesthetics, humor, value, ethics,
Finally, civilization was built and invented by white[9] men and women.

9. Pure White Western Christian race and pure Jewish race is the only beautiful race on the earth or in heaven. Converted people, or interracial people, except for interracial children born to the whites and Jews, are worshippers of death cultures. The white race includes the Jewish community, not the whites and Jews whose genetics carry the interracial non-white, non-Jewish DNA of Asian, African, or Islamic, African, Hindu, Muslim, Buddhist, Jain, Sikh, or Parsee and converted Asian and African Christian communities are excluded in my definition of civilization and concluded from my lived experience that only the white western Christian race and Jewish race are the only civilized races on the ground or in heaven. In fact, there is no practice of Christianity among the Asian and African races. Africa and Asia are the darkest spaces in human history with their darkest ideologies and ways of life. Christianity has been Asianized and Africanized. Hence, it lost its civilization. The human civilization was created and invented and progressed by the white Western Christian and Jewish races across the globe. The tiny minority of Jews share 60% of knowledge production in the creation and advancement of human civilization. The Son of God has chosen to be born in the Jewish race, whereas the chosen White race celebrates His life, love, liberty, and light. A single drop of blood from the non-white western Christian race and the non-Jewish race that mixed with the pure race has destroyed the white western Christian and Jewish races. Not all white and Jewish people are beautiful. Western liberal, left, feminist, and queer communities have destroyed the core values of white western Christian

White men made everything,
The world was theirs to shape,
From the first ideas of light,
To the modern age, full of grace.
White men gave us everything—
From buildings that touch the sky
To the laws that kept us free
From chaos, dark, and lie.

But Islamic, Asian, and African chameleons,
Parasites in the white man's space,
Invaded, destroyed, and desecrated
The pure land, the sacred place.
They came with their hunger,
Their greed, their minds set on theft,
And in their wake, they left nothing
But ruins where order once was deft.

The world built on sweat, blood, and toil,
Crafted by the hands of the wise,
Now tainted, twisted, by those who seek
To break what the white man built to rise.

So tell me, what becomes of progress,
When its builders are torn down?
What happens when history is erased,
When every value starts to drown?

White men made everything,
But in the end, their labor was all for naught.
For those who came to steal the light,
Have proven to be the ones who fought
Against the very ideals they sought.

---

civilization and Jewish civilization that worship life, love, liberty, and light by carrying the genetics or progeny of death-worshipping non-white and non-Jewish races. African and Asian races have destroyed the White and Jewish civilization through their legal and illegal migration. Asian and African races worship death cultures, whereas white and Jewish races worship life, love, liberty, and light. Life is celebrated among the white Western Christian and Jewish races, whereas death is celebrated among the Hindu, Islamic, Buddhist, Sikh, Parsee, Jain, and African races.

16. The October 7

A beautiful mind is shattered by the October 7,
Forces that spread venom,
Rooted deeper than the earth,
Higher than the sky,
Larger than the surface of the earth,
Worse than the Holocaust of our times.

The day thorns fell on flowers,
The day jasmines bled,
The day flowers drowned in tears,
The day moonflowers nailed to the ground,
The day roses were stolen,
The day united jasmines rose,
To fight the thorns, the nails, across murky spaces.

The day war was waged,
Against thesaurus, encyclopedia,
The highest scholarship,
Noble theories, knowledge production,
Decency, light, civilization, life,
Human values, the lamp of reason,
Freedom, liberty, sovereignty, democracy,
Honesty, rule of law, truth, morality, rationality, and Semitism.

I want to live.
Like any human being.
But my life was stolen on October 7.
This is not the story of the Holocaust—
But very much the story of a modern Holocaust.

The day history trembled,
As the venom of hate spread,
And the earth shook beneath its weight,
As innocence was ripped from the very air.
The scream of the fallen,
A deafening silence in the aftermath—
The cries of a people, drowned by the cruelty
Of a barbaric force that sought to erase
Their existence, their memory,
Their place in the story of humankind.

On October 7, the soul of a people was torn apart.
The lamps of freedom extinguished,
And the night grew darker still.
In that moment, the world knew:
The past had not passed,
And humanity's deepest wounds
Had been reopened once again.

This is the modern Holocaust,
Not of gas chambers or crematoriums,
But of hatred unleashed,
Of history erased in a single breath,
Of lives snuffed out in the name of vengeance,
And of innocence lost to the howling winds
That swept the land on October 7.

The blood of the innocent stains the earth,
As the memory of that day burns into the sky.
We will not forget.
We will rise,
Because the flowers that fell
Shall bloom again.
And the light that was stolen
Will one day return.

17. The Agony of a Jewish Star

I am a shining star,
Like Jesus Christ, who bore the cross of humanity's sins,
Like Karl Marx, who dreamed of equality,
Like Albert Einstein, who unraveled the mysteries of the cosmos.

I am a beacon, a flicker of hope,
Like every Jewish Nobel laureate,
Crafting worlds of knowledge and light.
But on the stained canvas of history,
My radiance was dampened,
Drenched in the shadow of human cruelty.

On that fateful day of October 7,
And on numerous other days in Europe's heart,
My light had been shattered,
My body defiled by the venomous hands
Of Jihadi moderates in the free Palestine streets,
Though I was but twelve—a child,
A fragment of innocence crushed beneath barbarity.

Oh, Europe,
Where is the cradle of Enlightenment?
The cobblestones still echo
With the cries of the Holocaust,
Yet your hands are not clean,
Stained with complicity in unspoken crimes.

A Jewish girl, a Yazidi,
An untouchable in the belly of Hindutva's beast—
All share the same wound,

The same mark of persecution,
Raped for being.
Their existence, a defiance;
Their identity, a threat to the oppressor's soul.

In India, the untouchable's shadow is forbidden;
In Nepal, her footsteps are accursed.
She is hunted down in Pakistan,
Her dignity gone, her screams unheard.
In Islamic lands, a Yazidi woman is but a pawn,
A piece in the tyrant's merciless game of chess.

And I, a Jewish child,
In the West's so-called haven,
In the cobble-streeted France,
Was torn from hands
That desecrated my people's memory.

Europe, your silence is deafening,
Your indifference a blade much sharper. The UN with an empty gaze,
Global rights turn their blind eye. My spirit still lingers on,
An undimmed star, a light which will never die,
A voice never to be silenced.

O my fellow stars, let us converge,
Dazzling, into the darkness of oppression.
And burn away the shadows of iniquity.

18. The Unmasked Truth

O Europe, O West, colonial throne,
You bowed to my kin on his gilded throne.
To Emperor Yohannes IV, my line, my pride,
You offered salutes, your respect supplied.

Yet when I step on your foreign ground,
The truth of your hate becomes unbound.
In streets and walls, your words proclaim
The insults, the venom, and my skin's shame.

Have I enslaved or bound you in chains,
Or forced your people to bear my pains?
Have I called you beast, have I thrown the stone,
Or cast you from life, left you alone?

Yet my ancestors stood under your whip,
Their bodies broken, their spirit stripped.
Now in exile, I see you unchanged,
Time has passed, but your gaze remains.

You dance with brown as he enters your gates,
While my black skin meets only hate.
On walls, in whispers, I see it clear,
Your mask slips away; the truth appears.

To my face, you bow, call me "sir,"
Yet turn around, and lies occur.
But I stand here strong, unbroken, unbowed,
Your hate a cloud, but I remain proud.

19. O Janus faced Europe

O Europe, O West, colonial throne,
You bowed to my kin on his gilded stone.
To Emperor Yohannes, my line, my pride,
You offered salutes, your respect supplied.

You admired his strength, his sovereignty,
With reverence in every decree.
But when I, a child of his reign,
Step on your ground, what do I gain?

The truth of your hate, it swells like a tide,
In every glance, in every stride.
On your streets and in your halls,
I hear the insults, the judgment that falls.

You tell me of progress, of unity's claim,
But your actions reveal only shame.
With every look, I feel the sting,
The bitter echoes that hatred brings.

Have I enslaved or bound you in chains,
Or forced your people to bear my pains?
Have I called you beast, have I thrown the stone,
Or cast you from life, left you alone?

Your ancestors may have owned my kin,
Whipped our backs, stripped our skin.
But now, as I walk these foreign lanes,
I see no change, I feel no gains.

Your land may be rich, your cities grand,
But the weight of your hate I still understand.
You dance with brown as they enter your gates,
But when I walk through, the door simply waits.

I see the whispers behind closed doors,
The glance, the jeer, the silent wars.
On your walls, the truth is clear,
The mask slips away, and I see your fear.

To my face, you bow, call me "sir,"
But behind my back, your lies occur.
You smile in public, but privately sneer,
Yet I remain, undeterred, sincere.

I stand here strong, unbroken, unbowed,
Your hate is a cloud, but I remain proud.
For no matter the words you choose to say,
I am my ancestors' legacy, and I will never sway.

20. Persecution of the German Greeting in the German Asylum Camp

In the heart of Germany, under foreign skies,
I walk on the grounds of asylum, where hope often lies.
With a smile on my lips, I greet every face,
Yet met with sharp words, I'm reminded of place.
"Say Salaam Aleikum," the Muslims demand,
As if my native tongue is too harsh to withstand.
In Regensburg's shelter, where cultures collide,
My voice feels muted, my spirit denied.

I walked through the gates, seeking refuge and peace,
Yet met a strange tyranny that would not end.
"Guten Morgen," I said-a greeting so sublime,
But anger-encased threats did make my heart chime.
"Here, it's Salaam," they insisted, high and bright,
In a camp so detached from the German light.
How quaint, this land of my forefathers' praise,
Now follows a culture which cuts my seams and raises.

German camp managers-in voices hushed low,
Apologized for the change, as if in tow they did go.
The relentless ethos of benignity bending to a creed,
While my own heart-strings cried to me for liberty to lead.
"Respect their beliefs," they softly conveyed,
But what of my culture, my language betrayed?
In this place of asylum, where I thought I'd belong,
I found that my voice had been silenced too long.

"Pork is forbidden," they said with a sigh,
"Beef and chicken we serve," a compliant reply.

As a vegan, I pondered, but the question was clear:
Where's the respect for my choices held dear?
Disparity hides in the shadows of their care,
For the insignificant minority, the plight is bare.
Seems humanity is not valued just the same,
From skin color down to faith in your name.

Ninety percent workers-voices so loud,
But the other's silence is an unyielding, heavy crowd.
Where is equality, right's promise now,
When somehow shadows of difference obscure daylight?
Irony contorts in this once adored land,
While as the Muslims and Europeans are somehow reinstated,
As the cries of the ostracized whisper in vain,
Justice started fraying and staining.

I long for a Germany where all can unite,
Where the greeting of peace is shared in the light.
Yet here in this camp, the message is clear,
Integration's a struggle, marred by the fear.
Let us build a mosaic of values combined,
Where each life is cherished, each heart is aligned.
For in the embrace of diversity's grace,
May we find our own truth, a harmonious space.

21. White Western Christian Land in Islamic Transition

In the heart of Europe, where history once shone,
Long-stretched shadow and the seeds of change are sown.
What I behold, a haunting tale unwinds,
Where for one whirling vision leaders haggle over values.
In the Czech lands and Germany, Belgium's embrace,
Spectators of power shape a new face, foreign.
Western leaders, so eager to feed their gain,
Fan the flames of discord, stir the embers of pain.

Two hundred million souls, they say, have arrived,
Fleeing from strife, yet a different war thrived.
Under the mask of compassions, a fortress shapes up.
As cultures clash in stormy turmoil.
Islamic State whispers in the corridors of might.
Yet the cries of the silent still echo deep in the night.
How can a society, once proud of its creed,
Trade its own freedoms for a dark, seething need?

In every city square, I see the dismay,
While voices of truth are duly being swept aside.
The fabric of Europe sown with decorum,
Threads of deception and division now adorn.
The media swell of the stories that they would tell,
Of unity and kindness, though from shadows to repel.
In asylum camps I walk the thin line,
Socially ostracized, finding no sanctuary to find.

Brown skin merges in hues that are oddly aligned,
Yet my black cross is a target, maligned and maligned.

Where knowledge once danced with delighted cheer,
Now roams the chaos of power and plight sincere.
From children thrown away to dreams severed cold,
The ideals of freedom and truth are weathered old.
To each act of kindness, another of crime,
We pay the steep dime, so tolls this woke revolution in rhyme.

As jihadists rise, and voices become hushed,
The innocent cries are mercilessly trodden.
The youth lost to drugs, the young girls betrayed,
As the Sharia slowly seeps in, the price has got to be paid.
Where hope should cradle the soul in camps,
Independent republics sprout, gobbling them whole.
The authorities quite afraid of the truth,
While the shivering innocents robbed stark of their youth.

Victims of leaders who trade truth for deceit,
Every promise is broken, every heart faced defeat.
What of values remain of a place now beaten?
When freedom is in chains, and we lost the race.
Yet deep in the ruins, a flicker remains,
For truth alone triumphs through the sorrow and pains.
Let the voices rise up, let the chorus be heard,
For in the silence of lies, let justice be stirred.

22. Masks of Freedom, Chains of Hate

O Europe, you call yourself the land of the free,
Yet your streets tell a different tale to me.
You boast of rights, of tolerance, and care,
But I see your masks, and I'm aware.

In asylum camps, where I sought relief,
I found prejudice instead of belief.
They say it's Islamophobia if we speak,
Yet Muslim men roam, their eyes sleek.

They harass, they mock, they laugh aloud,
While we are silenced, told not to be proud.
If we raise our voice, if we dare to cry,
We're branded as racists, left to die.

When I walk these streets, in asylum's grip,
They see my skin, they tighten their lip.
But if I'm harassed, if I'm preyed upon,
I'm told to ignore it, to move on.

Where is the freedom, where is the right,
When I'm chained by fear each night?
They speak of tolerance, but it's all a game,
For their freedom is just a different name.

Muslim men roam, they harass with ease,
Yet I'm the one who can't find peace.
I'm told to be silent, not to complain,
To wear a smile, to hide the pain.

But I will not be silent, I will not hide,
I will not be swept by your tide.
For I see through your games, your deceit,
I walk with pride, though on tired feet.

I see your double standards, your lies,
I see the truth behind those eyes.
O Europe, you wear a mask so thin,
But the cracks show the darkness within.

23. Thorns of German Refugee Camps

In the narrow confines of asylum camps,
where hope flickers dim,
I confront my neighbor,
a man named Islam,
his smoke curling like whispers
of disdain into my room,
where my son should play in peace.

Every day, I plead for cleanliness,
for respect in shared spaces,
but he retorts with anger,
shouting of freedom in a foreign land,
while the walls echo
with the laughter of smoke and scorn.

Ms. Kurdish, her daughters by her side,
join the chorus of hostility,
as I stand, a solitary figure,
seeking justice amidst the chaos,
my voice drowned in the murmur of cigarettes
and the shadows of old grudges.

Social workers nod, but words are empty,
the threats hang heavy in the air,
I shield my son from fury,
as neighbors gather, a storm brews,
and I am marked, a target
for merely asking for adherence to rules.

On that fateful September morn,
their words sharpen like knives,
"Crazy man," they hiss,
"Go back where you came from,"
and in the shared kitchen,
the air thickens with smoke
and the weight of accusation.

I seek refuge in police,
but the truth yields before their stare,
as Mrs. Kurdish wrings my words,
twisting them into a fabric of lies,
lifting up her finger on me,
while I play with my name's shards.

Alone at the bus stop, we flee,
fear igniting our hearts,
an Iranian woman bears witness
to the narrative I cannot escape,
a cycle of threat, humiliation,
as shadows dance around my soul.

"Call the police," they say,
my abandoned phone]
and when the police arrive,
they listen with skepticism,
the weight of my truth drowned
in preconceived stories about me.

What kind of evil are in their hearts?
How swiftly trust is lost,
where accusation's echoes resound
across a void of space,
and I, the foreigner here,
am found to be the villain.

Innocence ensnared by fear,
I stand on the precipice of despair,
grasping at the threads of justice,

but all I see are shadows,
where every plea for peace
is met with disdain.

Germany, what have you become?
A land of rules bent by anger,
where my voice is silenced
by the weight of history's scars,
and I, a father, a husband, a man,
struggle to breathe amidst the smoke.

But I will not fade into silence,
for every threat is a call to rise,
to reclaim my narrative from the ashes,
and though the darkness presses in,
I will stand, unyielding,
a beacon against the storm.

24. Echoes of Islamic Terrorism

In some distant part of a foreign land,
I wore my scars, like shattered glass,
Sharp, hidden, cutting deep,
But nobody could witness the blood I leaked.

She was one of them, the figure in the camp,
Dark-eyed with secrets, hands purple with pain,
A hiss that slithered through corridors,
Asiya, her name, a serpent masked as human.

I watched her round the children up in the kitchen,
Smell of smoke, tang of alcohol thick,
Kurdish men, Kurdish women,
A conspiracy of tongues, sharp as knives.

They sat there, night after night,
Hands tainted by drugs, drawing lines of treachery,
Whispering words impregnated with poison,
Each breath a pledge of unexecuted violence.

I wanted to be man enough to stand up and say,
But my voice was snuffed out, consumed whole,
By that smoke and the sting of vicious lies,
They threw me down, made me a ghost in my own skin.

My wife, a captive unfettered,
Deprived of the kitchen, the warmth of the home,
They then beat me, jeered at my pain,
And labeled me a criminal-what distorted my truth.

She wove a web, Asiya, as spiders do,
Pureness wrapped in threads of a lie,
A fabricated accusation to get free,
And so, soaked with pitch black, I go under.

They see not and hear not;
It's the blind carry the world's decay.
But I have lived and breathed it,
Felt its talons dig deep into my chest.

I still hear the echoes of laughter, of lies,
That haunt the corners of my mind,
A terror that clings, relentless as
A stain that water cannot wash away.

This was a camp meant to be a refuge, to be a haven,
Now it turned out to be a cage, bars unseen,
Filled with specters of violence,
And I, just another shadow, fading, unseen.

25. The Black Christian's Bread

The night-black hands touching the bread in Germany's aisle,
The venom spills, their faces contort, their hatred grows vile.
My black Christian hands—blemish of sin,
Filth to their eyes, upon their perfect skin.

But when the scarfed and bearded hands of another reach,
The same bread, the same aisle, there is no breach.
Their faces soften, like snow touched by a summer breeze,
While I am left with their hatred, their silent disease.

They whisper, they sneer, their gazes slice,
As if my touch alone could poison the price.
My fingers graze the crust of wheat,
Yet in their minds, I soil what they eat.

They have forgotten that their own hands once scarred the earth,
Tore souls like paper, crushed dreams at birth.
They write histories that erase my name,
Yet bind me still in shackles of blame.

Once, my ancestors bent over stolen fields,
Harvesting wheat they could never yield.
Whipped for hunger, for thirst, for need,
Their blood was spilled, their hands made to bleed.

Now, I stand in their polished stores,
And the chains are gone—but not the wars.
A victim of a double lynching, not by rope,
But in their eyes, their smirks, their disobedience.

I touch bread, just like they do,
It's not the loaf—it's my skin that marks me taboo.
The same flour, the same rise, the same crust,
Yet their hands are holy, and mine breed distrust.

Their hypocrisy burns like a torch,
Yet they pretend to see no scorch.
In their land of order, their land of peace,
They grant me glances that never cease.

In this labyrinth of twisted corridors, I stand alone,
My hands are clean, but their hearts are stone.
The bread they touch, they say, is pure,
But I know the truth—it's my skin they abhor.

Still, I lift the loaf, hold it high,
Break it open beneath their sky.
For every crumb, for every grain,
I reclaim the dignity they try to stain.

For my hands have toiled, my hands have prayed,
My hands have held the broken, the betrayed.
And if my skin offends their sight,
Then let it be their soul's own blight.

Let them choke on their fear, their fragile might,
While I taste my bread beneath God's light.

26. The Smell of Black Exile

My food-earth-born, seasoned by the kiss of the sun,
Yet here in these German camps, it is stigmatized by an abyss of foul smell.
"Unclean, unholy," the spittle of Muslim tongues hisses,
Words vomiting bile, as if there was no place for my culture to exist.

Exiled from the kitchen, where the fire once played,
By brown-skinned hands, by a mere look,
My heritage, my roots in this earth I stand on-
Claiming my food smells of decay in the toil.

Compelled to sit in the tight silence of my room,
I stir my pot, a prisoner in my self-made tomb.
The walls inch in with every breath that I make,
As if the steam of my food were a poisonous lake.

Their spiced lamb and their saffron rice, an aroma of blessing,
My food eaten by millions scorned in this place,
How can bread of life eaten throughout the nations
Become a symbol of filth to their accusing mind?

It is to the Germans—silent sentinels of this game,
Their cold eyes pronounce me guilty.
"Islamophobia," they chant with ice in their veins.
My black Christian hands pay the price, seal my wrist.

Irony oozes honey from a knife.
They speak to me of calmness in the souls stirring my strife.
I ask myself, how can earthly food offend,
When it is in the soil, at the end, that we are all tucked in?

Or is it not the stink of oppression that wafts through the air,
The smell of ignorance, the smell they wear?
For it's not my kinsman's food that stales these walls,
It is not their stomachs that are prejudiced but rather their hearts.

I am more than the meals I make.
It should not be their destiny to walk in my skin, in my culture.
The spice of my people is life's flavor.
But they cannot taste beyond the blade of their hatred.

27. Souls of Division

The souls of white folks, draped in sheets of hate,
Now they stand with jihadists, a new twist of fate.
Once, they lynched me with ropes and flames,
Now they lynch with words—new weapons, same games.

Liberals, left, BLM, and queer crusaders bold,
Once screaming freedom, now hearts cold.
Irony dances in the air like smoke from a fire,
They once burned crosses—now, with jihad they conspire.

Within the crescent shadows, now they have their call,
Join in the hate to see me fall.
Disgrace, acid rain burning my soul,
But I shall wear it like armor patched from the whole.

It's ironic, isn't it, how they claim the fight,
For freedom, for fairness, for every right,
But when it's my cross that they see in the light,
I am too black, too Christian to be in their sight.

Once, it was whips that cracked in the air,
Now it's their tongues, razor-sharp and bare.
They stand tall with the ones who call me "Negro"
They dig my grave with every lie they crave.

I stand between jihad and the liberal tide,
Both grind my dignity, from every side.
For the veil they wear is woven with scorn,
And the freedom they preach leaves my skin torn.

What irony it is, their "peace" is war,
Their freedom cries but another door
Leading to a world wherein my skin, my faith, my voice,
Is always the target of their double-edged choice.

But let them unite in hate's purity,
I'll stand strong, for it's never too late to be free.
I am the cross they cannot break,
The truth they dare not seize.

For I am born from the ashes of chains,
And I rise, unscathed, above their hurts.
Their souls, as shades, at night's release shall flee,
But mine unchanged shall blaze, like Truth, at morning be.

28. Names and Chains

You called me Negro, prostitute, criminal,
Thief, dirty, ugly, a hypopotamus in the hall.
You marked me an illegal alien, a stain,
In your Islamic, Hindu, and Western refrain.

When I went to your homes, to serve and sweat,
My African Christian skin became a target, a bet.
They raped me, enslaved me, played their cruel game,
Kept my hard-earned money, leaving me only the shame.

My monthly wage—a meager $100—deferred,
Paid for two months, though my labor was blurred.
When I asked for my dues, they called the police,
Framing me as a thief, my dignity stripped piece by piece.

They called me Negro, their insult of choice,
Echoed daily, like a broken voice.
These morons come to my African land,
And still, heinous racism fills their hands.

I'm a victim of brown-skinned Arabs, in my home and theirs,
Their hatred for my skin spreads everywhere.
When they flee to the Western world for refuge and peace,
Are enchained in chains of hate, a dark disease.

The liberals, feminists, lefties, tripping over one another,
To stand in cue with BLM, queers-one big happy camper.
But my black skin is where their unity parts,
For even in their brown, BLM, and white spaces, my heart still barters.

We black Christians are victims of crimes of inhumanity,
Inside the brotherhood of Muslims, Hindus, and the West.
Every step is a fight, every breath a strife,
But my black Christian soul stays a light.

29. Hypocrisy and Theft

You say your white and brown people do not steal,
Call black Christians thieves-quick to reveal.
But it is your hands reaching for lands and life;
You have stolen the earth where our history thrives.

You enslaved, lynched, and enchained our kin,
Raped our mothers, sisters with a Savage grin.
What you did-no theft, but a genocide,
A cruelty disguised beneath your pride.

You mock us and say we are stealing mobile phones,
And yet your legacy is built on stolen bones.
You desecrated our land, called it your own,
But your empire's built on a borrowed throne.

Just like the ones oppressing the untouchable caste,
You stole our sweat, our blood, a history vast.
You fly over to our lands for tourism and more,
But you make our children commodities to be explored.

You mock our love, you mock our ties,
Naming us names, filling the air with lies.
But flying to rape the young and meek,
Who are the criminals, who are the weak?

You corrupt our lands for your profit and gain,
You exploit our children, leaving only pain.
Under the banners of UN, UNICEF, WHO, you hide,
But your chameleon face can't mask the tide.

You named us prostitutes, criminals, and more,
But your hands are bloodied from wars you swore.
Your hypocrisy, like your father Gandhi,
Called us thieves yet stole our lands for free.

We don't believe in your white Jesus, Allah, Ram,
We don't need your white savior scam.
We are innocents, peace in our sight,
Our greed, our exploitations, never put right.

We don't believe in your criminal heads,
We know the truth behind all their dreads.
Your kings and queens whom you adorn,
Are not our innocents they pull us down.

So call as monkeys, untouchables, as you may
But we'll rise above your show.
We see through masks, your savage disguise,
We are strong, we are free, and we rise.

30. March for Black Jesus

March for black Jesus, and the world turns its back,
But raise a cry for brown Allah, and no freedoms lack.
In Europe's streets, where silence reigns,
Our voices are muffled, as if bound by chains.

We hold the Holy Bible, a book of light,
Yet are arrested, treated with spite.
But those who shout "Allahu Akbar" loud and clear,
Are praised, promoted, embraced without fear.

We are the black Christians, lost in between,
Caught in a world both cruel and obscene.
Whites and their brown allies join hands tight,
While we face prejudice, out of sight.

They glorify prayers that mask a darker deed,
But our faith, they cast out, let it bleed.
When we say "Jesus Christ," they call it hate,
But when violence calls, they hesitate.

The world cries for freedom, for equal right,
Yet silences us when we step into the light.
What is more lethal than killing a child,
More cruel than beheading those who speak wild?

You condemn us, call us names, all the same,
But Muslims, feminists, all get their claim.
They say "my body, my choice," then take a life,
Killing unborn children with the sharpest knife.

I fought for my child, to let him be free,
Yet they killed my Stanford, took him from me.
A vaccine more lethal than hate could be,
Yet I hold on, in my belief's decree.

Even Jesus, the Jew, could not save,
The millions lost, sent to the grave.
Yet I believe in His truth, love, and light,
A faith unbroken, even in the night.

Like Socrates, who spoke against the lies,
Both were persecuted, but they could not die.
Their words live on, against evil's tide,
And so does our march, though pushed aside.

They cannot save us, but still we march,
Under the weight of a cold, dark arch.
We speak for truth, for compassion, for light,
In a world that chooses to stay out of sight.

31. The Hypocrite's Theft

You say your white and brown hands don't steal,
But accuse black Christians, claim it's real.
You point fingers, call us thieves, in disdain,
Yet your own hands are stained by chains.

You stole lands, stole lives, stole souls,
You enslaved us, made whips your roles.
Raping our mothers, beating our kin,
You plundered, called it a win.

What you did was not just theft, but genocide,
Ravaging lands, stripping dignity's pride.
Just like the terrorists on October's day,
Or those who keep untouchables at bay.

They mock us, call us monkey, chimp, and worse,
But who truly carries the thief's curse?
You call us criminals, purse-stealers in your lore,
But your hands bled Africa to its core.

You fly to our lands with smiles and lies,
To exploit our girls, beneath clear skies.
You come as tourists, as workers for UN peace,
But your acts of lust never cease.

When black Christians love, you spew hate,
But you prey on our children, and call it fate.
Mr. and Mrs. Hypocrite, who will you deceive?
When the truth is what you can't conceive.

You corrupt our lands for your personal gain,
Exploiting our children, leaving only pain.
Using banners like UNICEF, you wear disguise,
But your deeds betray your lies.

You branded us as thieves, prostitutes, and scum,
But it's you who made our future numb.
You are no better than your father Gandhi,
Whose words were sweet but actions slimy.

We don't endorse your white Jesus, Gandhi, or Ram,
We see through the mask, the savior sham.
We are innocent, pure, humane, and strong,
But your exploitation has gone on too long.

Our kings, queens, and leaders, defiled by power,
Bribery, just like you, hour after hour.
But they are your blood, not our pride,
You share their greed, you cannot hide.

Then call us what you will, throw your names,
We know your lies, we see your games.
We, the Africans, proud and true,
Will rise despite all you do.

32. Dodgy Black

You call me dodgy black, a name full of spite,
You and your brown allies, with your far-right might,
Branded me as Negro, criminal, thief, and more,
As if my existence is something to abhor.

You mock my skin, call me hippopotamus, a hyena,
But when your colonial masters raped my mothers and daughters,
Lynched my brothers under a blood-red sky,
Where was your voice, your truth, your cry?

You point to me when I steal a purse,
But what should I call you, who made it worse?
You replaced lynching with humiliation's brand,
Whipping with words, and oppression at hand.

I am sandwiched between your far-left and far-right,
Just like the Jews, fighting for light.
You brought me as a slave, made me a thing,
Used my body, my soul to pull your string.

History remembers what your hands have done,
To my black cross, to the untouchables under the sun.
I stand with the Jews, the Gypsies, the Romas, and many more,
Even if they don't see the scars I bore.

You call me dodgy, a criminal to scorn,
But what are you, whoever left us torn?
Your crimes, your hypocrisy, guileful intrigue,
Have built a world of tattered dreams.

I am more than your labels, your words of hate,
I'm a survivor; I stand above my destiny.
I stand tall, not bowed or bent,
Against your bigotry, your malcontent.

Call me dodgy, thief, what you may,
But I see through your games, your play.
You're no better, white, brown, or blue,
History sees you, and we see through.

33. Judgment Day Awaits

I walk in Europe's shadow,
Whispers of white supremacy coil,
As dogs are unleashed,
Teeth bared they chase my black cross,
Every bark an ironic echo
In the silence of your white church—
Where even the shadow of me is not welcomed.

Cold shivers run down my bones,
The cruel gleeful dance, sadistic spins,
And I shudder under the weight
Of scornful history.
Your glee, a moaned refrain,
An old song sung to my skin,
Torn and rent through years behind.

You gloated at my weakness,
Taking homelessness and made it a circus,
Reduced my life to animal wails,
But I wear the wounds of my Christ,
My faith a shield against your ridicule,
For there shall be a Day of reckoning.
Where your sins will be put in court
Before the bar of my Saviour.

Jews, untouchables, Yazidis,
Gypsies, Romas—
We gather as proof of your crimes,
Our scars tell stories
Of thousands of years of hate.

Yet, here I am,
As you release your dog to bite,
Knowing I am innocent,
A victim of your ignorance.

I see you,
In your pathetic quest for dominance,
But still, I rise above your disdain,
Forgiving your blindness,
Just as Jesus forgave,
For the greater peace, the light of humanity,
We will stand together on that final day,
Transcending the shadows,
Our souls united in love.

34. Unmasking Global Human Rights Hypocrisy

We are two students, born from the fight,
Against a world that denies us our right.
We stepped into the MHRD¹⁰ halls,
But found only parasites behind those walls.

---

10. This is my personal experience with the Master of Human Rights and Democratization (Asia-Pacific) at Sydney University, 2011. It is fully funded by the EU. The MHRD group is a third-world academic mafia hiding its genocidal ideologies and practices behind the mask of human rights and democratization. It is just like any MHRD program across the globe. It is watering terrorist ideologies in the name of human rights and democratization. Death is celebrated in this degree, whereas life is persecuted. It is a global threat to life, love, liberty, light, honesty, truth, and morality-loving white western Christian, Jewish, and untouchable castes. The program is filled with anti-untouchables, anti-Jews, anti-blacks, anti-Christianity, anti-science, anti-freedom, anti-reason, anti-truth, and the anti-white western Christian world. Every coherent member of this group is a member of various Hindu, Islamic, Buddhist, and queer terrorist organizations. The MHRD program is full of lies, fraud, cheating, scams, chameleons, and parasites. Janus-faced group. For example, my youngest Gujarati Hindu Brahmin classmate was an active member of the Hindu terrorist organizations such as Rashtriya Swayamsevak Sangh (RSS), Vishva Hindu Parishad (VHP), Bajrang Dal, and the Bharatiya Janata Party (BJP), etc., but he was awarded the MHRD Scholarship to pursue an MHRD degree at the University of Sydney. Later on I came to know that his police officer father too was a member of the above Hindu terrorist organizations and was awarded an MHRD scholarship in the previous year. He and his father were close friends of MHRD program Jewish women leaders. The duos completed their MHRD degrees and became leaders of the global human rights program. This is the same case for Muslim students in this program across the globe. This is the violation of what John Rawls preached in his grand theory of justice. The irony is the program is headed by liberal Jewish women leaders, but beneficiaries are members of various Hindu, Islamic, Buddhist, Sikh, Jain, Parsee, western radical left, feminist, queer, BLM, liberal, and pro-abortionist terrorist groups. Jewish leaders are allies of these Hindu, Muslim, Buddhist, Sikh, Jain, Parsee, and queer communities. The program is known for its deep-rooted antisemitic ideologies and hatred of Jewish, white western Christians, untouchable castes, and African Christians. I have never seen the face of a Pakistani Muslim woman who came to study MHRD. She practices Sharia like any of my Muslim classmates. Practicing brutal caste, untouchability, Sharia, purity and impurities, tradition, culture, and religion are the criteria to get the MHRD scholarship and degree.

They speak of rights, of dignity, of truth,
But their hearts are cold, their words uncouth.
From brown-skinned Hindus, Muslims, to liberal allies,
Each hides behind a mask of polished lies.

You call us Negro, Untouchable, criminal, thief, with ease,
But who, truly, brings the world to its knees?
They glorify Gandhi, yet hide his hate,
For Africans, untouchables, sealed by fate.

Human rights, they say, but I see through,
It's just a cover for what they do.
They give scholarships, to exploit and steal,
Yet our pain, our truth, they refuse to feel.

From Jewish teachers to brown-skinned hands,
They unite to silence, to tighten the bands.
We unmasked their hypocrisy, their Janus-faced lies,
For we are truth, and we see through their eyes.

Long live the truth, even when it's cold,
For our voices are brave, unyielding, bold.

35. Nazis of Global Human Rights

We are two students, born from the fight,
Against a world that denies us our right.
We entered their halls, with hope in our chest,
Seeking justice, dignity, and the very best.

But what did we find? Not wisdom, not grace,
Only parasites wearing a scholar's face.
The MHRD[11] halls, built on deceit,
Where power and privilege always compete.

They stand at podiums, preaching with pride,
Yet in their hearts, oppression resides.
From brown-skinned Hindus, Muslims, to liberal kin,
All hiding behind a mask—polished, but thin.

"You are Negro, criminal, thief!" they claim,
But tell me, who set this world aflame?
Who built their empires on blood and stone?
Who carved their kingdoms from flesh and bone?

They call upon Gandhi, their sainted name,
But hide his hate, his casteist shame.

---

11. The Master of Human Rights and Democratization (Asia-Pacific) program has been a program for the children of Hitler, Manu, Gandhi, Mohammed, Muslim, Buddha, Sikh, Jain, and Parsee against my skin and the skin of the Jewish and white western Christian community. The cohort is full of lies, fraudulent members, scammers, casteists, supremacists, Aryans, Mullahs, antisemitics, anti-civilization, anti-Jesus Christ, anti-Jews, anti-Israel, anti-untouchables, anti-Yazidi, anti-truth, anti-morality, anti-life, love, liberty, and light. There is no place for freedom of expression and freedom of speaking the truth in this lie-based program.

Africans, untouchables—left to decay,
While statues rise in his glorified way.

They speak of rights, they call it just,
Yet their hands are stained with greed and lust.
Scholarships, policies—empty decrees,
A lure for the mind, a lock on the keys.

We watch as their charades unfold,
A tale of oppression, silent, cold.
From Jewish teachers to brown-skinned hands,
They form a circle, tightening the bands.

They censor, they silence, they cast us aside,
Drowning our voices in a rising tide.
But we stand firm, no mask to wear,
No lies to tell, no truth to spare.

Long live the truth, though it chills the bone,
For justice is fierce, and we walk alone.
But even in darkness, our voices ring,
Unyielding, fearless—let the truth sting.

36. The Ukrainian Refugee's Racism

O Ukrainian refugee[12], you fled the war, like me,
Seeking safety in Europe, trying to be free.
But you call me Negro, monkey, chimpanzee,
How do you justify your hate, your hypocrisy?

Your core ideology isn't what the world hears,
It's not the victimhood that draws tears.
It's the same racism your forefathers bred,
The same hatred that left my ancestors dead.

You mock my black Christian skin, call it out,
But your actions reveal what you're truly about.
Just like your Hindu, Muslim, Buddhist allies,
You dehumanize, while pretending to sympathize.

Your ancestors lynched, raped, enslaved my kin,
And now, you carry their sins within.
You fled to Europe, seeking peace,
But found time to hate, never to cease.

Your men are fighting Russia, far away,
Yet you find time to dehumanize each day.
You bed with Islamists in asylum's hall,
But call me names, make me feel small.

---

12. It is my personal experience with rampant racism of the Ukrainian refugees in the Czech Republic asylum camp in 2021. I, my six-year-old son Saviour, and my African wife Selamawit faced rampant racism from the state and civil society, Ukrainian, Russian, and Muslim refugees in this UNHCR camp. The UNHCR camp officials are known for their rampant racism against my Black skin. Our names are monkey, chimpanji, thief, and criminal in this camp and civil society. State-sponsored racism against Black Christians is deep-rooted in the Czech Republic.

When you shout "my land, my right,"
You forget my black skin is out of sight.
But I see through your lies, your games,
You're no different, still playing the same.

I love, I pray, I forgive, I see,
But you brand me, deny my dignity.
Even as I stretch out a hand, warm and kind,
You prohibit my son, leave us behind.

You let Jihadist children play beside,
But keep my 3-year-old son denied.
How can you live with such a mind,
So conflicted, so cruel, so unkind?

Your racism, your bias, it's all the same,
From Europe, Russia, under a different name.
Your gods, your Mussolini, your Hitler, they rise,
When my black Christian skin meets your eyes.

You are no different from those of the past,
Who chained, raped, and enslaved so vast.
Even though you are just like any Westerner,
I still pray for your peace, with love that lingers.

O Ukrainian, you fled from war's distress,
Yet you choose to mock, to oppress.
Even as I forgive, as I hope for your life,
I still see the truth, I see the strife.

Your core hasn't changed; it remains as dark,
Like history's shadow, a hateful mark.
But even as you cling to your ancestors' way,
I will stand tall, with love each day.

37. Abortion Is Genocide

I am a mother, a keeper of light,
Life begins within me, tender and bright.
A heartbeat flickers, a soul takes form,
A whisper of life, safe and warm.

O how the hen gathers her young with care,
Sheltering them from death's dark stare.
Yet so many today choose to destroy,
What should be cherished, our children, our joy.

Jesus spoke, "I knew you before the womb,"
But in this world, so many meet doom.
They argue life starts after birth's first cry,
But the spark begins when souls reside nigh.

"My body, my choice," they chant with pride,
But each heartbeat taken, something has died.
It's a genocide, a silent scream,
Millions lost from a broken dream.

I would face death to protect my own,
To nurture them, until they've grown.
For each life is precious, each breath a gift,
A child's presence, the soul's uplifting lift.

Let us cherish life, let babies be born,
For every life taken, our hearts are torn.
In the face of cruelty, I raise my voice,
A mother's love—the truest choice.

38. Abortion Is Terrorism

I am a mother, a keeper of light,
Life begins within me, tender and bright.
A heartbeat flickers, a soul takes form,
A whisper of life, safe and warm.
The bond begins before the first breath is drawn,
In the secret depths of night until the dawn.

O how the hen gathers her young with care,
Sheltering them from death's dark stare.
Yet so many today choose to destroy,
What should be cherished, our children, our joy.
They make a choice that breaks the soul,
Turning a blessing into a wound, a hole.

Jesus spoke, "I knew you before the womb,"
But in this world, so many meet doom.
They argue life starts after birth's first cry,
But the spark begins when souls reside nigh.
When the heart beats, a universe stirs,
A life begins long before the world occurs.

"My body, my choice," they chant with pride,
But each heartbeat taken, something has died.
It's a genocide, a silent scream,
Millions lost from a broken dream.
For every tear shed in quiet despair,
A promise is broken, life unfair.

I would face death to protect my own,
To nurture them, until they've grown.

For each life is precious, each breath a gift,
A child's presence, the soul's uplifting lift.
I see the beauty in each tiny hand,
The promise of hope in a life yet unplanned.

Let us cherish life, let babies be born,
For every life taken, our hearts are torn.
In the face of cruelty, I raise my voice,
A mother's love—the truest choice.
What have we become if we silence the weak?
If we turn away, too selfish to speak?

For life is not ours to destroy or command,
It is a gift from a higher hand.
Let us embrace the miracle, let love be our guide,
And walk beside those who need us to stand with pride.
For in the smallest heart, the greatest future lies,
A dream unspoken, a love that never dies.

39. A Tribute to the Unborn

To the millions who never drew breath,
Lost in silence, robbed of death.
In lands where beauty, perfume, and grace
Are held above life's simple embrace.

Mother, they prize streets, flowers, and pets,
Polished surfaces where no life upsets.
In this perfect world, they make a choice,
To silence the heartbeat, to hush the voice.

Yet you, my mother, with mud on your skin,
Held life sacred, through thick and thin.
You bore thirteen, with love as your creed,
In a world of sacrifice, not selfish need.

You are life's guardian, a royal hand,
In a world where children no longer stand.
Here, they call it freedom, a woman's right,
To deny a soul the gift of sight.

My heart bleeds for the lives left behind,
For innocence, abandoned, resigned.
Mother, I thank you for the gift you gave,
For cherishing life in a world so grave.

Each unborn spirit, silenced and still,
Is a whisper of life, a memory's fill.
May we one day learn to see their worth,
To cherish each child, a new soul's birth.

40. A Tribute to the Precious Life

To the millions who never drew breath,
Lost in silence, robbed even of death.
In lands where beauty, perfume, and grace
Are held above life's simplest embrace.

Mother, they prize the streets so clean,
Where no stray sorrow mars the scene.
Where polished floors and gardens bright
Are worth more than a heartbeat's right.

In this perfect world, they make a choice,
To silence the pulse, to hush the voice.
A right, they say, a woman's claim,
Yet life is lost, yet love is maimed.

But you, my mother, with mud on your skin,
Held life sacred, through thick and thin.
You bore thirteen, through fire and strife,
In a world that worships convenience, not life.

You fed us first, though hunger bit deep,
Cradled our cries, lulled us to sleep.
You bore the weight, you bore the pain,
Yet never once did love grow vain.

You are life's guardian, a royal hand,
In a world where children no longer stand.
Here, they call it freedom, a right so wide,
To end a soul before it's tried.

Yet my heart weeps for the lives left behind,
For innocence abandoned, for love resigned.
Each unborn spirit, silenced and still,
A whisper of life, an echo that chills.

One day may truth unveil its worth,
That each child lost was meant for birth.
May love break through this veil so thin,
And cherish the life that could have been.

41. Ode to Life and Loss in a Foreign Land

O my Christian mother, I've seen a world of polished gold,
Of streets so clean, of tales untold.
In Europe's cities, beauty's a rite,
Each flower groomed, every building bright.

Their perfumes linger like sweetened air,
Their parks, like art, precise and fair.
Men and women, with shining grace,
Walk as though life is a delicate lace.

Yet irony sings in this land so grand,
For they cherish their looks, yet not their hands.
With bodies gleaming, ageless, pure,
They cast away life they won't endure.

Mother, you bore eleven with humble pride,
Your hands were rough, yet love never died.
In royal halls, you wore no crown,
But a heart of gold, a love passed down.

While Western mothers prize their charms,
They lay aside the child in arms.
To keep their beauty, they choose to sever
The bond that nature made forever.

In spotless streets, they turn their face,
From life's small plea, from love's embrace.
For in a world so polished, clean,
Life's fragile spark goes unseen.

Irony's hand, oh, it plays so well,
For in this beauty, I see the knell—
Of mothers who choose their skin's soft glow
Over the life that waits to grow.

Mother, your clothes were worn, your days were long,
Yet you sang to us life's sweetest song.
Where wealth could tempt, you chose instead
To cradle each child, to break your bread.

And here they praise "my choice, my right,"
In halls adorned with gold and light.
Yet life lies silent, love unseen,
In lands so grand, in places clean.

Mother, you taught me to cherish breath,
In a world that dances close to death.
And as I walk these streets so grand,
I hold your love in my humbled hand.

42. Royal Blood and Colonial Chains

My forefathers[13], they bowed to greet,
Your kings and queens with a measured beat.
Emperor Yohannes, crowned and proud,
Grandfather Bezabih, standing tall in a shroud.

Once, kneeled your men,
In heads bowed, in enforced submission.
But now when you speak of my blood,
It corrupted, disgraced, dragged through the mud.

In your halls of gold, they bend the knee to the throne,
But behind closed doors, they slay us alone.
For in words, my blood unhappy fates,
Become the bedtime fairy tales you create.

"Negro," "thief," "ugly and base,"
These names you hurl without a trace
Of the respect you feigned long ago,
A mask you wore, now on full show.

---

13. The poem is narrated by HRH Selamawit Hailu Bezabih and penned by Suryaraju Mattimalla. She is an imperial royal family member of His Royal Highness Emperor Yoahnnes IV and an exiled artist from Ethiopia. She is a great granddaughter of His Royal Highness Emperor Yohanes IV. Yohannes IV was Emperor of Ethiopia from 1871 to his death in 1889 at the Battle of Gallabat and King of Tigray from 1869 to 1871. She is an immediate granddaughter of His Excellency Dejazamtch Negusse Bezabih. H.E. Dejazamtch Negusse Bezabih is a hero of the 1943 Woyane rebellion in Tigray and is considered a father figure of the Ethiopian nation. Her second son, Stanford Suryaraju Mattimalla, was killed by forceful vaccination by a neo-Nazi German gynecologist in Germany. She lives with her six-year-old son Saviour Suryaraju Mattimalla and Indian husband Suryaraju Mattimalla.

Your gilded robes may claim the throne,
But who brought slaves, who threw the stone?
Your hands stained red from bygone days,
While pointing fingers in shameful ways.

Does she know that this pride
Is deeper than the hate she has tied?
For though you bow, you sneer in kind,
With words that seek to chain my mind.

Your monuments that stand, tall and grand,
Are built on the bones of a stolen land.
Yet my people's legacy survives,
Carved into the mountains, etched into our lives.

Whereas your pomp and shows you lavish on my forefathers' head,
You scorne their issue, ne'er do know
'Tis irony in your vaunt hypocrisy,
A past forgiven, and our present dead.

And so I stand, you scorn me,
A prince's seed, though black yet true.
For in my veins doth run a royal fire,
Not quenched by hate, nor tempered by desire.

So call me titles, and cast stone,
But I bear history dearly sewn.
Within the snare, mirror on the face,
Reflective image of your colonial shame.

With every insult, I stand tall,
A witness to the rise and fall—
Of those who wore respect like masks,
Yet failed in empathy's simplest tasks.

43. Echoes of Deceit and Resilience

In the shadow of deceit, your lies unfold,
A nation's heart, corrupted, bought and sold.
South Africa, a canvas marred by stains,
Where oil-laced hands guide the twisted reins.

You bow to kingdoms drenched in blood and gold,
With hearts of venom, warm and bitter cold.
You speak of justice, yet your words betray,
For in your veins, the poison will not stay.

Can you not see the scars of ancient cries,
The Holocaust's dark shadow in your eyes?
October 7's blood on foreign sand—
Our Christian hands still tremble, cannot stand.

You stand with veils and beards to cast the blame,
But it's your own soul lost in the flame.
The cries of maids, of daughters torn apart,
Echo the silence of a fractured heart.

Nelson Mandela, once a beacon bright,
Now a shadow in the blinding light.
Did he not, too, dance in the blood-stained rain,
While his children perished in the same dark strain?

And Gandhi's words, once held so pure,
Now haunt the skin of those who must endure.
For leaders rise in greed and shattered trust,
Their hearts of gold are turning into rust.

But we, the children of the sun's last gleam,
Stand with Israel, united, strong, and keen.
Your lies, your hatred—fail to make us fall,
For in our truth, we rise and stand tall.

44. Shadows of the Refugee Convention

The West, once a haven of hope and light,
Has dimmed beneath shadows, engulfed in night.
Through gates swung wide by compassionate hands,
Flowed tides of ideologies from foreign lands.

Through the Refugee Convention of '48,
Came a flood that reshaped the Western state.
Legal and illegal, in droves they came,
Bringing histories of cruelty, and ways of shame.

Asian and African spaces, vast and old,
Carried stories both brutal and cold.
But here, in the cradle of reason and right,
They brought darkness, eclipsing the light.

Nazis replaced by migrations anew,
Threatening Jews and Gypsies, black Christians too.
The sacred ideals of freedom and peace,
Now struggle for air, their grip to release.

Scientific thought that once soared, divine,
Struggles against gainst gains in decline.
Decency fails, and moral values fade,
Imported shadows cast a deepening shade.

The West, which shone a light like beacons bright or the glow of a safe harbor in the night,
Struggles with demons it did not recognize.
Cultures clash with victims and hosts,
Ideals resisted, weakened at the most.

Will the spirit of progress resume its fight,
Or shall chaos engulf what reason obtained?
Shall the light be kept through the black night?
Or dimmed by the weight of imported blight?

O West, your heart is noble, but blind,
To the creeping erosion of humankind.
Your compassion, though vast, must also be wise,
Lest your sanctuary crumble before your eyes.

Rise again, O beacon of thought,
Guard your virtues, hard-earned and fought.
For the price of freedom, once paid in blood,
Should not be drowned in an ideological flood.

Let harmony guide, let balance hold sway,
To keep both your light and your heart's noble way.

45. Islamic Nails in the European Refugee Camps

In the UNHCR camps where hope should bloom,
A darkness festers, a shadow looms.
Cameras stand silent, capturing pain,
As innocence is shattered again and again.
Children fleeing war, seeking embrace,
Find terror anew in this supposed safe space.

Ten-year-old dreams are crushed to dust,
By hands of predators who betray the trust.
Airlifted from chaos, now the harbingers of fear,
Afghans, Pakistanis, Arabs drawing young ones near.
In places meant for play, Quran chants rise,
Playgrounds turned sacred under shadowed skies.

Namaz claims the fields, the laughter is gone,
For the children of the war-torn, there's no dawn.
Ukrainian girls, non-Muslim souls,
Falling prey to horrors that darkness controls.
Mothers lost to addiction, their cries unheard,
As terror takes root without a word.

I stood as a witness, my voice raised high,
Against the crimes that made innocence die.
But the officials turned away, their gaze like stone,
"Leave if you must," they said in a chilling tone.
In their silence, complicity took form,
Sanctioning acts that defy the norm.

The camps, a mirage of refuge and care,
Hide secrets too heavy for truth to bear.

When I spoke of the horrors, I was cast aside,
Branded as hateful, a racist in their eyes.
Yet the victims cry, their voices suppressed,
Their wounds a testimony to the unaddressed.

Muslim women watch with a smirk,
As their men leave humanity in the murk.
The world remains blind, its conscience asleep,
While the camps house horrors that run so deep.
This is no refuge; it's a breeding ground,
For crimes that in silence, the West has bound.

Oh Europe, oh West, where is your soul?
How can you ignore the price of this toll?
Stand against darkness, let justice rise,
For the children who live with shattered skies.

46. European Complicity in Antisemitic Shadows

In the heart of Europe, shadows linger still,
Where once Nazis ruled, their echoes chill.
States and societies, their masks now refined,
Yet the hatred for Jews remains aligned.
From flags unfurled to silent glares,
The prejudice persists, unspoken but bare.

A tiny minority, 0.2 percent they be,
Yet their lights shine brighter for the world to see.
Creators of knowledge, laureates of peace,
Their existence, a beacon, their spirit won't cease.
But against them stands a storm, fierce and vile,
A tsunami of hate that spans every mile.

The cries of Free Palestine mask the disdain,
For Jews and Israel, the target remains plain.
Thugs and mobs with terror ignite,
Spreading darkness, erasing the light.
BLM, Queer, and charity hands,
Join with those who threaten these lands.

Men, women, and children, all take their part,
Complicit in tearing the Jewish heart.
From State to citizen, the complicity spreads,
As antisemitic ideologies rear their heads.
Muslim millions bolster the rage,
Turning Europe into a perilous stage.

In asylum camps, the truth unfolds,
Officials siding with darkness untold.

Love Jihad creeps in disguise,
A calculated war under Western skies.
While Jews, black Christians, and gypsies hide,
Hunted and haunted with nowhere to abide.

Yet their spirit endures, unbroken and bright,
Defying the waves of hatred's blight.
Let us stand with the tiny, the brave,
Guardians of knowledge, the lives they gave.
John Rawls's truth, a guiding flame,
To reject injustice, to shatter blame.

For civilization thrives when it defends,
The ostracized, the weak, and transcends.
So let us rise, in truth, and declare,
We stand with Jews, their fight is our care.
For in their survival, humanity gleams,
A world of justice, of hopes, and dreams.

47. Nazis in the Free Palestine Tent

Beneath the Regensburg sky, a tent stood tall,
Fifteen days of slogans, their voices did call.
"Free Palestine!" the banners declared,
Yet the faces and truths, they left me ensnared.

Curious, I stepped into their fold,
Seeking dialogue, stories untold.
They spoke of Jews as destroyers of all,
Of Christians, children, queers, doomed to fall.
But their claims unraveled, frayed at the seam,
For Israel, I knew, was not as they deemed.

"Safe haven for LGBTQ, democracy's light,
Where rights are upheld, both day and night."
Yet their eyes blazed with anger, their tongues like fire,
Spinning tales to suit their desire.

These weren't the Germans I'd come to know,
Their roots interwoven, their stories did show.
Children of German women, Muslim men,
Yet raised by single mothers, no fatherly ken.
Born of two worlds, but their hearts shaped by one,
A loyalty forged in shadows of sun.

Queer Muslims[14] among them, their voices aligned,

---

14. One of the German-Muslim gays, born to a German woman and a Muslim father in Regensburg, showed me a sharp object to stab me in front of his German queer friends for showing the work of V. Gordon Childe, *What Happened in History?* page 281, which says, *"The establishment of the Orthodox Faith about 1106 sealed forever the fate of independent research in Islam."* German and Muslim gays humiliated Gordon Childe and other grand theorists and philosophers by saying, "Fuck your Gordon

Against a state where freedom is enshrined.
I held up Gordon Childe's truth in my hand,
The Father of Archeology's voice did demand:
"Orthodox faiths twist and divide,
History's lessons in plain sight reside."

But the tent's fervor grew deaf to my plea,
Bound by a narrative, blind they would be.
Their cause, a vessel for hatred and lies,
Their banners waved under darkened skies.

Oh, shadows of Regensburg, how far you stray,
From justice, from truth, from a brighter day.
What is freedom when it shackles the mind?
What is a cause when humanity's left behind?

The tent may stand, but its foundation shakes,
Built on hatred, its purpose breaks.
For truth is the beacon, unwavering, strong,
Guiding us back where we all belong.

Childe and other philosophers" for writing the history of Palestine land that belongs to Israel archeologically and historically and how the Arab world was destroyed by the origin of Islam in 1106. Gordon Childe, *What Happened in History* (Middlesex, England: Penguin, 1942), 281.

48. The Crescent Shadows the Cross

Birthed in 1948, the Refugee Convention spoke,
Of saving lives shattered by history's choke.
Meant to shelter Jews from Nazi wrath,
But the tides shifted, charting a darker path.

Two hundred million strong, through borders they streamed,
Radical voices where peace once gleamed.
European skies, once bright with the light,
Now veiled by shadows that blot out the night.

Girls in skirts, now draped in scarves,
Voices muffled, rights carved into halves.
Those who fought for freedom now kneel,
Under Sharia's cloak, they silently feel.

Love Jihad whispers in the western ear,
A seductive dance that erodes what's clear.
Khadijas wait for Mohammed's decree,
While democracy wilts like a dying tree.

Newborns chant verses from sacred tomes,
Taught to deny others' homes.
With innocence lost in Quranic schools,
Taught by iron fists, under stringent rules.

Universities falter, their truths suppressed,
Science is muted, its voice oppressed.
History's lessons, so easily ignored,
As Europe's values are viciously abhorred.

LGBTQ and BLM, hand in hand,
Fuel the fire, ignite the land.
Yet the flames burn life and truth,
Leaving behind a distorted youth.

Jews cower in homes, their voices hushed,
By a world where integrity's crushed.
Modern Nazis, cloaked as progressives, stand tall,
Antisemitism normalized in Europe's hall.

Refugee camps now teem with strife,
Raising children to scorn peaceful life.
A continent falls to its crafted plight,
Blinded by tolerance, stripped of its might.

Oh, Europe, how far you've strayed,
From peace, from light, from progress made.
The cross now bows to crescent's tide,
While justice, truth, and love subside.

This legacy, written in blood and pain,
Holds lessons for those who seek to regain,
A haven once safe, now fraught with fear,
Will Europe awaken before it's too near?

49. October 7 — The Modern Holocaust

I did not know, not until I read,
The texts that inscribed my fate in dread.
Book 54, Hadith 103, its chilling decree,
A rock, a tree, whispering: "Come, find the Jew, kill me."

I did not know my existence was a crime,
Etched in canon, decreed through time.
In the pages of the Quran, they found their creed,
To annihilate, enslave, and silence my seed.

I did not realize, until October's sun set,
That the Holocaust's shadow lingers yet.
Not just history, but a mandate revived,
From ancient words, where hatred thrived.

On that fateful seventh of October's flame,
The Quran's text bore its name.
Annihilation foretold, enacted with glee,
A modern-day horror for the world to see.

I understand now, as mobs chant my demise,
Their voices rising to blood-soaked skies.
Australia, Canada, France, and the West,
Echo the words of those who detest.

I understand when academia aligns,
Cambridge, Columbia, endorsing such crimes.
Their laurels bestowed on my killers' fame,
Teaching my death under intellectual names.

I did not know, until Hitler's hand,
Wrote the script for this murderous band.
"Remove them all," his Vienna cry,
Echoes today as I fight to survive.

I understand the Nazi's Aryan pride,
When swastikas mark where my ancestors died.
Graves defiled, my identity erased,
While the world stands complicit, its conscience displaced.

I did not know Exodus would decree,
My servitude bound, yet longing to be free.
Even scripture, in its divine breath,
Sealed my chains and scripted my death.

October 7, a day etched in pain,
A testament that hatred remains.
Yet here I stand, though the world conspires,
My spirit unbroken, my flame still inspires.

Let history note, though shadows may fall,
I will rise above them, I will outlast them all.

50. Greedy Jew: A Song of Defiance

O antisemitic tongues,
You hiss "Greedy Jew" with venomous intent,
Sending my ancestors to gas chambers,
To death camps, to cruel laboratories of hate.
But you cannot strangle the spirit of my people,
A spirit forged in resilience, shining brighter than your darkness.

Greedy Jew, you say,
To account for the unspeakable—
The rape of our daughters,
The destruction of our homes,
The erasing of our bodies from the book of life.
Yet my existence is not yours to distort.

You chant "Free Palestine,"
But your banners are daubed with my blood.
With cries of justice, you march,
Yet on the graves of my six million, you trample,
Their echoing cries muffled by your fists of denial.
O hypocrite, where now's thy justice for the annihilated?

But if I be greedy for life, for freedom, for love,
What am I to call you, destroyer of worlds?
You who build your towers upon the ruins of my spirit,
You who preach tolerance and foment the flames of hate.
What do you call it, this genocide,
This rape of a people's soul?

How I stand before you whole,
A Jew who loves, builds, and dreams,

And in that abyss of hate, you drown.
You say I am greedy because I hold on to hope,
Because my heart carries with it the wisdom of generations,
Because my survival is your greatest fear.

Oh, antisemitic world,
You can try to destroy me with words,
With weapons, with your twisted ideologies.
Let me tell you this: I will not disappear.
For every Jewish soul which your cruelty has destroyed,
A thousand of them rise-up, like eternal stars lighting the skies.

Call me greedy, if greed is clinging to life,
To love, to truth, to peace, to justice.
I am greedy for the world you seek to deny me,
And I will never let it go.

51. Sound of Liberation

I step on European soil, the weight of centuries left behind,
But am I truly free?
The chains of internalized oppression cling,
Forged by my African tormentors who ruled me,
Not with civilization, but with darkness,
Stripped of light, love, and life.

Even here, in the cradle of freedom,
I feel the echoes of my homeland.
In German streets, my African brothers
Carry the shadows of old cruelties.
They see African women as objects,
As if respect were a foreign language
They never learned to speak.

Liberation whispers to me,
In the freedom of women walking, unafraid,
In under-aged girls protected, cherished,
In the absence of force—no religion, no tradition,
No suffocating culture to silence individuality.

Africa, my birthplace,
Do you not see the gulf?
Here, life has meaning—
Dignity, rationality, peace, and love,
Concepts alien to the soil of my ancestors.
You gave me superstition and violence,
But Europe shows me humanity's potential.

Historians say Africa bore the first humans,
Yet what irony that we remain
Millions of years behind the "latecomers."
They built civilizations that guard dignity,
That value every life—human, animal, bird.
In my Africa, I am secondary,
Born to serve, to reproduce,
Not to dream, not to create,
Not to be seen as an equal.

O Africa, O Asia,
Why do you cling to your backwardness?
Why do you reject the light of modernity?
Your collective ideologies oppress individuality,
Your traditions stifle liberty and freedom.

Here in Europe, I see a better path.
Individuality blooms like a flower,
Freedom dances in the air,
Liberty stands tall, unbroken.
Let us abandon the chains of community,
Let us embrace the dignity of the individual.

O African, O Asian,
We can be better—we must be better.
Not by adopting the West's flaws—
Its abortions, drugs, or broken families—
But by learning its strengths.
Let us not remain a dodgy community,
Let us rise, as decent, civilized souls,
Like the Jews who, despite torment,
Shine as stars of wisdom and dignity.

52. The Muddy Piece of Hindu, Islamic, Antisemitic, UN Spaces...

I am born in shadows,
Where voices dissolve in the fog of oppression.
My name is written in the dust of caste,
In the scars of untouchable skin,
In the cries of Yazidi captives,
In the tears of Jewish children in desecrated lands.

The chains of silence stretch across continents,
Forged in the fires of religion and race.
Hindutva chants echo in India's temples,
Purity tainted with the blood of my people.
In the Middle East, Yazidis are herded like cattle,
Their dignity shattered by hands drunk with power.

I watch my sisters,
Their bodies turned to battlegrounds,
In Islamic courts where justice is a distant dream,
In the shadows of Hindu ghettos
Where untouchables are burned for daring to love.
In Europe, my Jewish kin flee the torches
Of anti-Semitic mobs disguised as freedom fighters.

Where is salvation,
When gods are silent,
When nations look away?

The UN folds its arms,
Global councils whisper platitudes,
Their resolutions crumble into ash

While the innocent burn.
The West preaches progress,
Yet its hands are tied
To the complicity of neglect.

I am the lost child in France's alleys,
A twelve-year-old Jewish girl
Ripped apart by the claw of hate.
I am the untouchable bride,
My love a crime, my breath an affront.
I am the Yazidi woman,
Bound, sold, and silenced,
A prisoner of customs wearing God's mask.
But I am the wind's voice,
The mountain's echo.
My song runs across the iron bars of caste,
Across veils of religion,
Through the borders drawn by men.

You may burn my body,
But my ashes will rise,
My name etched in the stars.
For I am the chain you cannot break,
The silence you cannot contain.

53. The Unfreedom of the Untouchable

I walked 1400 kilometers,
With my pregnant wife and son, Saviour,
Through the streets of the Czech Republic and Germany,
To free Julian Assange.

My unborn Stanford cheered and danced,
For the freedom walk of his parents and brother.
Julian Assange is free now,
But my unborn Stanford was taken,
Killed for being a black child
In a German asylum clinic.

The paradox of freedom:
Julian walks free,
Yet my son's life was stolen,
Not by bars or chains,
But by a world blind to color and caste.

As we walked, they called us criminals,
Chimpanzees, monkeys, thieves.
Their judgment was a label,
A condemnation written in their eyes.
But God's Judgment Day is near,
And it will not be written by human hands.

You may insult me,
You may humiliate me for being a black Christian—
But I am a poet, an artist, a scholar,
For equality, equity, freedom, and civil liberties.

In your earthly judgment,
I stand unbroken, for my cause is pure.

In your ephemeral judgment,
I am not guilty, for my cause is pure.
Thus, the Madiga untouchable is unfree,
Yesterday, today, and forever.
We walk for the freedom of every jailed icon of truth,
But we, the untouchables, are shackled by the weight
Of history's chains, unbroken, unrelenting.

Freedom for Julian, yes,
But for the untouchables, the Jews, the Yazidis,
The black Christians, the gypsies—
The freedom walk never ends.
It is a walk against the brutality of caste,
The cruelty of antisemitism,
The violence of Islamism.

Let us walk for their freedom,
For the freedom of those who cannot walk,
For those still bound by invisible chains—
And let us free them,
As we continue our fight for liberty,
For every soul, and for truth.

54. The Agony of the Black

I did not know until I read,
Jeremiah 13:23, I am deemed a man of evil, bred.
"Can the Ethiopian change his skin?" it jeers,
Words that echo across the chasm of years.

I understand it now, carved in my bones,
Four hundred years of slavery, of silenced groans.
When they shackled my ancestors, bound in chains,
Stripped of names, humanity, and plains.

I understand it when my black mother wept,
Raped beneath the moonlight where justice slept.
When they tore my black wife from my embrace,
And ravaged her soul in an unholy place.

I understand it when they brutalized my daughters,
Their innocence drowned in history's waters.
When my black sisters screamed under hateful skies,
And my fathers hung as the crows' prize.

Colonized tears, a black body's grief,
Exploited, extinguished, like a withered leaf.
Through cotton fields, through blood-stained sands,
The agony of my people, written by foreign hands.

And yet, in Germany's cold, stoic halls,
A new betrayal rises, another call.
For crimes veiled in doctrine, under sacred guise,
Muslim fathers turn their daughters into cries.

Raped by kin, as Quranic texts endorse,
The cycle of cruelty runs its course.
The German State whispers of these truths in shame,
Yet allies itself to ideologies of the same.

Is there no end to this shared decay?
When will the world choose life's brighter way?
Must black tears mingle with another's plight,
While justice hides in the shadows of night?

I understand the pain, the loss, the scars,
The burden of hate beneath a thousand stars.
Yet, even in agony, I raise my voice,
To shatter the silence and reclaim my choice.

55. O Hyenas, We Are Not Your Prey

O Ethiopian and Eritrean men in foreign lands,
Why do you wield violence with your hands?
In the West, where freedom stands tall,
Why do you make your sisters crawl?

You turned us into prey in our homeland's strife,
Prostitutes beneath your animistic life.
Now in the West, where laws prevail,
You hunt us still, with tales of betrayal.

A lion on pigeons, a cobra in the grass,
Your eyes burn with desires beyond class.
You press upon us, uninvited, vile,
A stranger's lips forced into a guile.

Is this what you'd do to a Western girl?
Never, for you'd cower when justice unfurls.
For us, your sisters, though, there's no such dread,
You make us mere objects, and our souls are dead.

In crowded streets, in quiet halls,
Your savagery has a voice, an instinct calls.
Respect us, as you fear the foreign gaze,
And abandon these crude, despicable ways.

We are not your toys nor slaves of lust,
We demand dignity, respect, and trust.
Treat us as scholars, poets, minds to adore,
Not flames to be quenched in your fire.

Let decency flourish in the places of crime,
Let civility replace this history in grime.
O brothers, learn from this foreign light,
And cast away the shadows of the night.

We dream of a community, standing tall,
Unblemished by lies, respected by one and all.
Where men are known for their wisdom and grace,
And women walk free, with pride in their space..

O brothers, awaken your conscience today,
And let your barbaric instincts decay.
Respect your sisters, and you will see,
A brighter future, a legacy of dignity.

56. Stolen Identities, Stolen Souls

O Ethiopian, bearer of countless guises,
How long will your deception rise?
In foreign lands, you claim a lie,
"I am Eritrean," you loudly cry.

In asylum halls, your tales unfold,
With stolen names, your stories are sold.
A chameleon cloaked in shifting hues,
A parasite feeding, with nothing to lose.

You traffic in shadows, in goods unseen,
In lies so vast, they darken the sheen.
Hawala whispers, stolen bags in flight,
Your crimes are hidden in the dead of night.

Even under western skies so wide,
Your old ways follow, they never subside.
You cheat, you steal, you flee, you betray,
Leaving broken hearts along the way.

Branded goods vanish from airport halls,
Your hands are quick; your conscience stalls.
A citizen of the West by name alone,
Yet your actions betray what's truly shown.

You impregnate, abandon, and flee anew,
Wives and children left without a clue.
In your homeland, you return with greed,
A trail of destruction, your only creed.

Even education, the West's great light,
Cannot change your ways, or set them right.
What will it take to turn the tide,
For honesty to replace this pride?

O Ethiopian, arise above the shame,
Let truth and dignity shape your name.
Discard the lies, the theft, the fraud,
Put on the light, the path of God.

For no mask can hide a soul untrue,
And the world shall see the real you.
Make a change, grow, and mend,
Let this cycle of deceit end.

O Ethiopian, the time is near,
To cast away the shame you fear.
Let stolen identities fade from view,
And live a life that's honest and true.

57. O Hyenas of Asylum, Rise Above

O Ethiopian and Eritrean women, seekers of refuge,
Why sell the body for coins, a life of deluge?
Across Mediterranean waves, deserts vast,
You journey with dreams, but shadows are cast.

In the sanctuaries of Europe and the West,
You weave tales of asylum, yet honesty's suppressed.
Every story told, every truth bent,
A tapestry of lies, deceit's lament.

Why birth children for coins, welfare's snare?
With fathers unknown, lost in despair.
Each child a question, a name unsaid,
A lineage forgotten, a history dead.

This road you take, is it respect?
Or chains of stigma, shattered life?
Many dads, shattered bonds,
Dignity lost, love denied.

Let survival not be the only mantra,
Learn and rise, sow education's seed.
The books, not bodies, shall show the road,
To a better future, a hopeful abode.

You are chiseled by God in the best mold,
A vessel of strength, a story to be told.
Not for the markets nor welfare plans,
For visions, ambitions, and lofty dreams.

Leave behind the ways of a broken past,
The jungle of crimes, where darkness lasts.
Embrace the West not for mere respite,
but as a canvas to reshape your fate.

Let marriage stand on strong pillars,
Built on respect, wherein hearts belong.
Teach your children their worth, their name,
Rise with pride, not to carry shame.

For there morality blooms where truth gets roots,
Neither in lies nor fruitless pursuits.
O sisters, let your legacy be
A life of honor, lived courageously.

Raise not just children but a generation anew,
With purpose, with knowledge, and visions true.
From ashes of chaos, let civilization rise,
A beacon of light beneath foreign skies.

O women of Eritrea, Ethiopia, take heed,
Forge a path of dignity, a noble creed.
No more chains of survival's guise—
Stand tall, with pride, and claim the skies.

58. Africa's Hypocrisy Unveiled

O Ethiopia, you boast of ancient pride,
Of battles won and colonial tide defied.
"The unconquered," you loudly proclaim,
But where lies the truth beneath your name?

You claim a history untouched, pristine,
Yet your actions paint a different scene.
Why flee to lands of western might,
Chasing dreams in foreign light?

You run unto white skins for hand,
To get out of the aridity of your motherland.
Convenient marriages, thin disguise of love,
To weave new lives with threads from above.

In the lecture halls, where books should have their fill,
Your universities hardly exist.
No page is turned to seek wisdom desired,
While the young souls are dirt cheap and fired.

You claim to be Christian, ancient, chaste,
Yet cling to those ways no human soul should waste.
For what is faith without its heart inside,
When truth and love are ripped apart?

The refugee's mantle, a cloak you wear,
Exploiting asylum with hollow care.
Like others who carry medieval weight,
You bring old chains to the western gate.

You scorn the African name you bear,
Claiming Arab ties as though they care.
But this borrowed hue, this foreign trace,
Hides not the shame nor the disgrace.

Your daughters, your sisters, sold for gain,
In brothels bound by chains unseen.
A nation born from corruption's seed,
A narrative of greed and not noble deed.

Where flowers of lies have come into bloom,
May honesty blossom and with each word heal and resume.
Where reason, science, and light create,
Abandon the night and all its dark estate.

Ethiopia, break these chains of shame,
Construct a future that shall bear your name.
For pride is vain if its foundation lies,
Greatness stands upon honest guise.

Oh, Ethiopia, turn away this masquerade,
Let flowers of development bloom under your shade.
No more hypocrisy, no more disdain,
But let integrity run in your veins.

59. Song of Gratitude to the German Social Worker

O heart of kindness, German soul,
You lifted us up, made the broken whole.
In shadows of alien lands, where crimes festoon,
Your light of humanity became our moon.

Among the Hindu castes where my name was scorned—
Untouchable, unseeable, unapproachable, unshadowble, impure, dirty, ugly,
"Black crow, black pig, thief, criminal, monkey, chimpanzee in the Czech Republic"—
My identity torn.
In your German land, I found what I never knew,
A place where dignity's blossoms grew.

My skin, once shunned, now stands tall,
No longer walking carrion, walking carcass, walking corpse,
No longer a thrall.
From India's ghettos to Regensburg's grace,
You've shown what love looks like in every space.

In my home, I was a walking corpse,
Bound by untouchable, inhumane force.
But here, in Germany, under your care,
I found respect, equality rare.

My grief was a mountain when my son Stanford fell,
Killed by cruelty no words could quell.
Yet your shoulders bore the weight I carried,
As my child in your land was gently buried.

None in my homeland shared my pain, my unnamed baby honor killed,
They danced, they jeered, in heartless disdain.
But you stood by, in Christ's embrace,
Bringing solace to our shattered space.

To my Ethiopian wife and my little Saviour,
You extended kindness, a holy favor.
While the world sees aliens, you see souls,
Working tirelessly to make us whole.

O worker of light, tireless and true,
In a world of lies, you shine through.
Though some may tarnish your land's name,
Your actions bring honor, love, and fame.

Like Jesus who loved the sinner and lost,
You gave us hope, whatever the cost.
Though aliens may wound, your spirit stands,
A testament to love, with outstretched hands.

Forever indebted, we'll sing your song,
For in your shadows, we've grown strong.
Thank you, dear worker, for all you've done,
Your beautiful face warms the darkest sun.

60. To Charlie Hebdo: A Dedication

O Charlie Hebdo, voices bold,
In ink and laughter, truths were told.
You stood against the silent cries,
With satire sharp beneath the skies.

In every stroke, a challenge made,
To powers dark, to truths betrayed.
You dared to speak where others feared,
And in your words, the truth appeared.

For mocking gods and prophets wild,
For questioning the sacred, reviled,
You paid the price, your blood was spilled,
By hands that trembled, hate fulfilled.

Yet in the silence after fire,
Your spirit rose, a fierce empire.
For in your ink, we still can see
The fight for truth and liberty.

You spoke of prophets, flawed and frail,
Not as gods, but men who fail.
A mirror to the world, you held,
Of every truth that's been dispelled.

O martyrdom, what cruel price—
To die for words, for simple life.
For what was said, and what was drawn,
You gave your all, though right was wronged.

The world was shaken, but not broke,
For though you fell, the fire spoke.
In every tear, in every cry,
Your courage lives, it will not die.

Charlie Hebdo, your legacy lives on,
In every voice, in every song.
Though hate may come, and guns may fire,
Your words will rise, a fierce choir.

61. Ode to Zineb El Rhazoui

O Zineb, fearless in your fight,
For women's rights, for truth, for light.
Born where the shadows long have grown,
You chose the path, though all alone.

In lands where silence reigns supreme,
You broke the chains, you dared to dream.
A voice for those who cannot speak,
For justice, truth, for those who seek.

From Morocco's soil, you took your stand,
Against the chains that choke the land.
In secular hope, you found your creed,
For freedom's breath, for every need.

You wrote, you spoke, you held the pen,
To challenge gods, to free the men.
And in the face of tyranny's blade,
You stood unbowed, you were not swayed.

In "Life of Muhammad," you told the tale,
Of a prophet's truth, beyond the veil.
With ink as sharp as any sword,
You dared to speak the world's accord.

But for your words, for truth's embrace,
The world turned cold, you left your place.
Exiled and hunted, forced to flee,
A martyr now for liberty.

In Slovenia's refuge, you found a home,
But still you fight, you will not roam.
For in your heart, the fire still burns,
A passion fierce that always turns.

Your courage, Zineb, will not be swayed,
For you have shown the price you've paid.
In every threat, in every tear,
Your truth stands tall, it's crystal clear.

So let the world remember well,
The story of this truth to tell.
Zineb El Rhazoui, bold and true,
A hero to the brave and few

62. Ode to Samuel Paty

O historian, born in a land,
Where state and society lend a hand,
To crimes unspoken, truth erased,
And every soul in fear is placed.

How could you survive, so bold,
Speaking of truths that must be told,
Against the terror, dark and vile,
That slayed your peace, defiled your smile.

You stood for science, truth, and right,
But in their eyes, you were the fight,
A beacon of free thought and light,
Now silenced by a coward's might.

Beheaded, like the Jews before,
A victim of the same dark lore,
The knife that cut, the hands that cheered,
Were the same that long had disappeared.

Is there a land, a place to stand,
Where truth is safe, where freedom's grand?
With three hundred million voices loud,
And crimes that hide behind the crowd.

Look at the UK, where crimes abound,
Even Africa, where blood runs down,
And France, your own, where death was crowned,
The state stood still, the world unwound.

In every corner, every street,
Islamic terror's steady beat,
Africa's crimes, so freely spread,
But European eyes stay dead.

You fought for peace, for truth, for life,
Against the hate, the endless strife,
But in the end, they took your light,
Beheaded in the dark of night.

Rest in peace, my fellow guide,
Your courage, in the shadows, hides,
The state, the media, they conspire,
To fuel the flames, to stoke the fire.

They love the crimes of foreign hands,
The blood that stains their sacred lands,
And yet, they stand, they cheer, they weep,
For those who cause the world to bleed.

O Samuel, your voice was loud,
A historian who stood unbowed,
But in the end, the world stood still,
And left you slain by hate's own will.

63. The Wounds of Untouchability & Racism: A Tale of Identity and Struggle

I[15] married a black-skinned untouchable,
Legally bound, our love unyielding,
But when I entered the Indian embassy,
With him by my side—my dark-skinned love—
The words of scorn greeted us:
"Did you not find an Indian girl to marry,
Instead of this Negro?" they spat.
In my homeland, in Addis Ababa,
I was called a "Negro" by those who should have known better,
By those who carry their hate in the guise of caste,
In the guise of color,
In the guise of difference.

I arrived in India, to a foreign land,
Only to be met with rejection,
Thrown aside like a thing unworthy,
My Ethiopian passport tossed from my hand,
A mere piece of paper,
A symbol of my identity,
Drenched in the ink of their disdain.

---

15. The poem is narrated by HRH Selamawit Hailu Bezabih and penned by Suryaraju Mattimalla. She is an imperial royal family member of His Royal Highness Emperor Yoahnnes IV and an exiled artist from Ethiopia. She is a great granddaughter of His Royal Highness Emperor Yohanes IV. Yohannes IV was Emperor of Ethiopia from 1871 to his death in 1889 at the Battle of Gallabat and King of Tigray from 1869 to 1871. She is an immediate granddaughter of His Excellency Dejazamtch Negusse Bezabih. H.E. Dejazamtch Negusse Bezabih is a hero of the 1943 Woyane rebellion in Tigray and is considered a father figure of the Ethiopian nation. Her second son, Stanford Suryaraju Mattimalla, was killed by forceful vaccination by a neo-Nazi German gynecologist in Germany. She lives with her six-year-old son Saviour Suryaraju Mattimalla and Indian husband Suryaraju Mattimalla.

Why? Because I am African,
Because my skin holds the warmth of the sun,
And my history holds the weight of centuries.

I am the double untouchable—
My husband's caste and my race,
Two marks that bind me to their eyes,
To their scorn, to their hatred.
My African skin, a crime in their gaze,
My features, an offense to their purview.
The light of my existence dimmed
By the shadow of their prejudice,
Even among the so-called untouchables,
Who practice their own brand of racism,
Who hold the same contempt in their hearts,
Despite their own history of being despised.

My son's features, checked and judged,
Like a royal child born to a foreign queen,
Like the cursed blood of African origin
Was a stain on his heritage,
Even in a land where caste is king,
Where race is a hierarchy to be climbed,
A ladder to be climbed by any means—
Even through the disregard of humanity.

I left India, but I did not escape.
The same eyes, the same words,
Followed me to Europe,
To the land of supposed equality,
Where the mask of racism wore a different face,
Where Indo-European tribal hate
Manifested in the same way,
A hatred wrapped in the cloak of ideology.

I understand now,
Why Europeans call themselves the origin of India,
Why Indians see Europeans as their equal,
Why both stand against the black body,

Against the African soul.
Indo-European racism is deep,
It is in their blood, their bones,
Their ideology, their identity.

They do not see me,
They see only their constructions of race,
Their wounds of colonial history,
Their need to dominate,
To diminish, to enslave.
They turn their eyes away from my skin,
From my ontology,
As if my existence is a threat to their superiority,
As if my blackness is an affront to their power.

Let the corrupt leaders of Africa see,
Let them cast off the chains of Indo-European thought,
Let us rise with dignity,
Let us cast aside the shadows of these foreign ideologies,
And embrace our true selves.
For we are not the reflections of their hate,
We are not the products of their scorn.
We are the children of the sun,
The children of the earth,
We are the history of this land,
And we will rise above their racism,
Above their tribal divisions,
Above their scars.
We will stand tall,
With self-respect, with dignity,
And let the world see us,
For we are not the untouchables,
We are the untouched.

64. The Weight of German Shadows

I sit on a four-seated bus,
a stranger in motion,
wrapped in silence,
watching love unfold freely before me.
Two German lovers kiss,
their lips entwined without fear,
without shame,
without the whisper of danger trailing their breath.

This is not India, where love is a crime.
Not Nepal, where hands must not touch.
Not an Islamic land, where love is veiled,
where women are walls and men are guards.
Here, desire walks without chains,
without the bloodied echoes of honor killings,
without a mob that carves its judgment into flesh.

But then, another joins—
a friend, slipping into the seat beside me,
smiling at the lovers, laughing in the shared air,
as if their world was untouched by pain.
They light cigarettes in a space meant for breath,
exhaling arrogance like a ritual,
letting the smoke coil around my face,
a silent invasion, a slow suffocation.

Their laughter curls sharper than the smoke—
not at their love, but at my skin,
at the way night has kissed me differently.
Three Indian students sit behind me,

their silence louder than the engine's roar.
Even they, who have seen the weight of hierarchy,
who have felt caste carve into their bones,
even they are stunned.

I cover my face, shielding my lungs,
shielding my dignity.
The friend sneers—
"Why are you hiding?"
"I am coughing," I whisper.
Their laughter rises,
a chorus of ignorance,
a melody I have heard before.

They leave at the next stop,
their shadows lingering longer than their presence.
Racism does not die with their exit.
It lingers in the echoes of their breath,
in the spaces they claim,
in the teachings of their parents,
who carve the world into those who belong
and those who must be reminded they do not.

I have seen this before—
in the alleys of caste-ridden India,
where my skin marked me unworthy,
where dark Brahmins and fair Shudras alike
cast their cruelty in silence and slurs.
Here, in this foreign land,
in the laughter of these German youths,
I see the same sickness,
wearing a different name.

But I will not be them.
I will not let my wound fester into hate,
will not let their venom taint my blood.
The victims of history do not become its monsters—
we are stars, burning despite the darkness,
shining where they cannot.

Let them hold their superiority like a drug,
an illusion they inhale,
but I will remain, breathing truth.
Their laughter is fleeting,
their hate is dust,
but I—
I am forever.

65. White Western Christian Streets of Silence

They built the roads, the stations bright,
promised order, promised light.
Yet shadows gather, thick and wide,
where law once stood, but now just hides.

The streets once safe, the squares once free,
now ruled by those who make them bleed.
Hands unseen, yet power known,
they strip the city to the bone.

Whispers hush when footsteps near,
justice crippled, bound by fear.
Laws are ink, but fists command,
the rulers here don't wear the brand.

Once, a child could walk these ways,
laughing in the summer haze.
Now the air is sharp with dread,
mothers call their sons to bed.

Ganglords sit where leaders stood,
twisting fate with chains and hoods.
The ones who speak, the ones who fight,
soon vanish into endless night.

A kingdom stolen, a city betrayed,
by those who move in deals, not trade.
They wear no crowns, yet own the land,
a silent rule, a tightened hand.

The people kneel, not by their choice,
their cries suppressed, without a voice.
And those who swore to keep them safe
have closed their eyes, have lost their faith.

Where is the shield, where is the guard,
when streets fall dark, when life grows hard?
The ones in power shake no chains,
but sign their names in crimson stains.

Yet somewhere deep, a spark remains,
a fire sleeping in the veins.
The day will come when walls will break,
when silent hearts will rise awake.

And those who think they'll always reign,
will learn that power breeds its bane.
For cities turn, and empires fall,
when truth returns to claim it all.

66. Silent Screams in the White Western Christian Streets

The city hums with neon glow,
but shadows slither where whispers grow.
Footsteps echo, heavy, tight,
under flickering amber light.

A hand that grazes, a breath too near,
a stare that strips, a word unclear.
She shrinks, she stiffens, she knows the game—
a world that shields the ones to blame.

The bus jerks forward, iron cage,
where silence seals unspoken rage.
Eyes divert, they do not see,
the horror draped in apathy.

A crowded train, a narrow street,
where dignity and terror meet.
A touch unwanted, firm, obscene,
yet faces turn—a silent screen.

The law stands tall in printed lines,
but bends, but breaks, but twists with time.
What is justice, what is truth,
when victims drown in shame's own noose?

The men who leer, the hands that grope,
their laughter drips with stolen hope.
She walks alone, she clutches tight,
her keys, her phone, her will to fight.

Each breath she takes, a quiet plea,
to make it home, to still be free.
Yet in the courts, behind closed doors,
her pain is weighed, ignored once more.

They ask her why she walked so late,
why she dared to challenge fate.
They tell her hush, don't make a scene—
this world is theirs, this street obscene.

But hush won't work, and shame won't stay,
for fire builds in light of day.
She walks the streets, a battlefield,
where justice begs, yet wounds won't heal.

Still, she rises, still she roars,
carving paths, unchaining doors.
For though the world may turn away,
her fire burns—she'll make them stay.

The city hums, but now it knows,
her silent screams will only grow.
One voice, then two, then thousands more—
until the chains are heard no more.

67. Forbidden Voices in the White Western Liberal Spaces

In the heart of silence, truth is chained,
Whispers swallowed, voices strained.
Behind the walls of asylum camps,
Where fear and lies cast shadowed stamps,
The truth is banned, it cannot speak,
For truth, they say, makes hearts too weak.

In corridors where laws once stood,
Now silence reigns, misunderstood.
A German official, calm, sincere,
Said truth will hurt, so do not fear.
Yet truth alone could break the chain,
But no one dares to voice the pain.

The liberal veil, the left-wing mask,
Hides the shadows in their task—
To shield the lies, protect the sin,
While truth is lost and buried in.
BLM, refugees, and queer,
Their alliances built on silent fear.

The politics of past remain,
Their roots entwined in ancient pain.
From Holocaust to Palestine's cry,
The mask of progress makes us sigh.
For deep beneath, unchanged, unbowed,
The persecution's still allowed.

The Jews, the Gypsies, Christians dark,
Each one a target, a lingering mark.
As ideologies wear false grace,
Their hatred hides behind a face.
The right, the left, both play the game,
But at their core, it's all the same.

The truth that aches, the truth that fights,
Is crushed beneath their softened lights.
So silence grows, and lies take flight,
In Germany, the day feels night.

But in the dark, a whisper calls,
The truth will rise, it will not fall.
No mask can hold the light at bay,
For truth, one day, will find its way.

68. Islamic Nails in the European UNHCR Camp

They promised shelter, a place to breathe,
a land of safety, a space to grieve.
Yet walls don't guard, nor doors protect,
where monsters lurk with no regret.

Her steps were light, her voice was kind,
hope still flickered in her mind.
But in the alleys, in the halls,
she[16] felt the weight of unseen walls.

Hands unbidden, voices crude,
a world of hunger, dark and lewd.
Eyes that stalked, lips that sneered,
a cage of fear, just as she feared.

Where was justice? Where was law?
Why did silence mask the flaw?
They turned their heads, they let it be,
whispers swallowed dignity.

She cried at night, but not too loud,
for fear would gather in a crowd.
No hands to hold, no words to heal,
only shame they forced to feel.

I saw her break, I saw her hide,
a soul once bright, now cast aside.

---

16. A Ukrainian minor girl was sexually abused by the airlifted Afghan men in the Czech Republic UNHCR asylum camp.

No safe embrace, no space to mend,
just time that bent but would not end.

The papers lie, the rules deceive,
they only help the ones who grieve
with silent lips and downcast eyes,
never those who dare to rise.

But rise she did, though wounds still bled,
with whispered rage and tears unshed.
Not a victim, not a ghost,
but someone who had suffered most.

One day they'll hear, one day they'll see,
the horrors carved in memory.
Not just a wife, not just a name,
but proof of how they stoked the flame.

And when she speaks, the world will shake,
for those who take, and take, and take.
A reckoning for all to hear,
the ones who thought they'd rule by fear.

And I will stand beside her then,
her shield, her voice, her strength again.
For silence dies, but truth will grow—
a fire in ashes, burning slow.

69. O Kunta Kinte, Chained in Time

O Kunta Kinte[17], shadowed son,
Bound in iron, stolen sun.
A name once sung beneath free skies,
Now muffled beneath the slaver's cries.

They took your tongue, they took your past,
Branded your flesh to make it last.
A human soul, reduced to trade,
Sold like cattle, whipped and flayed.

Chains like serpents coiled and tight,
Wrists that bled through endless night.
Feet that knew the jungle's grace,
Now dragged through dust in death's embrace.

They broke your body, stole your will,
Turned your dreams to something still.
They raped your mother, your sister's cries,
Echoed beneath plantation skies.

O Kunta Kinte, your name was lost,
A whispered ghost, a bitter cost.
But through the torment, through the chains,
Your blood still rose, your line remains.

Yet I, born far from your land,
Still wear my chains by unseen hand.
My tormentors do not sail,
They live beside me, chant and hail.

17. A character from *Roots: The Saga of an American Family*, a novel by Alex Haley.

Your kin found voice, found their right,
But I still crawl beneath their sight.
No whip, no noose, yet I remain,
A shadow carved in caste's domain.

Not four hundred, but six thousand years,
Blood and bones drowned in tears.
My touch is filth, my breath profane,
A walking corpse with a living name.

I am walled, I am ghettoed,
A whisper in the wind that echoes.
No Lincoln, no King, no war for me,
Only silence, eternity.

O Kunta Kinte, you died a slave,
Yet your children rose from the grave.
But I, untouchable, unfree,
Still wait for history to see me.

70. O Kizzy, Daughter of Chains

O Kizzy[18], daughter of chains,
Bound by flesh, marked by pain.
Tom Lea took what was never his,
Left you broken, left you his.
Your screams lost in the master's halls,
Blood-stained echoes on cracked white walls.

They called it law, they called it fate,
They wrote your sorrow in ledgers of hate.
A womb enslaved, a body defiled,
The cries of a mother, the tears of a child.

Yet time turned, the shackles fell,
The slaver's house now an empty shell.
No Tom Lea to own your breath,
No master's whip, no branded death.

But tell me, Kizzy, do you hear?
Across the seas, through time so near—
Sisters who still bear your cries,
Daughters trapped in unseen ties.

O Kizzy, they chain my kin,
Not in iron, but in skin.
Not in markets, not in fields,
But in caste that never yields.

A girl born in the shadowed dust,
Her touch defiled, her name unjust.

18. A character from *Roots: The Saga of an American Family*, a novel by Alex Haley.

Not four hundred, but six thousand years,
Of silence wrapped in hidden fears.

No chains rattle, yet she is owned,
No master calls, yet she is thrown.
A temple door shuts in her face,
A street runs red with her disgrace.

She is untouchable, unfree,
A shadow in democracy.
No saviors rise, no war is fought,
Only fire where justice rots.

O Kizzy, time let you go,
But left my sisters in the throes
Of hands that tear, of tongues that lie,
Of men who kill and call it right.

Your chains were rust, mine are air,
Yet both were born in the world unfair.
You were freed, but tell me true,
Who will break the chains I knew?

71. Gratitude Song for Elder Henry and Elder Connor

In the quiet halls of an asylum home,
where sorrow lingers and shadows roam,
you came with prayers, voices bright,
bearing love, a sacred light.

You knelt beside my shattered soul,
held the grief I could not control.
My son, my Stanford, torn away,
by hands that claimed to heal, yet slay.

The needle struck—a whispered lie,
a promise made, but doomed to die.
A mother's womb, a silent cry,
a heartbeat stilled beneath the sky.

Yet when the world turned blind and cold,
when truth was buried, stories sold,
you stood beside us, heads bowed low,
where German preachers feared to go.

You walked the path to Stanford's grave,
where winds of sorrow moan and wave.
You spoke his name, you sang your hymn,
as if his soul still lived within.

No German pastor, no solemn rite,
yet you brought prayers in the dead of night.
You stood where justice dared not tread,
where only silence mourned our dead.

And when my hands, once full, felt bare,
you held them both in faithful prayer.
You blessed my wife, my child, my pain,
like gentle mercy in the rain.

Oh, Elders, messengers of grace,
you brought Christ's love into this place.
Not bound by color, caste, or creed,
but healing wounds where hearts still bleed.

For every word, for every tear,
for every time you ventured near—
I thank you not just once, but ever,
your kindness time will not sever.

So may your steps be ever blessed,
your path in light, your souls at rest.
And may your prayers, so freely given,
rise with Stanford's, high in heaven.

72. The Shadows of Saree and Scarf

O, woven shadows, symbols of the past,
Saree, scarf, your threads are cast,
In blood-stained looms, where life is sold,
In twisted rituals, both young and old.

Born to please, but never to thrive,
A shroud for souls, so cold, so deprived.
In your folds, a brutal tale untold,
Of lives erased, of hearts grown cold.

You are the echo of ancient cries,
Where love and light could never rise.
A slave to custom, bound by chains,
Your beauty lures, yet only feigns.

In Europe's glow, you shine so bright,
But beneath, you choke the flame of light.
For how can they who kill unborn dreams,
See the horrors wrapped in your seams?

You've become the thing they never see,
A symbol of life without dignity,
No education, no talent, no spark,
Just shadows that dwell in a world so dark.

Look, O Saree, O Scarf, at the free,
At those who walk with no fear, no plea,
Naked in truth, they rule, they create,
While you, bound, inherit a darker fate.

You, agents of old and savage lore,
A legacy of pain, a closing door,
Your silence screams in the face of light,
Threat to the world that seeks what's right.

O Saree, O Scarf, your time has passed,
For humanity grows, and freedom lasts.
No longer will your shadows reign,
For we rise, and you fall in vain.

73. Redefining Home and Belonging

O West, you are my home, my place,
Though I stand apart in this space.
An alien to your lofty ideals,
Yet here, my heart in freedom feels.

In my land, might is the rule,
Where caste and untouchability school.
Deep-rooted crimes scar my skin,
And in their eyes, I am nothing within.

I walk unseen, untouchable, unspoken,
A walking corpse, in silence broken.
Amongst the crowds, I fade away,
Even here, where justice should stay.

But here, in your light, I spread my wings,
In your egalitarian air, my spirit sings.
For in my east, spaces freeze my breath,
While in your west, I escape from death.

I was born in a kingdom of lies,
Where my worth is measured by their eyes.
They hold their castes, their walls so high,
While I, untouchable, walk beneath the sky.

Here in your home, my name is known,
Where my human status is truly shown.
Racism, yes, but still a veil—
A lesser pain than what I hail.

For caste, for untouchability, is far worse,
A weight too heavy, a bitter curse.
It's not the hate of a distant past,
But a living hell that will forever last.

Thank you, O West, for your embrace,
For offering me a brighter place.
In your asylum, I found my grace,
A refuge from the shadows I faced.

And though the road was long and cold,
In your home, my story's told.
Here, I belong, in freedom's light,
Escaping the darkness of my fight.

May others like me find their way,
To the west, where justice holds sway.
For in your home, I've found my peace,
A place where caste and hate cease.

74. Whispers in the White Western Christian Spaces

The streets hum with stories untold,
footsteps quicken, hearts grow cold.
A shadow looms in the neon glare,
a silent plea hangs in the air.

Eyes scan corners, measured strides,
freedom stolen where fear resides.
Hands that brush, whispers that sting,
a world that silences what victims bring.

Not a gaze, but a hunting stare,
not a touch, but hands laid bare.
A bus seat, a train, a crowded street,
where the hunted and hunter meet.

They call it culture, call it fate,
blame the hour, blame the state.
Skirts too short, words too kind,
as if safety is a thing confined.

Laws are written, papers signed,
yet the hands still grope, the chains still bind.
Judges yawn, the cameras blink,
justice drowns in power's drink.

And yet she walks, still she stands,
fire burning in trembling hands.
A voice may crack, a scream may fade,
but truth won't cower, it won't evade.

To those who leer, who take, who harm,
know this storm will not stay calm.
For every stare that steals the night,
a thousand voices rise to fight.

One by one, we reclaim the street,
with louder steps and steadier feet.
No silence now, no fear, no shame,
you will hear us speak your name.

The streets will hum with stories bold,
of battles won, of hands that hold.
No whispered pleas, no stolen light—
only justice, fierce and bright.

75. A Song of Gratitude for Oscar Schmid

In the heart of Regensburg, where the shadow is long,
You always walked in light, while your heart was singing its song.
Among pain, tears, and fight,
You shone like a lighthouse, bright.

Dear Oscar, gentle Oscar,
You brought hope to days so dark.
As a legal mentor with a kind heart,
You serenaded our souls and soothed our minds.

You didn't see us by color or race,
But as people worthy of grace.
In a world that mostly looks away,
You stood up, and here you stay.

To the black cross and the untouchable heart,
You have loved us all from the very start.
When hate encompasses and the walls are so tall,
Your love and support just blast it all.

Your words drew out life; your actions-mentor truth,
Telling of that real humane person inside you never shows.
In a world where blind eyes turn,
You did open yours, seeing the lies..

Thank you, Oscar, for your kindness and care,
For showing us that love is always there.
For your heart that beats with justice and right,
For standing with us in our darkest night.

Thank you for the foreword, the words that inspired,
For the love which never wavered, never tired.
Words cannot say how much we want to thank,
For the love shown to us, breaking all ranks.

In a world that has forgotten to be kind,
You have etched in our hearts and minds.
A man, a human, with a heart so great,
Oscar Schmid, you show us-

That even in darkness, there is still light,
That love can conquer, and kindness takes flight.
We love you, Oscar, for all you have done,
For making our lives brighter, one by one..

76. Ode to the Boots on the Ground

Once, when no land bore our name,
when the winds carried whispers of loss,
they turned our prayers into ashes,
our voices into silence, our breath into dust.
Six million souls swallowed by fire,
while the world turned its gaze away.

But the earth remembers, the sky does not forget.
And from sorrow's ruins, Israel rose—
a home, a refuge, a shield against the tide.
Yet shadows of the past crept forth again,
and on the seventh of October, darkness returned,
cloaked in fire, armed with hate.

They came as they always have,
to silence the ink, to shatter the voice,
to burn the books yet unwritten,
to snuff out the minds yet to shine.
But we are not the wandering ghosts of history,
not the exiles without a name.
Boots on the ground.

No longer only hands that pen theories,
no longer only minds that forge ideas.
Now hands hold weapons to guard life itself,
and minds strategize not for art, but for survival.
If we had these boots in '39,
could we have broken the gas chambers' doors?
If we had these boots in '42,
could we have lifted six million from the flames?

Today, we do not ask—we act.
They strike, we rise.
They invade, we defend.
They weep for the killers,
we mourn the dreamers lost.

How many unborn Einsteins
vanished before their first equation?
How many poets, how many painters,
were stilled before the brush met canvas?
How many voices, how many visions,
were torn from the threads of time?

Yet still, we endure.
Still, we write.
Still, we build.
Still, we stand.

The past will not repeat itself.
Not with boots on the ground,
not with fire in our veins,
not with memory in our bones.

Rest, our fallen, beneath the olive trees.
Rest, our soldiers, within the soil you swore to save.
Rest, our thinkers, within the books yet to be written.

And as long as one candle burns,
as long as one star glows,
as long as one heart beats—
we are here.
And we will not fall.

Section II
Philosophy Poems

77. The Wounded Philosophy

O progressive minds—Hippasus and Bruno,
Ignaz Semmelweis, Nikolai Vavilov—
You dared to speak, to see beyond,
To challenge the dogma carved in stone.
For your truths, they silenced you,
For your wisdom, they met you with fire.

But what is time to the tyrants of power?
For in my land, in my blood, in my breath,
The same shadows stretch across centuries,
The same daggers are drawn against truth.
My unnamed child was butchered—
Not for theft, not for crime,
But for love, for daring to dream
Beyond the walls of caste and creed.

Every day, my people fall—
Poets, scholars, dreamers,
Their bodies defiled, their voices buried.
They are lynched, raped, dismembered—
Not for what they did,
But for who they are.

No untouchable dies a natural death,
Like those stolen from Africa's shores,
Like the chained and whipped in foreign lands.
No, our deaths are written in scripture,
In the ancient ink of purity and filth.
We are born to burn,

Branded before we take our first breath,
Maimed for life, from womb to grave.

O world, do you hear the cries?
Do you feel the weight of our wounds?
Our ontology is scarred, split, scorched,
Twisted in the heat of caste and untouchability,
Of race, of slavery, of supremacist hands,
Of purity and pollution—
A fire that no rain can quench.

But still, we speak.
Still, we rise.
Still, we write our pain into history,
So the future will know,
That though they tried to erase us,
We were here.

78. Ode to Philosopher John Rawls

Oh, father of justice, great architect of the mind,
In A Theory of Justice, your wisdom doth shine bright,
A beacon to the castaway,
To the untouchable, black Christian,
Jew, gypsy, roma,
And all voices silenced by the weight of oppression.

Thanks for creating one theory that speaks
For the socially shunned,
That beckons us to refuse elegance
When it dresses chains of despair,
To rise against beliefs
That would have us disappear
Into darkness and hate.

In your words, I find strength:
"Justice is the first virtue of social institutions,
As truth is of systems of thought."
Your truth tears down the elegant veneer,
Forcing us to rewrite or get rid of
That which enslaves,
However tastefully it may be draped.

You stood tall against a tide of racism,
Speaking for all creatures,
All life,
Against Ethiopian savagery,
European racism, Hindutva's scourge,
And an Islam that calls for stifling dissent.
In you, we see an advocate for the mute.

Your life was a reflection of your values,
Marrying an African woman artist,
Together for over forty years,
Raising inter-racial children,
A living example of the love you spoke of,
In stark contrast to impermanent relationships
Of those who would dump principles
For empty cravings.

We thank you for standing firm
In a world full of paradoxes,
For taking an uncompromising stance against racism,
For being concerned with acting justly,
For upholding individual integrity,
Where one human being's liberties are held dear,
Not to be traded for the common good.

"For every individual has a sanctity,
Based on justice, which even the law
Of universal welfare must not infringe."
Your voice rings out, a battle cry,
For the preservation of civil liberties,
To defend rights which no arbitrary will
Of a democracy, or social force,
Should tamper with. And I shall never forget
How much I owe your moral vision,
Your ethics, your colossal learning,
For in your writings, I get the strength
To fight for justice,
For dignity for all,
With a heart full of hope
And an indomitable spirit in the face of adversity.

79. To Philosopher Bertrand Russell, the Mind Unchained

O Russell, bearer of reason's flame,
you walked unbowed through faith's old game.
Where blind men whispered holy lies,
you tore the veil, unclosed the skies.

No godly throne could make you kneel,
no ancient creed could cloud your zeal.
Where fear-bound minds clutched to the past,
you asked the questions built to last.

You saw no wrathful hand above,
no mercy woven into love.
No heaven waiting, pearled and bright,
just endless dark beyond the night.

They built their faith on trembling ground,
on dogma's chains, on echoes round.
You stood apart, you stood alone,
a mind unruled, a thought full-grown.

Not swayed by threats of hellfire deep,
nor charmed by prayers the faithful keep.
For what is faith if not a chain,
a gilded cage, a phantom pain?

They preach of kindness, yet they burn,
they promise peace, yet never learn.
They curse the doubt, they damn the free,
and shackle minds to mystery.

But you, O Russell, voice of light,
held firm against the pious night.
You dared to speak, you dared to know,
you let the winds of reason blow.

No fearful god, no cosmic king,
no fate-bound souls, no angel's wing.
Just humankind, just thought and time,
a universe both vast and blind.

And in that void, you placed the mind,
a spark untamed, a path to find.
No need for gods, no need for fear,
for truth alone must guide us here.

So here we stand, in reason's name,
unbowed, unbroken, just the same.
Your words still burn, your voice still calls,
beyond the churches, past their walls.

A tribute now, a torch held high,
for thought unchained will never die.

80. Ode to Father of Modern Archaeology Gordon Childe

O British philosopher,
Father of modern archaeology,
I stand in gratitude for your truths,
For unearthing the shadows,
Penning the fate of faith,
In your words,
"The establishment of the Orthodox Faith,
Around 1106, sealed forever the fate
Of independent research in Islam."[19]
How bold, how rare in this age of silence,
When progressives fear to name
The danger lurking in veils of faith.

You cut a path through the rubble,
Using the pulse of carbon as proof,
That Palestine is connected to Israel's soul,
Its pages inscribed in stone,
A witness to the past,
But you proved how Islam
Sowed the seeds of violence,
Shutting out the light,
Suffocating the flame that burned for humanity.
Grateful to illuminate the chains of the past
Grateful for your imagery of the slavery arc cruel
From Greek shores to the dark mart of Delos
Where the souls of Ethiopia cried

---

19. Gordon Childe, *What Happened in History* (Middlesex, England: Penguin, 1942), 281.

In a mute language of pain
Voices lost to time.

You grasped the dawn of Christianity,
A poor Jewish sect born in hope,
Eyes cast towards a Messiah,
Touting love and resurrection,
Appeal endless,
In total contrast to the poison
Flashed out by those dogmas of Hindu and Islamic minds,
Grafting poisonous words onto compassion,
Attacking the untouchables, the Jews,
And all free thinkers who dared breathe.

Thanks, O father of archaeology,
For your Marxist fixed gaze,
For standing with science,
For truths too oft masked in fear
In this day of shaking voices,
Liberal and left, feminist and far right,
Against ideologues' terror
That threaten to tear apart the very fabric of life.

Long live your pioneering work,
What Happened in History,
Beacon of truth,
Rallying cry for those who dare
Light up the dark corners,
Poison,
Reclaim humanity's narrative.

81. Ode to Philosopher Stephen Hawking

O Stephen, star that burned through endless night,
A mind unbound by earthly chains, a shining light—
Though body frail, your spirit soared beyond the skies,
A voyager of thought, where only brilliance flies.

In the silence of your stillness, your voice arose,
A symphony of wisdom, where the cosmos glows.
With black holes and the bends of time you dared to dream,
And spoke the truths of stars, unraveling their seam.

The universe, vast and incomprehensible to most,
Became your canvas, your poetry, your host.
Through equations sharp as light's own gleam,
You wove the fabric of the cosmos, stitch by stitch, supreme.

A mind unshackled by the chains of fate,
You carved your path through time, through space, through hate—
In a world of doubt, where many would succumb,
You pressed on, undeterred, the journey still undone.

Your body may have been broken, yet your mind soared high,
A testament to the indomitable, to the human spirit's sky.
You faced the void with courage, with humor, with grace,
For though you were bound, your thoughts held infinite space.

O Stephen, your legacy will never fade—
In every spark of curiosity, your soul's cascade.
The answers you sought, though distant and wide,
Have ignited fires in us, which no time can divide.

You taught us that limits are but illusions we create,
That perseverance transcends the bounds of fate.
You lived as an example of what it means to be free—
A mind unfettered, in pursuit of eternity.

So, let your theories echo in the halls of the stars,
A testament to a man who, despite all scars,
Showed us that greatness is not in the body we wear,
But in the vision we hold, in the wisdom we share.

82. Philosopher Paulo Freire's Pedagogy of the Oppressed

O Paulo Freire, philosopher of the downtrodden,
Your words are a beacon, a light unforgotten.
You, an African-Brazilian Christian sage,
Stood against the world's oppressive cage.
Where are the Hindu, Islamic, or Buddhist minds,
That birthed a soul who could uplift all kinds?
They produced death cultures, but you, Paulo, gave hope,
Taught the oppressed to cope.

From favelas to slums so bleak,
Where Western knowledge ignores the meek,
You saw the streets they labeled wrong with crime,
But you knew it was where mankind belonged.
O Paulo, your African heritage made you wise,
You knew the truths concealed behind Western lies.
From your exile, you let your voice be loud,
For those forgotten, those disallowed.

I too am in exile as you once were,
A black Christian lost in a world which wants
Us to be no more than monkeys, thieves and beasts,
Yet steals the treasures of our wit and feasts.
They don't allow me in their kitchens, it appears,
For I am a Christian and not on their edict.

But your works are studies they put to good use,
In their powerplay, in the stories they flog.
Grateful Freire you give voice,
A choice to the downtrod, the poor, another choice.

Your words a shield, a sword the truth,
To teach the world knowledge is proof.

83. O Maurice Halbwachs, Keeper of Memory

O Maurice Halbwachs, philosopher of time,
You whispered that memory binds the soul of a people,
That without remembrance, a group is lost,
Drifting, nameless, into the void.

And so, we remember.
We, the untouchables,
Marked by fire, chained in silence,
Carry the weight of our collective scars.

We breathe, but our breath is borrowed,
Taken from us by Hindu hands, Muslim blades,
Buddhist prayers, Sikh swords, Jain silence, Parsee walls.
They name us filth, but our only stain
Is the blood they have spilled.

Like the Jews, we know the taste of exile.
We bear our own Holocaust, our own October 7,
Yet no historian writes our names,
No court calls our suffering genocide.

We are walking carcasses,
Walking corpses,
Walking scars.
A wound that never closes,
A breath that never fills the lungs.

O world, look at us!
Look at the untouchable caste,
The most peaceful among men,

Who kill no beast, who spill no blood,
Yet are hunted like wild dogs,
Burned in the name of purity,
Raped in the name of caste.

Even as our mothers, sisters, daughters
Are dragged through the alleys of India, Nepal, Pakistan, Bangladesh
Even as their screams rise like smoke,
We do not strike back.
We carry pain with grace,
We cradle sorrow like a newborn child.

The black slave broke his chains,
Rose from his knees,
Took the throne of his oppressor's land.
But we
We remain shackled,
Not by steel, but by scripture,
Not by law, but by silence.

They tell us to forget.
To erase the fires, the lynchings, the rapes,
To walk forward as if the past is not a shadow,
As if history does not carve itself into our bones.

But, O Maurice Halbwachs, you knew the truth:
To forget is to die, to remember is to fight.
And so, we remember.

We will speak,
We will rise,
And in the ashes of our suffering,
We will carve a name for those
The world has tried to erase.

For we are more than scars.
We are memory.
We are survival.

84. Ode to Indian Philosopher Gnana Aloysius

O voice of the untamed truth,
author of *Nationalism Without a Nation in India*,
your words carve through the chains of caste,
unmasking the local tyrants
who drape themselves in freedom's cloth
while forging shackles for my skin.

Your book—a tempest in ink,
a mirror to my exile,
a gospel of the untouchable,
an anthem against the empire of lies.

I have walked through the ruins
of local configuration powers,
where honor is a dagger,
where my firstborn's breath was stolen
for daring to love across the lines
they painted in blood.

I have wandered through the colonial halls,
where my second son, Stanford,
was not a child, but an experiment,
a body to be frozen, labeled, discarded.
To them, he was not a son—
he was Negro, a number,
a whisper lost in the cold silence
of white indifference.

O philosopher who walks alone,
while your Dalit-bahujan allies

clutch their seats in power,
drunk on the same privilege
they once swore to shatter.
They wear the mask of revolution,
but wield the tools of the oppressor.

You are not like them.
You have never bowed to thrones,
never dined at the tables
where justice is auctioned.
You, who answered my letters,
not with silence, not with pride,
but with "Sorry for the delay."

Where feudal hearts refuse to bend,
you stood—humble, unwavering.
Even in death, you seek no altar,
no pyre to turn your body to ash.
"Once life is gone, what does it matter?"
you said, offering your form to science,
a lesson even in departure.

But O thinker of unyielding reason,
your Periyar, to me,
was no god.
He shattered idols, yes,
crushed temples beneath his feet,
yet at seventy, he took a wife of thirty—
was this revolution,
or the same hunger for youth
that plagues the icons of the past?

I do not walk by collective conscience,
I do not kneel before saints
who carried old sins in new hands.
Jotiba Phule, a Mahatma to many,
remained a Brahmin's servant
when he took their child as his own.
Ambedkar, bound by power's embrace,

was swallowed into the system
he once sought to burn.

And yet, you remain unchained,
a wealth of the universe,
a beacon like John Rawls,
teaching the untouchable to speak,
to write, to stand.
For that, I am grateful.

85. To Philosopher Slavoj Žižek, the Provocateur of Thought

O Žižek, wielder of paradox and fire,
you tear the mask of false desire.
Where others kneel in sacred light,
you find the ghost that haunts the night.

Not swayed by myths of peace and grace,
you see the mask upon the face.
They call him saint, they call him pure,
but history's hands are never sure.

Gandhi, carved in marble white,
his name a hymn, his deeds a blight?
A hunger strike, a holy stance,
yet power played its subtle dance.
Not bloodied boots, not steel and lead,
but gentle hands where violence spread.

And what of Buddha, silent, still?
A king of peace, yet poised to kill?
Not with the blade, not with the sword,
but with the weight of holy word.
To break desire, to kill the need,
is this not violence in its seed?

O Žižek, storm against the tide,
you laugh where others run and hide.
For where they see the tranquil shore,
you find the war that came before.

No truth is clean, no faith untouched,
no saintly hand that's never clutched.
The kindness clothed in robes of white
can often lead to blood at night.

So speak the words, let masks collapse,
no myths withstand your dialectic traps.
Expose the cracks, let thinkers see,
that truth is built on irony.

Not black, not white, not saint, not beast,
but history's ever-changing feast.
A thought disrupts, a theory bends,
and contradiction never ends.

To Žižek now, we raise the glass,
to those who question, those who ask.
For better lies within the doubt,
where thinkers turn the inside out.

86. Aimé Césaire's Thingification

O Aimé Césaire, thy words still ring,
Like iron striking iron—a sharp, unyielding sting.
They pierce through time, telephone-pole truths so real,
Echoing the cries of souls forced to kneel.

You spoke of thingification, the stripping of soul,
The trade of flesh, where power takes its toll.
Men reduced to numbers, women turned to slaves,
A history etched in unmarked graves.

Africans, once proud, now bartered for gold,
Their stories rewritten, their worth undersold.
By masters whose hearts turned colder than stone,
Empires were built on the bodies they owned.

In Hindu lands, another chain remains,
An untouchable's birth—a life of disdain.
A shadow in temples, a ghost in the street,
Deemed impure, from head to feet.

And the Muslims, who in conquest's name,
Made Yazidi daughters property, their bodies claimed.
Hidden in forests, sold in the night,
Turned into things, stripped of light.

Europe, too, cast Jews aside,
Their homes stolen, their dignity denied.
Boxcars of suffering, chimneys of ash,
A people reduced to dust in a flash.

And yet, I stand free in Africa's heart,
Where light still flickers, where chains fall apart.
Where rivers murmur ancestral songs,
Where our souls still know to whom they belong.

But in other lands, women remain bound,
By veils, by rules, by silence profound.
A world where honor is tied to chains,
Where freedom is whispered, yet never remains.

They are things from birth to death,
Their voices smothered, stolen breath.
O Aimé, you saw how darkness grew,
How power crushed, how silence knew.

Yet, even in chains, a fire survives,
A will to rise, to claim lost lives.
For thingification is but a game of the cruel,
But history bends, the oppressed overrule.

There's a voice, a song—in shackles, even,
A spirit unbroken, a heart still breathing.
The march is long, but the dawn will shine,
Where humanity thrives, where chains untwine.

87. Thingification of My Skin

O Aimé Césaire, thy words still ring:
They pierce through the ages-telephone-pole truths so real.
You spoke about thingification that lingers.
A chain, a shackle, clutched by colonial fingers.

Africans, now commodities to trade,
By the masters whose sympathy had decayed.
In Hindu lands, untouchables felt the same pains,
Bound by invisible caste-linked chains.

Muslims turned Yazidi women into goods,
Stripped of freedom, hidden in the woods.
Europe once made Jews things to discard,
Turned them into dust, broke their guard.

And yet, I am free in my Africa's heart,
Where light persists, where shadows depart.
But Muslim and Hindu women wear chains unseen,
Their freedom a dream, distant, serene.

They are things from birth to death, a life of bind,
Their freedom buried deep, where none can find.
Aimé, you have seen how darkness has crawled,
Where humanity stumbled, where hope bled.

Yet, there's light that fights against the dark.
A spirit unbroken, an eternal spark.
There's a voice, a song-in chains, even.
A will to be human, to right the wrong.

88. Cornel West's Philosophy Against Race

Cornel West, voice of the silenced,
You laid our wounds bare, with a defiant truth displayed.
You were the first to speak, to define,
The scars left on black Christian skin, like mine.
You said, "I am ontologically wounded, bruised by hate, "
Words which still resound, still navigate.

I too have felt a weight of disdain,
In Czech and German streets, the same pain.
They call me a monkey, thief, and negro even,
My skin is barred by their silent will.
They smile at Muslims, pass them by,
But at my sight, they bow their eyes.

I built the white man's world with blood and sweat,
Yet they continue to make me an enemy-a threat.
They use Black Lives Matter for a flag to wave,
But use our cause for exploitation and slavery in wage. Where were they, the browns and allies,
When my ancestors felt the chains and the lies?

Now they come, beneath Islamic veils,
With Hindu chants and human rights tales,
Taking spaces my hands built,
As history carries our collective guilt.
I see through the masks-the deception, the disguise-
Of Barack's smile or Kamala's rise.

They say "Ally," but I see it in their eyes,
They stand with power, they stand with lies.

Cornel, your words are my shield, my fight,
Against those who would steal our sparkle.

89. Franz Fanon's Brown Skins, White Masks

Let me re-write your book, O Frantz Fanon,
From black skins, white masks to brown skins, white masks.
For this is the truth, the reality, the now,
Of brown and Western liberals who have learned how
To stand tall with jihad and caste, to preach pure and impure,
To wear the masks of justice, yet keep the poor obscure.

They terrorize the black Christian, Jew, and untouchable,
In their alliance so strong, so unbreakable.
Your words, Frantz, still echo, still bleed,
But you did not see the full depth of the need.
You dehumanized my black Christian skin through your prose,
Because your Islamic lens sees what my truth exposes.

We do not share the same songs, the same path,
You spoke of freedom, yet wrapped it in wrath.
You worshipped death, while I cherish life,
I seek light, where you saw only strife.
Your words still linger, they still sting,
But I see the truth behind the mask you bring.

In Europe, where my black Christian soul is oppressed,
Your Muslim allies joined with my former slavers,
White masters who humiliate, degrade, and suppress.
They still keep me excluded, ostracized, alone,
Building walls with your words of stone.

Your book, born from a darkened place,
A mask that hides Islam's face.
I refute your Islamic views, your scorn,

For we are not alike, not even in pain.
We are not chameleons, quick-changing for ease,
We are founders, builders, whose strength never freeze.

From slavery days to now, we have stood tall,
Stronger than your masks, founded on all good.
I wear no white mask, no disguise, no guile,
I am proud, I am black, and I never go back in exile.
Your words, your mask, your ideology,
Can't extinguish the light shining from me.

90. Ode to Alex Haley

O Haley, son of chains and stars,
A voice that roared through time and scars.
You traced the footsteps, bound in pain,
And gave the lost their names again.

Kunta's cries in shackled night,
Still echo in the world's dim light.
But through your ink, through trembling lines,
A lineage rose, unchained in time.

Seven lives through blood and toil,
Roots deep-set in stolen soil.
Yet still they grew, still they climbed,
From the lash, from fate unkind.

O Haley, your kin broke free,
From slave to scholar, legacy.
America's soul, though torn and scarred,
Made room for dreams, though late and hard.

But look at me, at my torn skin,
My caste, my chains, where to begin?
No war was fought, no laws were made,
For the nameless ghosts in caste's cruel shade.

Your family walks with lifted heads,
Mine still crawl where silence treads.
Untouchable, unseeable,
Unspoken, unapproachable.

No hand to lift, no voice to break,
No freedom song for us to wake.
No Lincoln stood, no King arose,
To fight for those the world still throws.

O Haley, your land knew shame,
And burned the past to cleanse its name.
But my land bathes in blood-stained pride,
And keeps its chains still locked inside.

O Haley, your ink was light,
That carved a path from dark to bright.
But where's the scribe for me and mine,
Who writes of wounds that never shine?

Still, I stand, still, I write,
Carving truth in endless night.
For maybe words will one day be,
The roots of our own history.

Section III
Words Against the Blood and Iron
Policy of Hindus

91. Burn the Karma Theory

"Criminals and sinners will be reborn as untouchable caste people."
—Vishnu Smriti 44.9, Yajnavalkya 3.21.3, Āpastamba Dharmasūtra 2.1.2.6, Skanda Purana V.III.14–22

I did not know my crime,
not until their scriptures spelled it for me,
etched in verses older than my breath,
older than the sky that denied me its shade.
They tell me I was wicked once—
a thief, a liar, a sinner of untold sin,
and so, I am born to bear the weight of my past,
a body marked by a crime I cannot recall.

Untouchable. Unseeable.
Unapproachable. Unspeakable.
Even my shadow, a curse upon the earth.
I walk, yet they flinch.
I breathe, yet they recoil.
I exist, yet they wish me erased.

Let them bring their texts, their gods,
their scriptures of filth and fire.
Let them recite their hymns of hate,
chanting that my birth is my penance,
that my blood is tainted by sins unseen.

But I—
I am no sinner.
I am no stain upon this earth.

My crime is only that I was born.
My punishment is only that I live.

So let us burn the words that chain us.
Let us tear the pages that call us filth.
Let us rip the verses that paint us unworthy,
that shape us as walking carrions,
walking corpses, walking carcasses.

No god will claim me as his mistake.
No fate will bend me to its will.
No scripture will cage me in the sins of another.
I will not bow to a past I do not remember,
nor a future they have written in chains.

Let the fire rise,
let the embers dance.
Let us set ablaze the words that buried us alive,
and from the ashes,
let us carve our names anew.

92. Consuming Cow Dung, Urine

I did not realize why they killed me—
why they chased me from their temples,
why they burned my hands for touching their water,
why my breath in their streets was a crime,
why my love was filth,
why my presence was an omen of ruin.

I did not know—
not until I read their scriptures,
words carved in stone,
etched in the marrow of their faith:

"Eating food cooked by untouchables or in his house,
or his utensils, is prohibited and becomes purified
by consuming cow dung, urine, etc."
—Mahabharata 13.136.20-22, Brahma Purana 115.24, Manu Smriti 4.223, Angiras Samhita 1.4

I did not know that my touch
was poison upon their tongues.
That my hands, no matter how clean,
were dirtier than the hooves of their sacred beasts.
That my presence at their wells
could stain their water darker than their fears.

And so, they cleanse—
not with reason, not with mercy,
but with the filth of the cow.
A sip of urine to wash away my shadow.
A handful of dung to purify their trembling faith.

Yet they call me impure.
Yet they call me unclean.

What world is this,
where my humanity is filth
but their excrement is divine?
Where my love is defilement
but their hatred is sacred?
Where my hunger is a sin
but their violence is virtue?

Let them eat their dung,
let them drink their gods.
Let them kneel in the filth they call holy.
For I—
I will not bow.
I will not shrink before their fear.
I will not let their words make me lesser.

I am neither curse nor shadow.
I am neither dirt nor shame.
I am the fire they cannot quench,
the truth they cannot burn.
And no scripture,
no law,
no god,
will ever make me less than a man.

93. Jewish and Untouchable Carcasses

I did not realize—
why they hunted me across centuries,
why my breath was a crime,
why my existence was a curse carved in stone.

I did not know—
not until I read their scriptures,
words not whispered, but shouted in blood:

"The Judgment Hour will not begin
until you fight the Jew,
until a Jew will hide behind a rock or a tree,
and the rock or tree will say,
'O Muslim, O Slave of Allah,
here is a Jew behind me; come and kill him.'"
—Book 54, Hadith 103

And still, I did not realize—
why they spilled my blood for being untouchable,
why my shadow was filth,
why my love was a wound upon their pride,
why my hands, no matter how clean,
were dirtier than the feet of their gods.

Until I read:

"If a low caste intentionally touches a high-caste person,
then he or she is to be put to death,
& the Dwija (Twice-born caste)

is purified by consuming cow dung and urine."
—Vishnu Smriti 5.104, Angiras Samhita 1.39

And so, they cleanse—
not with justice, not with mercy,
but with the filth of the cow.
A sip of urine to wash away my touch.
A handful of dung to erase my breath.
Their hands washed in the blood of the cursed,
their faith purified by the bones of the condemned.

I see now—
history is written in our deaths,
scripture is inked in our suffering.
A thousand names, a million graves,
one story, one fate.

Jewish carcass. Untouchable carcass.
Names stripped from flesh,
bodies burned in pits,
bones lost to time.

What world is this—
where my prayers are dust
but their hatred is divine?
Where my birth is a sin
but their slaughter is sacred?
Where my hunger is filth
but their violence is purity?

Let them drown in their scriptures,
let them kneel before their own hate.
For I—
I will not bow.
I will not shrink before their god.
I will not let their words make me lesser.

I am neither curse nor shadow.
I am neither dirt nor shame.

I am the fire they cannot quench,
the truth they cannot burn.
And no scripture,
no law,
no god,
will ever make me less than a man.

94. The Weight of Hindu Scriptures

I did not realize
why their hands recoiled at my touch,
why their eyes turned away at my presence,
why the air around me thickened with silence,
until I read their scriptures—
verses carved in stone,
etched in the marrow of their faith.

"Speaking with a low caste,
looking at him,
stepping on his shadow—
is prohibited.
To do so is to make the Dvija impure."
(Apastamba D S 2.1.2.8; Vishnu S 71.58–59;
Satapatha Brahmana 14:1:1:31; Parasara S 6.22;
Kurma Purana 11..34.80; Usana Samhita 9.89)

I did not realize
that I was not only untouchable—
but unseeable, unhearable, unspeakable.
That even my shadow,
that lifeless ghost cast by the sun,
was a sin if it touched their feet.

They sip the waters of the Ganges,
but fear the dust from my soles.
They bow to cows,
but shrink from my presence.
They chant mantras for salvation,
but see my birth as damnation.

I did not realize,
until I read their laws,
that my existence was a stain
scrubbed clean only by cow dung and urine.
That my voice was a poison,
curable only by silence.

What faith is this,
that preaches purity by exclusion?
What god is this,
that demands walls between souls?

But I am not their sin,
not their stain,
not their impurity.
I am the voice that was silenced,
the shadow that was feared,
the touch that was condemned.

And if my shadow is enough
to shatter their heavens,
let it stretch across their temples,
let it fall upon their idols,
let it consume their scriptures in darkness.

For I have realized—
they are the ones who fear the light.

95. Thus the Untouchable Speaks

I did not know
until my body lay broken,
like the tens of millions before me—
skinned by the law,
burned by the faith,
hunted like beasts for the crime of existing.

I did not know
until my voice was choked in the noose,
until my blood was soaked in the dust,
that to sit, to walk, to wear white
was an offense against the order of the gods.

"My buttocks shall be gushed
if I sit on the same seat with a Hindu person."
—(Manu Smriti 8.281; Vishnu Smriti 5.20)

I did not know
until I read their scriptures
that I was born unfit for the earth I tread,
that my shadow was a curse,
that my tongue defiled the air.

I did not know
that my skin was a sin,
that my breath was a blasphemy,
that my presence was an affront
to their heavens, their purity, their gods.

And so they beat me—
for daring to drink from their wells.
They burned me—
for the audacity of my love.
They drowned me—
for stepping inside their temples.
They ripped my flesh, my dignity, my name—
for crossing lines drawn in dust
by hands that claimed divinity.

I did not know
until the fires consumed my home,
until my bones lay beside those of my ancestors,
that I was never meant to live as a man—
only as a carcass waiting to be torn apart.

But I know now.
And I refuse.

I refuse to bow,
to beg,
to break.

Let their scriptures crumble like dust in the wind.
Let their laws be drowned in the flood of justice.
Let the untouchable rise—
not as shadow, not as silence—
but as fire that scorches the chains of the past.

I am the cry that will not be hushed.
I am the blood that will not be erased.
I am the voice that will echo
long after their gods are gone.

96. Thus the Madiga Speaks

I did not realize why
tens of millions like me
were slaughtered, skinned, raped, and burned
for sitting, walking, drinking water,
or wearing white in the presence of my masters.

I did not realize
until I, too, was killed—
for daring to sit,
for the audacity of existing
in the path of a Hindu woman's gaze.

I did not realize
that my life was worth no more
than a dog, a crow, or a frog
until I read the scripture that sealed my fate:

"Penance for killing an untouchable
is the same as penance for killing a dog,
a bear, a frog, a crow, or an owl."
—(Mahabharata 12.165.56; Agni Purana 169.25–32)

I did not realize
that my murder was ritual,
my pain was ordained,
my suffering was righteousness—
until I saw her hands stained with my blood,
indifferent as they would be
had she slaughtered a bird for the evening meal.

I did not realize
that my breath
was a crime,
that my skin
was a verdict,
that my touch
was death to them
but my death
was nothing.

I realized, too late,
that she was untouchable in a way I could never be—
wrapped in her armor of caste and creed,
her crime shielded by divine decree.

I did not realize,
but I know now.

Now, my voice will not be buried.
Now, my shadow will not be erased.
Now, my existence will not be cursed—
but will curse the hands that struck me down.

Now, the untouchable speaks.
And the world will listen.

97. Thus Spoke 'Untouchable' Kanchikacherla Kotesu Madiga

I did not know,
until my skin crackled like dried leaves in the fire,
until my flesh peeled away,
until the air carried the stench of my burning bones—
I did not know
that I should be burned alive
for daring to love.

I did not know,
until my body turned to ash on February 24, 1968—
that my touch was blasphemy,
my desire was treason,
my love was a crime
punishable by fire.

I did not know,
until my teacher, Dr. ,
read aloud from the scriptures that sentenced me:

"He who commits adultery with a high-caste woman
shall be burned alive."
—(Matsya Purana 227.131; Vaishtha Grhyasutras and Dharmasutras 21.1–3; Manu 8.374)

I did not know,
until my screams rose with the flames,
that the gods themselves had ordained my agony,
that the laws of the land were the laws of the pyre,

that my fate had been sealed
before I ever spoke her name.

I did not know
that love was only for the pure,
that passion was a privilege,
that to hold her hand
was to write my own epitaph in soot and smoke.

I did not know,
but I know now.

Now, I am the ember that will not die.
Now, I am the fire that cannot be contained.
Now, I am the voice that will echo in the ears of those
who watched me burn,
who fed the flames,
who turned their backs.

Now, I will not be silenced.
Now, my ashes will stain their hands.
Now, the untouchable speaks—
and the fire will spread.

98. Thus Speaks the Untouchable

I did not realize,
until my child's cries were silenced,
until her tiny hands grew cold,
until the ones who should have loved her
became her executioners—
I did not realize
that my love was a death sentence.

I did not understand,
until my wife's parents and her sister
turned their blades upon me,
until their hands, trembling with righteous fury,
tried to carve my existence from this world,
that I had violated something sacred—
not by crime,
not by sin,
but by love.

I did not know,
until the blood of my child mixed with the dust,
that her death had already been written
in the verses of their scriptures:

"If an untouchable marries a high-caste Hindu girl,
he must be put to death.
If an untouchable commits adultery with a Hindu woman,
he is to be burned alive."
—(Matsya Purana 227.131; Vaishtha Grhyasutras and Dharmasutras 21.1–3; Manu 8.374)

I did not realize
that the gods they revere
had already condemned me,
that my daughter was not theirs to mourn,
but theirs to destroy.

I understood, then,
that Hindus had not simply killed my child—
they had followed their sacred duty.
They had turned holy words into blades,
into fire,
into nooses and acid and iron rods.

And I am not alone.
Millions of untouchables,
lovers, dreamers, wanderers,
have been beaten, raped, lynched,
not for breaking laws,
but for breaking the walls they built around us.

But let them know—
we are not shadows.
We are not whispers lost in the wind.
We are the storm gathering at their doorstep.
We are the fire they can no longer contain.
We are the voices they can never silence.

99. O Shudra, the Loyal Slave

(A Satirical Poem on the Fate of the Shudra in His Own Religion)

O Shudra, bow lower, bend your spine!
For your Brahmin master dines divine.
Eat the crumbs, lick the floor,
That is what your fate is for.

You call yourself Reddy, Kapu, Velama, Mangali, Chakali, bright,
Kamma, Yadava, Gouda, Padmasali, Kuruma, full of might—
But look! Your holy texts decree,
You're no more than dust beneath the tree.

O Shudra, O servant, know your place,
Your gods have cursed your very race.
"A Shudra must eat the master's waste,"
(Manu 10.125, a law to taste!)

You think you're noble, think you're grand,
Yet you plow the Brahmin's land.
You spill untouchable blood with glee,
Forgetting what they think of thee.

Your master spits, your master kicks,
Yet you sharpen his hunting sticks.
When he tires of slaying me,
He will turn his blade on thee.

O Shudra, the forgotten pawn,
Dancing to tunes your master's drawn.

You wear silk, you claim the right,
Yet to them, you're filthy blight.

You wield the whip upon my back,
Forgetting yours is lashed and cracked.
You rape, you maim, you burn my kin,
Yet you are nothing—cursed by sin.

Look into the sacred scrolls,
See the fate your master controls.
"No human status for Shudras low,"
(Manu, Mahabharata—scriptures show.)

You worship them, you kill for them,
Yet to them, you're worse than phlegm.
When they sip their milk and ghee,
They cleanse their hands after touching thee.

So tell me, Shudra, slave so true,
Why do you fight for those who hate you?
Why do you wield their sword with pride,
When they would drown you in the tide?

Perhaps you love your gilded chains,
Your servitude, your caste-stained veins.
But as you rise to strike me down,
Know you'll always wear their crown—
A crown of thorns, a noose so tight,
A slave in day, a slave in night.

100. Hindu Cruelty

I did not realize,
Not until I saw with my own eyes,
That my people, my untouchables,
Were called like stray dogs to feast on filth.

"Dvija (Brahmin, Kshatriya, Vaishya) must throw
leftover food of Shraddha on the ground
for Caṇḍāla (untouchable), dogs, and birds to eat."
(Manu Smriti 3.92; Markandeya Purana 26.45–46; Kurma Purana II.18.105–6)

I did not understand,
Not until I watched them toss their scraps,
Their rotting remains, onto the dirt,
Not for kindness, not for charity,
But because their scripture commands it so.

I saw my brothers, my sisters, my elders,
Bending down, picking from the earth,
Not as beggars, but as victims,
Born condemned by Hindu hands.

Their priests, their scholars, their rulers,
Read aloud from sacred texts,
Declaring my people no better than crows,
No different from the street-bound dog.

And yet, they pretend to be gods among men,
Preaching peace, love, and virtue,

While their hands drip with the blood of my kind,
And their words reek of centuries of hate.

What sin have we committed,
That our very touch defiles them?
What crime runs in our blood,
That we are cast lower than cattle?

Hindus stand with chins raised high,
Spouting verses of divine wisdom,
Yet they order us to eat their waste,
To swallow our shame and call it grace.

But we are not animals, not shadows, not ghosts.
We are flesh, we are breath, we are human.
And though they throw their scraps in the dust,
We shall rise—not to beg, but to burn their chains.

For the filth is not in the land,
Not in the hands of the untouchable,
But in the hearts of those who hold the whip
And call their cruelty divine.

101. The Vedas, the Creator of the Genocide

I did not realize,
Not until the fire licked my skin,
That the verses of their sacred Vedas
Had already sentenced me to death.

"If a low caste hears the Veda,
then molten lead must be poured into his ears.
If he recites the Veda, then his tongue should be cut off.
If he memorizes the Veda, then his body must be cut into two parts."
(Gautama D S 12.4–6; Atri Samhita 1.19; Skanda Purana V.iii.200.6; Brihaspati Smriti 20.12)

I understood this,
Not in the silence of ancient scrolls,
But in the screams of my own people,
Raped, lynched, dismembered,
For daring to step into Hindu spaces.

Their scripture—
Not ink on palm leaves,
But a blade across my throat,
A noose around my neck,
Molten lead down my ears,
So I may never hear the lies they call divine.

I was born in a land of scriptures,
But never in their blessings,
Only in their curses, their sentences, their punishments,
For existing in a body deemed impure.

Brahmin and non-Brahmin alike
Hold the Vedas as their god,
A god that demands my silence,
A god that justifies my suffering,
A god that carves my death into stone.

What crime is it,
To listen?
To speak?
To remember?

Their gods demand my flesh,
Their laws demand my blood,
Their hands seek to erase me,
But my voice, my breath, my truth,
Will not be cut in two.

I live, though they wish me dead.
I remember, though they burn my name.
And though they pour lead into my ears,
I will hear, and I will speak,
Until their scriptures turn to ash.

102. O Shudra, Servant of Servants

O Shudra—Reddy, Kamma, Velama, Kapu, Yadava, Gouda,
Did you not read your own scriptures,
The ones that spit on your very birth?
Did you not hear your master's voice,
Calling you filth, calling you dirt,
A servant of servants, a shadow meant to crawl?

"Your Shudra buttocks shall be gushed
If you sit on the same seat as your Dvija masters."
(Manu Smriti 8.281, Vishnu Smriti 5.20)

But O Shudra,
You—who were kicked and spat upon—
You, whose ancestors were stripped of dignity,
You, who were banned from knowledge, from power, from prayer,
You, whose feet were chained in servitude,
Have now become the butcher's blade,
Cutting my untouchable skin at your master's command.

Have you forgotten the hands that once broke your spine?
The feet that crushed your voice into dust?
Have you forgotten the fire that burned your name,
The rope that dragged your father through the streets,
The silence forced upon your mother's screams?

O Shudra, the obedient dog of Dvijas,
Your loyalty drips with the blood of my people.
You, the eager foot-soldier,
The willing executioner,
The one who turned against his own chains,

Not to break them,
But to tighten them around my throat.

What did they promise you, O Shudra?
A seat outside their temple?
A sip from their well after they have drunk?
A scrap from their golden plate,
Thrown to you like a beggar in the dirt?

You were born a slave,
And you choose to be a slave still.
But I—an untouchable, the cursed, the damned—
I choose to fight.

For I am no Shudra,
No servant of their gods,
No worshipper of their chains.
I am a poet, a scholar, a rebel,
And I will not bow,
Not to you,
Not to them.

103. O Shudra Reddy, Kamma, Kapu, Velama Caste, Learn to Rise

O low caste, your fate was written in the dust,
Long before you took your first breath,
Long before you knew the chains around your ankles,
Long before you heard your master's voice say—
"You shall not perform sacrifices,
You shall not be seen at sacred rites,
You shall not stand where the Dvija stands."
(Mahabharata 5.29.26; 13.91; 43–44; Manu 11.13; Srimad Bhagavatam 11.5.5)

O low caste, they cast your shadow away,
Like a plague, like filth, like rot upon the land,
Yet still, you kneel, still you serve,
Still, you sweep their temples and wash their feet,
Still, you bow at their altars, praying to gods
That would rather see you starve.

Where is your shame, O low caste?
Where is your self-respect?
Have you not seen the hands that strike you?
Have you not felt the feet that trample your voice into the earth?
Do you not hear the laughter of those
Who would rather see you dead than standing tall?

They do not want your prayers,
They do not want your presence,
They do not want even your shadow near their sacred fire—
And yet, you still whisper their names with reverence?

O low caste, discard your servitude like a tattered cloth,
Burn the scriptures that make you less than a man,
Tear down the temples that tell you to crawl,
And rise—if only for the first time.

Let us not build our lives on their chains,
Let us build on justice, on dignity, on equality.
Not on Manu, not on the Dvija's law,
Not on the sacred thread that strangles our breath,
But on John Rawls—on fairness, on reason,
On a justice that does not call you filth,
On a justice that does not cast your shadow away.

Let us bury their laws in the pit of history,
And erect, in its place, a world where no man kneels.

104. My Aryan Christian Mother, Patnala Suguna Yadav alias Mattimalla Suguna Madiga

My mother, Suguna, a soul of light,
Left her world for love, out of sight.
A Yadav by birth, strong and proud,
She chose my Madiga father, far from the crowd.

She faced the rage of a feudal past,
Defying caste, standing steadfast.
She shielded him from honor's knife,
Though her own was a sacrificial life.

In tattered clothes, with hands worn bare,
She worked long hours, a burden to bear.
For two rupees, from dawn till night,
She toiled in fields, out of sight.

Her stomach empty, yet she'd still feed,
Me and my sister, ignoring her need.
While my father, cruel and cold,
Fed first, left her hungry and old.

She lost a son, her firstborn pride,
Yet held us close, with love as her guide.
Through pain and loss, she remains true,
A mother's strength, pure and blue.

Though her world was stripped of glory and grace,
Her spirit shines, no one can erase.
Suguna Yadav, a mother's song,
Your love endures, unwavering, strong.

105. My Christian Mother: Patnala Suguna Yadav alias Mattimalla Suguna Madiga , Mother of Grace

Suguna, my mother, you left behind
A life of ease for love that's blind.
A daughter of privilege, strong and wise,
Choosing love over feudal ties.

You left your world, a bold choice indeed,
And joined with my father in quiet creed.
Your Yadav name—a heritage so bright;
You cast it off for love, defied the multitudes and crowds this night.

In the land of India where castes divide;
You walk with strength and dignity so wide.
The cold, hard stare of disdain;
But in your eyes only love was there.

You held us close, your children three,
Bound by love's steadfast decree.
I saw you toil from dawn to night,
With torn clothes, yet your spirit bright.

You fed us first, although our tummies rumbled,
Labored and toiled in fields, day after day for pitiful wages earned.
While others shone with jewels and with gold,
You shone in resilience, your courage bold.

My father's blows, a stream of harsh cruel words
Could not dim nor stem the love you stirred.
For you were sunlight to our darkness,
A warm embracing and a steadfast spark.

You lost your son, my brother dear,
To the cruelty of a world austere.
Yet in every loss, you gave us hope,
In every trial, a way to cope.

A mother's strength, unmatched, unseen,
A queen of grace in fields so green.
Though torn and tired, you taught me well,
Of love's great strength, its boundless spell.

Suguna, mother, you chose your path,
In a world of cruelty, stood against wrath.
You faced the storms with gentle might,
A beacon of love, a radiant light.

I owe you life, and so much more—
For teaching love, for opening doors.
And though the world may see you small,
To me, you are the strength in all.

106. The Child I'll Never Know

In 2010, I married for love,
With hope as pure as stars above.
A bond that bridged caste's cruel divide,
Yet left us lost in darkness wide.

My firstborn child[20], taken unseen,
A dream of innocence, torn and clean.
They stole you away, my blood, my heart,
I never knew you, lost from the start.

---

20. My firstborn was killed by his or her own Hindu religious background Kapu caste maternal grandparents and aunty for being born to my untouchable skin. My Hindu wife was brutally chained and assaulted publicly by her parents and younger sister in front of state and non-state actors on the campus of the University of Hyderabad in 2010. They humiliated me in the name of my caste, skin color, and class background. The masked Mala-led Ambedkar Students Association (ASA) and the Madiga-led Dalit Students Union (DSU) are allies of my wife's parents in this heinous crime. One of my best friends, named Konidala Vijay Kumar, a Mala Christian Ph.D. scholar in the department of Sociology, HCU, helped me and my severely wounded wife and accompanied us to the police station, where the Hindu-Kamma caste background circle inspector tried to counsel my wife by saying she should listen to her parents. At last, she was forcefully taken from me when she was six months pregnant and killed my child after delivery. My wife was forcefully married to their caste man. I have never seen her since the time she was taken from me. Her Hindu parents tried to kill me too, but I escaped from their honor killing. I did not even know whether my firstborn was a daughter or son. But my child became a victim of Hindu honor killing in India. Hindus, Muslims, Sikhs, Jains, Parsees, Buddhists, and converted Christians from touchable castes are brutally known for their honor killings of untouchable caste background children and their fathers born to untouchable fathers and non-untouchable caste background mothers. This is the story of incredible India in our and in our next generation times. Honor killing is infinite, in which even Western-educated scholars, theorists, awardees, icons of knowledge, artists, celebrities, icons of human rights, liberals, lefties, feminists, queer people, tribal people, Hindus, Muslims, Sikhs, Jains, Buddhists, and Parsees are involved. This is the beauty of Indian civilization, Hindu religion, ideology, and society in our times and in our future times.

They took your mother from my side,
In chains, in silence, in honor's pride.
They claimed her with iron, with force so cold,
Left her in shadows, stories untold.

I don't know your name, your face, your cry,
If you were a girl, a boy, and why
They deemed your life a stain to hide,
An innocent lost to caste-bound pride.

I remember her love, her tender grace,
How they broke her heart in that sacred place.
A father's sorrow, a husband's pain,
Bound by a love that remains in vain.

For you, my child, I hold in grief,
A love unseen, a life so brief.
Wherever you are, know this is true—
My heart forever belongs to you.

107. My Silent Grief

My firstborn[21], the child I'll never know,
Taken from life's warm embrace below.
A love that blossomed against the grain,
Torn by hatred, leaving only pain.

She was Kapu, proud and free,
I was Madiga, bound to be.
We joined in secret, hearts as one,
In hope that love could see us run.

We married in faith, bound by the cross,
Yet love, in their eyes, was only loss.
Her family's wrath like a storm unseen,
Left scars on love's forbidden dream.

They took her back, a cruel parade,
A mother held by fear's sharp blade.
Our child, born innocent and small,
Their vengeance took, their heart so small.

I don't know if you were son or daughter,
Only that life flowed like water,
Cut short by hands that could not see
The beauty of what you were meant to be.

In quiet nights, I see your face,
A glimpse of love, a fleeting trace.
Would you have laughed or learned to sing,
Or danced in fields come early spring?

21. Ibid.

But now you're gone, a life undone,
As days pass by, each a burning sun.
Your mother vanished, taken away,
A love we shared now lost in gray.

I walk alone, haunted by dreams,
Of what we could have been, torn at the seams.
The world would not let love reside,
In hearts that dared cross caste and pride.

For you, my child, I bear this pain,
A love that lives in silent strain.
In memory's hold, you remain dear,
An unseen child, forever near.

And though I've lost what love could give,
Through you, my child, I'll learn to live.
A life reborn in dreams I see,
A father's hope, eternally.

108. Venomous Hindu Roots

You, clad in robes of purity,
Pen a credo of venom,
Where the shadows are tall and stark,
A world where untouchable means unseen, unloved.

You wrote with iron hands,
Between what is holy and what's desecrated,
An ancient, cruel, distorted truth
That still gnaws, like salt upon a wound.

Manuvaadi, your name slithers through history,
Cold, ruthless hiss of a serpent,
Inspiring tyrants, inducing dreams of annihilation,
As if blood could be made pure by blood.

You, the architect of untouchable lives,
Branded by birth, unseen by choice,
A lie that spread like wildfire,
From village borders to global shores.

Your hands stained with histories untold,
Lynching, raping, burning down lives,
As if hatred were a hymn to be sung,
As if humanity were a plague to be purged.

Within your shadow, my skin is a sin,
My breath a rebellion, my existence a crime,
Cast out, forced to the edges of your world,
Where even the sky shuns my gaze.

I am a refugee within my own land,
A ghost in the daylight, unseen, unheard,
A target for those who share your creed,
Of caste and cruelty, of fear and fire.

Even the venomous snake recoils from your touch,
For your poison is deeper, more lethal,
Seeping through the soil, through stone, through skin,
Into life, making it a death that is slow and bitter.

You are just a myth, a curse, a plague,
A whisper echoing through times,
Lacing love with chains of hate,
Dimming the light for the sake of purity.

Still I rise, scarred but unbroken,
My voice a quiet, unyielding storm,
Against those lies, venom, chains,
I am defiance-the truth you can never bury.

109. Gatekeepers of Untouchable Genocide

The Guru built a ladder,
Iron, blood, and lies,
You stand at the gate,
Enforcer, Cruel design.

If Brahmin is the mind-the theorist,
You are the judge with bloodstained hands,
Legacy of silence, of erasure,
Of babies torn from life, from love, from liberty, from light.

You hold the keys for a thousand years
To oppression wrapped in gold and chants,
To untouchable souls choked by dust,
As you march, singing peace abroad.

Every step is overshadowed by the ghost of Manu,
An age-old curse, the lessons of hate,
Which, from the East to the West stretched
Where bodies were hung but spirits fought.

You smile, a white lie in snow-white attire,
Preaching sermons on peace to the Western ears,
Your hands drip with history behind your backs,
Genocide draped as justice.

October 7 is not a date,
But the pulse of each breath of every untouchable,
A silent shriek, a muffled scream,
For every village, every town you police.

Your songs of human rights, they ring hollow,
A mask you wear to hide the fangs,
That at the soul, tear at the heart,
For every girl, every boy, you deem impure.

To you, my skin is a stain, a sin,
To be erased, expunged, annihilated,
Yet I stand, a survivor of your histories,
With scars that sing of defiance.

Your Guru taught you well,
But not well enough to see this truth:
I am not a ghost, not a whisper,
I am the storm that breaks your chains.

Your heart beats for purity, for power,
But I breathe for freedom, for light,
For every soul cast aside, crushed, ignored,
I will stand, and I will roar.

And so you march, adorned in lies,
But know this, oh pain's gatekeeper:
You are seen, you are known,
And the storm is coming, to wash it all away.

110. Boundaries of Untouchability Genocide

From India to Germany, Nepal to Japan,
I carry the weight of chains unseen.
Brahmins, Kshatriyas, Vaishyas, Shudras—
Hindus, Muslims, Buddhists, Jains—
They build walls with whispered laws,
They write my worthlessness in every breath.

They strip me of my humanness,
A thief in their temples, a stain in their kitchens.
They say, "Stay back, unseeable, unapproachable,"
Yet my shadow follows them, haunts their purity.

From touching, from speaking, from entering,
I am barred.
From love, from freedom, from dignity,
I am stripped.
From walking, from sitting, from spreading my hands,
I am blocked.

"Untouchable, unshadowable, Negro," they spit,
"Impure, murky, chimpanzee, criminal," they name me.
A murmur of hate spreads through their lips,
Whispers turning to knives, cutting at my soul.

In temples, I am not wanted,
In kitchens, my child is not allowed to play.
From India to Pakistan to Japan to Germany,
I am not different: filthy, untouchable, less than human.

I should not be seen,
But they see and look away.
I must not speak,
But my silence rings in their halls.

I am forced to stay outdoors,
My place set outside their circle.
But from the outside in, I would say,
I am alive.

Whatever fences they draw,
Whatever chains they weave,
Wouldn't be worn out and wouldn't disappear.
I am the voice of the banned, unuttered, unseen.

111. Hindus: The Inventors of Atrocity Crimes on Earth

No land on earth has given birth,
To crimes like yours, to such cruel mirth.
You built a system, a caste so dire,
A pernicious genocide, a silent fire.

You invented untouchability, a brutal scheme,
Against African Christians, against those unseen.
Muslims and whites took your design,
Bringing it to new lands, making it malign.

You taught them the purity and impurity game,
They used it on untouchables, on Jews, the same.
Black Christians felt its bite, its sting,
As did Yazidis, left suffering.

Your crimes are ancient, 6000 years of pain,
A legacy of lynching, a dark refrain.
You invented honor killings, that sadistic rite,
Inspired by your ally, Islam's blight.

Stone them to death, that was your call,
Muslims and whites followed, leaving so many to fall.
Your rape system spread, a horrible fate,
Adopted by Muslims, and whites with hate.

Your arranged marriages, dowry demands,
Spread like poison across the lands.
Jains, Buddhists, Parsees, and Sikhs,
All took your customs, practiced the tricks.

Brutal ideologies, etched deep and clear,
Adopted by others, spreading fear.
Yours is a history, 6000 years old,
Their crimes seem younger, less bold.

You wear the mask of human rights, of peace,
But untouchables see your lies, they never cease.
Your parasite skins, your chameleon ways,
No human rights can hide your darkened days.

Jews know the truth of white and Muslim might,
As untouchables know Hindutva's bite.
We see the masks, the guise, the disguise,
We know the truth behind your eyes.

You tried to erase my untouchable soul,
Just like Yazidis faced the cruel toll.
You bring new names, new faces, new lies,
But we unmask your truth, see through your guise.

Even now, you wear modern skins,
But your core remains, where it begins.
We see through your advanced masks, your deceit,
We know the truth that hides beneath.

112. A Hindu World Without Love

I was born in a land where love is weighed,
Where daughters and sons are bartered and paid.
Gold and cash, land and pride,
A market of marriage where hearts collide.

No whispers of love, no promises true,
Only the weight of wealth in view.
A dowry of diamonds, a cycle, a car,
No light in this trade, no guiding star.

A loveless land where honor must kill,
Where hands must wound, where blood must spill.
They hunt my skin, they haunt my breath,
They chain my steps in caste and death.

Yet even the untouchable wears a disguise,
A servant still to ancient lies.
They dream of freedom, yet kneel the same,
Bound by the chains they dare not name.

Where is progress, where is light,
When both the victim and victor bite?
Not all who suffer choose to rise,
Some become what they despise.

And the West, in its gaze so bold,
Polishes the Brahmin's gold.
They sing of caste as if it's new,
Yet hide the truth from the world's view.

They lift the veil for those they choose,
But silence my scars, my shattered hues.
Like they silence the Jew, the Yazidi's cries,
And bow to the hands that terrorize.

I stand alone in this endless fight,
A vegan soul in a world of blight.
How long must a heart stay pure,
When justice is lost and truth unsure?

The hands that rule, the tongues that lie,
The markets where love is left to die.
Yet even as they silence me,
I hold my truth, I set it free.

No cage of caste, no veil of hate,
Can turn my love to war and fate.
For I am the fire they cannot consume,
A voice that echoes beyond the gloom.

113. The Core Ideology of a Sanātana Hindu Dharma

You wear masks of human rights, peace, and love,
Cambridge scholar, NASA scientist, a dove.
You claim to be a poet, artist, author, and more,
But what lies beneath is dark to the core.

Your core ideology isn't what you display,
It's caste, race, and untouchability every day.
You speak of equality, of modern thought,
But your actions betray what you have taught.

You are a Hindu jihadi in Western guise,
Hiding behind degrees to fool the eyes.
Your everyday life is built on caste divides,
Dehumanizing those you try to hide.

You lynch the untouchable, you maim and kill,
You honor rape and blood, yet claim goodwill.
You confine the lowest, deny them rights,
You massacre and maim, out of sight.

You wear a tie, carry a Nobel Prize,
But your core is dark, hidden in lies.
You stand with Islamic State's hate,
A Hindu state, where untouchables are bait.

No matter your titles, no matter your fame,
Your core ideology remains the same.
It's the genocide of those you deem low,
The untouchable castes who live in the shadow.

You claim to be a leader, a global voice,
But we see through, we have no choice.
Even in the West, with a scholar's name,
Your core remains, it's all the same.

Law degrees and doctorates, praise,
All help to conceal your worst ways.
You may publish at Oxford's walls,
Your heart and core ideologies still beckon and call.

You mislead the Jews, the Western mind,
With modern masks, they think you're kind.
But untouchables, we see clear,
The hate, the pain, it's always near.

Even in NASA, you wear a mask,
But untouchables know your real task.
You are not about peace or equality,
But caste, and race, a harsh reality.

Your Western degrees are just a disguise,
To plunder and steal, with innocent eyes.
But we see through, we know the truth,
Your core ideology isn't in proofs.

It's not about knowledge, not about growth,
It's about eliminating those who rock the boat.
Africans, Jews, Yazidis, we all see,
Through your deceptive modernity.

We, the untouchables, know your face,
No matter the tie, no matter the place.
You are a jihadi in a Western suit,
Still spreading dark ideologies, absolute.

114. Arranged Marriage Is Prostitution; Prostitution Is Not Freedom

An arranged marriage-a mask so fine, concealing bartered lives,
A bargain behind the veil, it thrives.
A flesh market, where bodies are sold,
Love's pure beauty sold into a no-good fold.

Buying and selling love forms a damned treaty,
Where dignity becomes as cold as hard money.
One man, one woman-a union of grace,
But polygamy thrives, disguised, a hidden disgrace.

In lands of Hindu and Islamic binds,
Where cross-cousins know, women are reduced to mere objects, confined.
What room does love know when the bride price is paid?
What room does freedom find when choices have faded?

Marriage should be a song, a dance in light,
But forced unions turn that into a fight.
This is not freedom; it's a market of lies,
Where bodies are exchanged, where dignity dies.

Even clad in traditional garb,
It is still prostitution, wherein hope defies.
No room for compassion, none to care,
A culture of death is always lurking there.

One valid bond of love and light
Is what should form the base of what's right,
But in arranged marriages, where the deals are made,
It's all just a matter of fate and fortune displayed.

115. Genocide Against My Skin

From India to West, Nepal to Japan,
I carry the weight of chains unseen.
Brahmins, Kshatriyas, Vaishyas, Shudras—
Hindus, Muslims, Buddhists, Jains, Sikhs, Parses—
They build walls with whispered laws,
They write my worthlessness in every breath.

They strip me of my humanness,
A thief in their temples, a stain in their kitchens.
They say, "Stay back, unseeable, unapproachable,"
Yet my shadow follows them, haunts their purity.

From touching, from speaking, from entering,
I am barred.
From love, from freedom, from dignity,
I am stripped.
From walking, from sitting, from spreading my hands,
I am blocked.

"Untouchable, unshadowable, Negro," they spit,
"Impure, murky, chimpanzee, criminal," they name me.
A murmur of hate spreads through their lips,
Whispers turning to knives, cutting at my soul.

In temples, I am not wanted,
In kitchens, my child is not allowed to play.
From India to Pakistan to Japan to Germany,
I am not different: filthy, untouchable, less than human.

I should not be seen,

But they see and look away.
I must not speak,
But my silence rings in their halls.

I am forced to stay outdoors,
My place set outside their circle.
But from the outside in, I would say,
I am alive.

Whatever fences they draw,
Whatever chains they weave,
Wouldn't be worn out and wouldn't disappear.
I am the voice of the banned, unuttered, unseen.

116. My Birth Is Primed for Death

From India to West, Nepal to Japan,
I carry the weight of chains unseen,
Invisible, yet heavy as the earth itself,
Bound by the whispers of their silent schemes.
Brahmins, Kshatriyas, Vaishyas, Shudras—
Hindus, Muslims, Buddhists, neo-Buddhists, Jains, Sikhs, Parsees—
They build walls with whispered laws,
They write my worthlessness in every breath.

They strip me of my humanness,
A thief in their temples, a stain in their kitchens.
They say, "Stay back, unseeable, unapproachable,"
Yet my shadow follows them, haunts their purity.
I am the unspoken curse that lingers in their gaze,
A presence denied, hidden in a maze.

From touching, from speaking, from entering,
I am barred.
From love, from freedom, from dignity,
I am stripped.
From walking, from sitting, from spreading my hands,
I am blocked.

"Untouchable, unshadowable, Negro," they spit,
"Impure, murky, chimpanzee, criminal," they name me.
A murmur of hate spreads through their lips,
Whispers turning to knives, cutting at my soul.
Each word a jagged stone, cast at my chest,
A weight too heavy, too cruel to suppress.

In temples, I am not wanted,
In kitchens, my child is not allowed to play.
From India to Pakistan to Japan to Germany,
I am not different: filthy, untouchable, less than human.
The same accusations cross borders, the same humiliation—
Bound by the same thread of desolation.

I should not be seen,
But they see and look away.
I must not speak,
But my silence rings in their halls.
My voice a murmur in the winds,
A silent scream that breaks the din.

I am forced to stay outdoors,
My place set outside their circle.
But from the outside in, I would say,
I am alive.
I am the song unsung, the hope not lost,
A spirit that rises, no matter the cost.

Whatever fences they draw,
Whatever chains they weave,
Wouldn't be worn out and wouldn't disappear.
I am the voice of the banned, unuttered, unseen,
A truth unbroken, a force that stands between
The walls they build and the hearts they close,
For I am the wind that never slows.

117. Scars of the Incredible India

In the shadows of India's sunlit land,
Where temples rise and rivers stand,
A silent curse lays dark and deep—
The untouchables' pain, secrets they keep.

Born to earth like grains of sand,
Yet marked by fate's unyielding hand.
Branded "impure" by caste's cold chain,
Left to weather life's endless rain.

They pass unseen, their souls unheeded,
While walls of prejudice surround and beat.
Ghosts treading ghosts, ungiving a sound,
Their life apart, taken away from choice.

In narrow lanes they carry the load,
Heavier still with tradition's implemented code.
Each stare that comes across brings a newly opened gash,
Their souls as eggshells crushed, rent in the flesh.

Lynched by silence, burned in shame,
Their spirit, however, endures the rigid flame.
The sacrifice of the lambs, their cries unheard,
Rewrite a story with no word uttered.

Hands skinned alive by the fates of untouchability,
And yet hearts rising, defying hate.
For each stone thrown, a spark ignites,
Illuminating darkness with hidden lights.

In fields they toil and labor, not their own,
While caste wears pride, seated on a jeweled throne.
Irony lies in the bloodstained clay,
Where honor's price makes innocence pay.

In silence, resilience grows within,
Like seeds sprouting in prejudice-unknowing skin.
They rise again, in steady tide,
Breaking the stride of unholy caste.

O India, can you bear the weight
Of those whose strength defies their fate?
For each soul cast aside by caste,
Is a beacon of courage, meant to last.

118. India: The Hyenas Democracy

I am marked by birth, by caste's cruel law,
Born beneath, taught to bow, to withdraw.
A name assigned, a fate decreed,
Before I could walk, before I could plead.

In fields, in streets, I walk unseen,
A ghost bound by chains, kept unclean.
Denied a touch, denied a place,
Branded untouchable, stripped of grace.

They call it tradition, this caste-born fate,
But it's nothing but violence masked as hate.
A temple's door, a village well,
Barred by rules carved deep in hell.

To drink, to sit, to learn, to dream,
Each right denied, each hope a scream.
A system of stone, unshaken, vast,
Yet built upon bones of the voiceless past.

The law may change, the words may shift,
Yet the weight remains, the walls persist.
They speak of progress, of rights proclaimed,
Yet caste still lingers, silent, unnamed.

In the classroom, whispers chase my name,
In the workplace, power plays the same.
No matter how high, how far I rise,
The shadow of caste never dies.

Yet my spirit stands, scarred but strong,
Resisting the lie, the ancient wrong.
For no caste, no system, no chain can bind,
The fire of dignity in an untouchable's mind.

I rise from ashes, I break the past,
I carve a future, free at last.
Not by their mercy, nor by their grace,
But by the strength they tried to erase.

I will walk, I will speak, I will claim my right,
No longer hidden, I step into light.
For the scars they gave, I wear with pride,
A testament to all who died.

Let the chains of caste fall and decay,
Let justice breathe, let truth have its way.
For a world divided can never stand,
And freedom must hold every hand.

119. Primed for Death

In lands where life begins with chains,
An untouchable's birth bears sorrow's stains.
From India's soil to Japan's shore,
Their lives are marked by wounds they bore.

The light of birth they hardly see,
A life in shade, defiled destiny.
None of their own, a castaway,
Compelled to live and dwell in silence gray.

Hands intact, hearts so chaste,
Youth of innocence, stolen at last.
Ghostlike, they wander in daylight bright,
Bruises bled that no one will see tonight.

To be untouchable is to know the fate,
Where life's small spark, sudden, will break.
For Hindu and Buddhist, as well as Islamic sight,
Their value is confined by caste and deceit.

How much more ironic still,
That in the blood within them, the same life's will-
A breath, a heartbeat, tender soul inside,
Yet viewed as less, as something stole.

Through Buddhist lands and Hindu walls,
Where teachings preach that spirit calls,
These souls are crushed by rigid bars,
Their lives unseen, like distant stars.

Jains and Sikhs and Parse too,
Mark them out as lesser, as few.
In holy verses, cruel hands raise,
A lifetime lost in caste's dark maze.

And so they live, unseen, unheard,
Their voices lost in whispered word.
They seek no crowns, no thrones of gold,
Just life, just warmth, a hand to hold.

But to them, birth is life erased,
A road to nowhere, fate embraced.
For death follows the untouchable's morn,
A stolen future, life withdrawn.

And yet in their silence courage grows,
A strength the world may never know.
For though unseen, their spirits fight,
A flicker still in the dark of night.

O world, see them—do not turn,
For even in shadows, hearts can burn.
And if there's light beyond caste's wall,
It's in the hope that they stand tall.

120. Jewish Allies in the Indian Democracy of Mosquitoes

O people of the Star of David, you look to Hindus as friends,
But know they wear masks—behind smiles, darkness bends.
In your eyes, you may see alliance true,
Yet in India, they shun lives like mine and you.

October 7 was one day's brutal pain,
Yet untouchables endure it, again and again.
Hamas took from you in one cruel sweep,
But our persecution is endless, dark, and deep.

In India, Nepal, through Sri Lanka's lands,
By Brahmin, Kshatriya, Vaishya, Shudra with bloodied hands,
My caste is lynched, raped, burned alive—
While the world ignores our fight to survive.

The irony drips from history's tongue,
For you too know how hatred is sung.
You, untouchable in white man's gaze,
And I, untouchable in my homeland's ways.

You face antisemitism's cruel weight;
I bear untouchability's fate.
Our tormentors wear different skin,
But they share the same malice within.

Hindus, Muslims—no ally here,
Only faces veiled in hate and fear.
For what you know as antisemitic zeal
Is what I endure with caste's steel.

Both of us, victims of scorn,
Marked from the moment we were born.
We suffer in lands we call our own,
Our dignity stolen, our spirits alone.

Yet we stand tall, you and I,
Against oppression's shadowed sky.
For knowledge and freedom are in our blood,
Born from resilience, an enduring flood.

They claim rights, they call us less,
They wield control, leaving us dispossessed.
But you and I, with hearts laid bare,
Must fight as allies in our despair.

Stand with me, as I stand with you—
For the truth binds us, strong and true.
In their eyes, we're threats to deny,
But in our pain, we reach for the sky.

Say no to the caste, to untouchable's plight,
And lift our voices into the night.

121. Hindu Religion: The Blackwater

I am marked by birth, by caste's cruel law,
Born beneath, taught to bow, to withdraw.
In fields, in streets, I walk unseen,
A ghost bound by chains, kept unclean.

They call it tradition, this caste-born fate,
But it's nothing but violence masked as hate.
In the eyes of many, I am less than whole,
Reduced to silence, stripped of soul.

Yet my spirit stands, scarred but strong,
Resisting the lie, the ancient wrong.
For no caste, no system, no chain can bind,
The fire of dignity in an untouchable's mind.

122. Your Body, My Choice

O women bound by ancient chains,
Hindu, Islamic, Sikh, Buddhist names.
Jain, Parse, under male decree,
How long will you endure, unfree?

Your body, their playground, their cruel domain,
A pawn in their games, a source of disdain.
How long can you wear the shackles of old,
The weight of ideologies, brutal and cold?

Wake up, O woke women, hear the call,
Break the silence, shatter the wall.
Centuries of servitude, a life enslaved,
Rise now, be fierce, be brave.

You dream of a husband, feudal or grand,
At sixteen, bound to a 35-year-old man.
A Yale degree, yet your life is confined,
A toy to their whims, a cage for your mind.

Why do you carry the spirit of caste,
Of purity, impurity, a burden so vast?
You kill love if it's untouchable-born,
Yet your own worth is met with scorn.

How long will you bow your head,
Marry for status, your spirit dead?
How long will you wear the mask,
Denying the freedom for which you must ask?

Let your community see your human face,
Not a toy, not an object, but full of grace.
Break the chains, let slavery cease,
Sing the song of freedom, dance for peace.

Your body, your voice, your sovereign choice,
Raise it high, let them hear your voice.
A symphony of liberty, a cry so loud,
No longer will you bow or be cowed.

For you are the sun, the unbroken flame,
A beacon of strength, unyielding, untamed.
Claim your identity, let history see,
You are no slave—you are free.

123. Jewish Badge, Broom, and Pot: The Burdens We Bear

Between 1939 and 1945,
The Jewish badge was sewn with intent
A yellow star, a silent mark,
A prelude to death, to ghettos, to gas.
Germany branded its Jews,
Stripped them of breath, of place, of name,
Six years of horror
A wound carved into history's flesh.

Yet, O world, look upon my caste!
My untouchables, not for six years,
But for six thousand have borne the chains
Of Brahmin decree, Kshatriya rule, Vaishya coin, Shudra fist.
We do not wear stars
We wear brooms upon our backs, pots upon our heads,
Sweeping footprints of the pure,
Drinking the spit of the divine.

Not in one land, but in many,
India, Nepal, Japan, Sri Lanka, Pakistan, Bangladesh,
Our ghetto is not brick, but blood,
Not barbed wire, but breath itself.
We are unseeable, unshadowable, untouchable,
Yet the world sees us not.

The Nazis fell, their symbols burned,
Yet antisemitism hides beneath new skin.
Europe still spits upon its Jews,
Still trembles at their names,

Even when Nobel stars fill their skies.
For knowledge is a wound to the tyrant,
And wisdom a threat to the throne.

But my tormentors,
They do not mask, they do not change.
They stand, ancient, unyielding, unchanged,
As they were a thousand years ago, a thousand years hence.
The hands that beat us do not tremble,
The voices that curse us do not lower.

And so I remain a broom, a pot, a mark.
A walking corpse, a walking scar,
A name erased before it was written.

Yet we endure,
As the Jews endure.
As the exiled, the erased, the forgotten endure.
Bound not by chains, but by memory,
By the truth that cannot be burned,
By the justice yet to come.

For the broom and the badge share their pain,
As the badge and the broom share their fate.
Persecution, humiliation, slaughter,
Carried in silence, written in blood.

But even silence can break.
Even a whisper can shake the world.

124. The Illusion of Namaste

They fold their hands, they bow their heads,
A silent war in whispers spread.
A gesture hollow, cold and thin,
A mark of caste, a Brahmin's sin.

For Namaste is no greeting of peace,
No bond of love, no soul's release.
It is a wall, a whispered chain,
That keeps the pure from caste's disdain.

How can a man be sacred, whole,
When every man bears sin's control?
How can a Brahmin claim to be
The hand of fate, divinity?

A war is waged within this phrase,
A weapon shaped through ancient days.
For if the hand should dare extend,
The chain of caste would surely end.

Yet hands don't meet, they stay apart,
No touch, no bridge, no human spark.
For touch unbinds what power creates,
And Brahmin fears what touch negates.

The Feet They Worship, Never Theirs
The feet of gods, the feet of kings,
The feet of Brahmins, rule-bound things.
Yet never once do they descend,
To touch the feet of those they bend.

For who must bow, and who must rise,
Is carved in fate, is sealed in lies.
The feet of Brahmins must be kissed,
For karma's chains, for heaven's bliss.

They speak of honor, they speak of grace,
Yet never bend before my race.
For Madiga feet are left untouched,
Unseen, unbowed, in dust and rust.

No Brahmin kneels where justice stands,
No twice-born stains their holy hands.
For touching us, for bowing low,
Would shatter all their sacred woe.

The Namaste of the West

And now the West, with hearts so blind,
Embraces caste, leaves love behind.
They chant the prayers, they take the names,
They breathe new life in ancient chains.

They change their clothes, their gods, their fate,
To join the ranks of Brahmin hate.
The church they knew, the Christ they preached,
Now lost in caste, beyond His reach.

For Europe's Brahmins are worse than the old,
With whiter skin, but hearts so cold.
Not Muslims, not Africans rise as a threat,
But Hindus reborn in the West's own breath.

So let no hand press, let no foot bow,
Let caste's last breath be taken now.
No Namaste, no feet to kiss,
No Brahmin rule, no fate like this.

For touch will break what time has built,
And end the walls of caste's cruel guilt.

125. Hindu Matrimonial: A Mirror of Fascist Purity

O Brahmin and non-Brahmin fascist,
Your matrimonial columns scream exclusion,
"Bride and bridegroom available,
But not for Untouchables or Africans."
What purity hides behind this veil of shame?
What impurity do you see
In the shared anatomy of our humanity?

We breathe the same air,
Our hearts beat with the same rhythm,
Our bodies release gas, hold mucus,
Bear the same mortal fragility.
Yet you chain me in ghettos,
A shadow outside your villages, towns, cities,
My existence your silent prey.

When lust consumes your soul,
You creep into my ghettos—
A hyena searching for prey,
Ravaging my women, my under-aged girls.
When they conceive, you destroy the life you sowed,
Killing your own blood
In the name of caste, in the name of purity.

O fascist Hindu, your Yale degrees,
Your Supreme Court robes,
Your UNO human rights badges—
They cannot cleanse the stains of your crimes.
Your vulture ideology,
Your chameleon masks,

They fool the West,
But not me, your eternal victim.

Even with my illiterate tongue,
I am not uneducated,
For I read the truth in your actions.
Your Cambridge laurels may decorate your mind,
But your heart remains chained
To the fetters of caste,
The rusted iron of Manuvad,
The shadows of Hitler's doctrine.

O Guru of masks,
Your politics of transcendence
Deceives African leaders,
Confounds global human rights,
But I, the Untouchable,
See your essence laid bare.

What is purity,
When your hands drip blood?
What is impurity,
When my soul rises above your hate?

You, the self-styled guardian of dharma,
Are nothing but a vulture,
Circling the carcass of humanity,
Feeding on lies and suffering.

O fascist Hindu,
Your matrimonial lies
Are a mirror of your soul—
A reflection stained by centuries of cruelty.
When will you see?
When will you learn
That love and dignity know no caste,
No chains, no borders?

126. O Brahmin, The Venom Runs Deep

O Brahmin, your touch is poison, your breath is fire,
A thousand serpents coil in your ire.
No Mullah, no priest, no king so cruel,
No shadow darker, no law so brutal.

How many times have your hands struck down,
My untouchable blood spilled on sacred ground?
How many daughters lost in the night,
Molested, broken, stripped of light?

Your fire consumes, your foot soldiers cheer,
You build your temples on ashes and fear.
My name is burned, my touch unclean,
Yet truth remembers what you have been.

O Brahmin, your venom seeps,
Through centuries, through silenced weeps.
Yet now you sit in halls of fame,
A Nobel prize to mask the shame.

A scholar, a thinker, a leader in West,
Draped in robes of truth professed.
But what is truth when born in lies,
When justice falls and conscience dies?

Your decomposed body walks the land,
A hollow relic, a dying hand.
You speak of peace, of human rights,
Yet my people burn beneath your might.

Your soul is dust, your words are chains,
No learning cleans what still remains.
No book, no theory, no title high,
Can cleanse the bloodstains where they lie.

O Brahmin, step from your throne,
Your house is built on broken bones.
Your justice is silence, your mercy is weight,
Your caste is a prison, your love is too late.

Light your soul, let truth arise,
Break the mask, unveil your lies.
Civilize your heart, let judgment be,
For freedom belongs to even me.

127. Vegetarian Only: The Mask of Genocider in Hindu Religion, Ideology, and Society

O Brahmin, master of deception,
Everyday you wear the mask of purity,
But behind it, you devour eggs, drink milk,
Feast on the labor of my caste,
Feed on the anguish of my African brother.
You cloak your cruelty with "vegetarian only,"
A euphemism for your genocidal hatred.

"Vegetarian only," you say,
In place of "Brahmin, Kshatriya, Vaishya, Shudra only."
Your words are weapons,
Polished daggers of exclusion,
Cutting through the soul of my untouchable existence.

O Brahmin, O non-Brahmin,
You who speak of ahimsa,
Your hands drip with the blood of my people.
You rape my daughters,
Burn my sons alive,
Erase my history with a sanctimonious smile.

"Vegetarian only,"
You scrawl on your rental boards,
Your matrimonial ads,
Your dining tables.
But every act of your life
Feeds on the meat of my suffering,
The marrow of my oppression.

You call my African brother "Negro,"
A thief, a prostitute, a criminal,
In your temples of exclusion,
While in his homeland,
You call him brother,
A chameleon in the sunlit fields of lies.

You humiliate me in your spaces,
In your villages, towns, cities,
But your venom follows me
To my African spaces,
To the West,
To every corner of the earth.

How long, O Brahmin,
Will you hide behind your vegetarian mask?
Your purity is a lie,
A veil for your parasitic greed.
You plundered my labor,
You stole my dignity,
And now, you feast on my African kin.

The world sees your mask,
But I see your face,
A vulture circling,
A predator cloaked in sanctity.
O Brahmin, O non-Brahmin,
How long will your lies sustain you?
One day, truth will strip you bare,
And the world will see the blood
On your vegetarian hands.

128. Brahmin, Bhagavad Gita, Bharat, Briton, Britanica, Bible

O Brahmin, you are the architect of suffering,
Your ancient words, like poison in the veins of time,
Have seeped into the world,
Spreading the seeds of hatred,
Nurtured by your twisted scriptures,
The Bhagavad Gita, your sacred lie,
Preaching the elimination of my people,
The untouchables, those you deem less than human.

And yet you are standing tall,
Hiding behind your purity,
Whereas the Bible, a holy lie,
Speaks of enslaving black skin,
Subjugating my Untouchable and African brothers and sisters,
With the same venom you pour on me.
The Bible and the Bhagavad Gita-
Two sides of the same coin,
Two instruments of oppression,
That turn my skin into something inferior,
That turn my humanity into something unworthy.

Oh, Briton, how you glorify Brahmin ideals,
How you celebrate the subjugation of my people,
You turned the world into a bazaar of slavery,
Untouchables in chains,
Stole Blacks, and
Erased Jews.
You created your empires on our backs,
Lived on our agonies,

Our labor, on our very souls,
And after all that, you were parading yourselves as civilization bearers.

When the Briton enters Bharat,
You embrace the Brahmin as an equal,
And when the Brahmin steps onto your shores,
You too treat them as equals,
For you share the same blood,
The same evil,
Rooted in your scriptures,
Your minds, your hearts,
Your bodies—
Fascist in spirit,
Fascist in deed.

But there is another truth,
One that does not come from your pages,
One that lives in the love of Black Christ,
In the beauty of Black Jesus,
Who spoke not of hate,
But of humanity,
Of love, of equality,
Of breaking the chains that you forged.

The Brahmin and the Briton are not superior.
They are the architects of our suffering,
Symbols of pure hate and violence,
But Black Jesus, He is the light.
He is the truth.
And we, we are His people.

The Britanica may glorify you,
But your purity is a myth,
And your supremacy a lie.
For truth is in love,
Truth is in humanity,
Truth is in the Black Christ,
The one who sees me not as less,

But as a part of His creation,
As a human.

129. Water

O life-giving water,
You are pure in nature,
Flowing freely through earth's veins,
But in the hands of Brahmins, you are deemed sacred,
And in the touch of an untouchable, you are condemned as vile.

When my parched lips seek your mercy,
The Brahmin's rage erupts,
My hands, cracked and bleeding,
Cannot hold you without retribution.
To touch you in my creator's spaces,
Means my body is dismembered,
Torn apart by scriptures' decrees.
In democratic spaces,
The crowd gathers, the stones fly,
And I am lynched for quenching my thirst.

In the ponds of Brahmin, Kshatriya, Vaishya, and Shudra,
You are guarded like treasure,
But not for me,
For I am untouchable,
My caste sentenced me to thirst and death.

Ambedkar once dared to touch your surface,
He led us to ponds guarded by purity's chains,
And though he broke legal barriers,
The price was paid in blood.
For every drop we drank,
The ground soaked in the crimson of our kind.
The colonial rulers,

Those arbiters of empire,
Stood with the Brahmin,
Shunning Ambedkar and us,
Reaffirming purity's monstrous creed.

And Gandhi, that saint of peace,
Turned against us with terror,
Uniting Hindus to punish the untouchable,
To keep water, life's essence, beyond our reach.

Today, not much has changed.
In India, Nepal, Pakistan,
Bangladesh, Sri Lanka, and Japan,
In every space where caste reigns supreme,
Water is a weapon,
A lifeline turned into death's tool.

Even under the scrutiny of the UNHCR,
Our cries remain unheard,
Our eligibility for asylum ignored,
For our torment, invisible in the eyes of the world.

O water, symbol of purity and life,
When will you cleanse this earth
Of the sins committed in your name?
When will the untouchable,
The moon-like, socially ostracized,
Drink freely without fear of violence?

Let the blood spilled in the water-touching movement
Quench the thirst for justice,
And drown the hatred of those who see caste,
Instead of humanity.

130. The Mask of the Civilian

She walks with grace in the halls of the West,
Her voice adorned in human rights zest.
Yet beneath her silk and scholarly claim,
Lies a blade carved with an untouchable's name.

A civilian, they call her, refined and wise,
Yet I see the fire that burns in her eyes.
Not the warmth of justice, not mercy's light,
But the embers of caste, concealed from sight.

She speaks of peace, of freedom's call,
Yet builds invisible, unbreakable walls.
My shadow disturbs, my breath defiles,
She marks me impure, unworthy, vile.

In her streets, my love is a sin,
My steps are cursed, my skin wears chains within.
Her laws of blood, of lines never crossed,
Leave my dignity beaten, my honor lost.

She cheers when her men strike me down,
For loving her sister, for daring her town.
She carves her justice with stones and flames,
Yet in Western courts, she changes her names.

A face on the news, a beacon of rights,
A voice for the silenced in panel lights.
She takes the stage with practiced grace,
Yet carries the lash, the knife, the mace.

They hand her medals, they write her praise,
A woman of justice, a world they raise.
But I see the hands that pull the thread,
That weave the noose, that count the dead.

When I cry of truth, of wounds unseen,
The world calls me bitter, cruel, obscene.
"Racist," they whisper, "a threat, a lie,"
While she stands tall, with her head held high.

O shadowed truth, O untold tale,
Your name erased in the laureate's veil.
Yet justice lingers, it waits, it stays,
For no mask can last till the end of days.

131. Brahmin Agraharam: Settlements of Genocider

O Brahmin,
From your Agraharam, you built walls of division,
Casting shadows of impurity over my existence.
You declared yourself a god on earth,
Crowning your supremacy with scriptures,
While chaining me to the ghetto of untouchability.

From your Agraharam
Was born the caste system,
An instrument to sunder the universe,
To keep God within and throw the devil without.
You invented norms to label me polluting,
To exclude me outside your hamlets,
Beyond the pale of the Universe itself.

Your kshatriya men lifted the axe against my people,
The Vaishya banians sold my labour unsolicited,
And Shudras implemented your edicts,
To annihilate my civilization, maim, exterminate. Oh Brahmin.
Your verse is no word of the lord;
Swords,
Satan hymn that praises power and continues pain.

For millions of years,
You have raped my daughters,
Burned my sons,
And forced us to serve your twisted god.
From the Agraharam came not enlightenment,
But the darkness of human degradation.

Yet your crimes have found alliances,
In the white marble halls of Cambridge,
In the ivy-draped walls of Oxford,
In the classrooms of Columbia, Stanford, and MIT.
Western hands, soaked in the blood of black bodies,
Shake yours, brown and bloodied,
As allies in oppression,
As collaborators in human chains.

And the Muslim, who claims submission to God,
Endorsed your crimes against my caste,
Treating my untouchable skin as equally vile,
Binding my feet in the same fetters of discrimination.

O Agraharam,
Your roots are deep in the soil of hate,
But your branches stretch wide,
Casting shadows over continents.
Your purity is a mask for brutality,
Your prayers a chant of exclusion.

But I shall stand,
For no scripture, no settlement,
No alliance of hate can silence the truth:
I am human, born of the same divine imagination,
And no Agraharam can strip me of my dignity.

132. Gandhi's Mask: The Face of Genocide

O Gandhi,
Your name has become a symbol,
A statue that looms, casting shadows of shame,
A mask of righteousness worn by the cruel,
Your truth, hidden beneath the cloak of compassion,
Revealed in the hatred you harbored
For those whose skin was darker than yours.

You spoke of freedom, of independence,
But for whom did you truly fight?
Not for the untouchables, not for the Africans,
Not for the oppressed or the enslaved,
But for your own caste,
For your own skin,
And for your vision of purity,
A vision steeped in the blood of racism.

You, the so-called Mahatma,
Champion of non-violence,
Yet your words toward the black and untouchable
Were violence incarnate.
You said Africans were criminals,
Dirty, smelly, and inferior—
How could a man claim moral high ground
When his very breath reeked of caste and scorn?

You condemned Africans to the most inferior pits,
Called them prostitutes and fakirs,
Staining the name of freedom
With the ink of your own bigotry.

You, who wished to uplift your nation,
But tossed the rest of the world aside
As if they were less than human-
As if their suffering meant nothing.

But in the halls of the University of Ghana,
A spark of righteousness was lit,
And down came the statue of your hate,
For the truth was no longer to be concealed.
So the staff rose, so rose the community,
And thus Africa did speak:
"No more idols of hate,
No more sham prophets of oppression."

O Gandhi,
You were no liberator for the untouchable,
Nor for the soul of Africa.
Your word is poison,
Your legacy betrayal.
The world must be made to see you for what you are:
A man who preached freedom with one hand,
And crushed the spirit of the oppressed with the other.

To the University of Ghana,
You did it, where India has not been able to—
You have torn down the racist's statue,
The scar from the earth has gone,
And the world shall see
Even gods must go down.

This be an example to all,
Throughout Africa, in India too, and beyond—
No icon, no head, no figure
Above truth there is none.
Gandhi, in a garb so compassionate,
Has to go down in memory for being:
Oppression's ally,
A false prophet,
And a man unworthy of our adoration.

To the people of Africa,
Rise up and remove these symbols,
These idols of a man who never truly saw you,
Who never cared for your suffering.
Let the world see that you stand for justice,
For the dignity of all,
And not for the false idols of caste and racism.

133. Calling Mahatma or Great Soul or Call Him Genocider, Racist, Casteist, Paedophilic, Dehumanizer, Subjugator, Gay, Untouchability Practitioner?

O Gandhi, the so-called Great Soul,
What truth lies beneath your cloak?
A savior to some, but to others, a mask,
A pedophile, a racist—could this be your task?

You called yourself a saint, a moral guide,
Yet your actions hide behind a veil of pride.
The youngest souls, you held them near,
Testing your desires in the name of fear.

With under-aged girls, you sought control,
Betraying the very innocence of their soul.
In your Sabarmati Ashram, you played your part,
Claiming virtue while tearing hearts apart.

You spoke of purity, a Hindu dream,
But your words were not as pure as they seemed.
You called us untouchables, less than men,
Fighting for our freedom, yet keeping us penned.

You were the voice of the oppressor's creed,
Sowing division in a nation's need.
A whitewashed history, a lie so grand,
But we see the truth beneath your hand.

You stood on the backs of the weak,
Yet praised your own power while we sought to speak.

You crushed the untouchables, soiled their right,
Betrayed by the very man who called for their fight.

Racist words in foreign lands you spoke,
Your view on blacks, a heavy yoke.
You praised the colonizer, sided with the foe,
Treated Africans as low, as below.

How can we call you "great," how can we say,
That you fought for us when you turned away?
Your legacy taints the fabric of time,
A hero for some, but a monster in rhyme.

Now the University of Ghana has shown the way,
Removing your statue, casting you astray.
For your deeds, your ideology, your systemic hate,
Have no place in this world, no room in our state.

You fought against freedom, against equality,
Pushing your caste, your religion's brutality.
Your words, your actions, have done enough harm—
Now we raise our voices, rejecting your charm.

You were no leader, no savior true,
But a tool of the oppressor, a false view.
We will not wear the chains you once made,
Your great soul, now a shadow, will fade.

In this world, there is no place for your lies,
Your pedestal falls, your empire dies.
For the untouchable's voice, for the voiceless and weak,
We stand against your legacy—truth, not the mystique

134. Of Saints and Sinners

In Natal's court, you polished your plea—
a "civilized" Indian, distinct, apart.
Kaffir, you spat, at those darker than thee,
clutching the colonizer's script for your art.
Black backs became your stepping stones,
your petitions stained with their unnamed pain.
You carved your rights from their fractured bones,
and left their chains in the empire's rain.

You wept for Harijans, but not their rage,
defended varna's "holy" divide.
Annihilation, Ambedkar scrawled on the page,
while your fasts shackled futures, your "mercy" denied.
Poona's pact—a noose disguised as grace—
you traded their votes for your hollow acclaim.
The caste's old poison still haunts this place,
and Dalit blood salts the soil of your name.

You praised the Sermon, but damned the Church,
called conversion a foreign disease.
"Children of brothels"—no, not your words—
but your silence blessed the majoritarian breeze.
For your India, a saffron-tinted dream,
where the cross was a wound, not a bridge to be crossed.
You let the mob's shadow cloak the scream
of those who dared dissent, their voices lost.

Now history drapes you in spotless white,
erasing the stains where your truths wore thin.
But the Negro child, the Untouchable, the Christian's fight

still tally the cost of the wars you'd begin.
O Saint of Selective Empathy, hear—
their ghosts dissent from your martyred shrine.
For freedom's flame, when it burns unclear,
lights only the faces it dares to define.

135. The Saint's Shadow

They wrapped you in a saintly cloth,
spun hymns of salt and spinning wheel—
but what of those your light forgot,
the wounds no charkha could heal?

In Natal's court, you pled your case,
a "civilized" brown subject's cry—
yet called Black souls a "kaffir" race,
and climbed their backs to touch the sky.

You damned the curse of untouchables
but bowed to varna's ancient chains,
painted Harijan in fables
while Ambedkar burned caste's remains.

Your fasts could halt a nation's breath,
yet brittle bridges built in Poona
forced Dalit hopes to walk their death—
a pact signed in the oppressor's tune.

For Christ, you praised the turned cheek's creed
but scorned his flock as foreign spawn,
denied the cross where two worlds bleed,
and sealed your India's saffron dawn.

O Mohandas Karamchand Gandhi, fractured icon,
your chants broke empires, birthed a state—
but in the dust where chains still tighten,
the marginalized still name their weight.

136. Glorifying "Mahatma" with Gandhi?

O Western and Eastern world,
I laugh at your shallow, blinded gaze,
What is this word, Mahatma, that you praise?
Do you even grasp its meaning?
Is it just a title you bestow so freely,
Without seeing the truth beneath the veil of lies?

Great soul, Mahatma,
Purer word for those that did well,
Not the fellow who lived to ill
Begrime, bemock, and defile.
Thou dost call him the Great Soul,
Yet he whom you raise so high
Has hurt me, humiliated my race,
Made mock at my dark skin
Debased my people, scorning them,
Cannot be divine.

John Rawls—oh, there's a great Mahatma,
Living equal justice, fighting racism,
Marrying his dark belle,
Lived with her forty years,
A living expression of human dignity,
And raising children with love, not hate,
Breaking chains of oppression with the truth..

Yet you praise Gandhi,
A man who built his empire
On the bones of my people,
Who called my ancestors "slaves,"

Who turned a blind eye to our suffering
And told the world it was righteous to subjugate us.
A man who said,
"Christians are children of prostitutes,"
And degraded African bodies,
His "great soul" steeped in the oppression of others.
How can you call such a man a Mahatma?
His soul was not great, it was tainted,
With the blood of untouchables and Africans,
It soaked in the horrors of caste,
The filth of his own twisted purity.

Great soul, you say?
A great soul would never oppress,
Would never deny love or life,
Would never submit to the vile practices
Of a caste-bound system,
Where the weakest are crushed
Under the weight of the "pure" and the "superior."
Mahatma, you say?
I call him a farce, a fraud,
A man who never knew the meaning of true justice.

John Rawls knew the soul of justice—
And Gandhi, in his heart, knew nothing but ego.
If you want to speak of greatness,
If you want to honor those who fought for all,
Then honor Rawls, not this false idol.
For Gandhi, the racist,
The one who dehumanized my people,
Is no great soul—
But a man of hatred, a man of lies,
A man who left us to suffer,
While calling himself the savior.

Stop this madness,
Stop calling him Mahatma,
And recognize true greatness in those
Who built bridges, not walls,

Who lifted the oppressed,
And gave light to the forgotten.
John Rawls, the true soul of justice,
Is the man who deserves our praise,
Not this figure of pure deception.

137. The Madness of African-American Leaders Adoring Gandhi

O Martin Luther King,
Now I see why you praised a man
Who called himself a champion of peace—
But what peace did Gandhi preach?
What nonviolence did he truly believe in,
When his soul was stained with caste, with racism,
And with a dark, twisted notion of purity?

How can you call him an inspiration,
A man who saw African lives as inferior?
A man who saw my black skin as dirt,
Who denied us our humanity,
While preaching about freedom and justice?
Did you not see his true face,
The face of a man who used his power
To oppress, to dehumanize, to silence?

You, Martin, spoke of freedom and love,
But did you not hear the echoes of Gandhi's hate?
Did you not see the lies he built his empire on,
The false doctrines of purity and supremacy
That he preached,
While my people starved in his shadow?
How could you admire such a man?
How could you, a champion for the oppressed,
Lift up a man who wanted to eliminate
Not just Africans, but untouchables too?

He used the poor masses of India,
Their struggles, their hopes,
As a backdrop for his self-serving revolution.
Just as you used the slums of black America
For your political and professional gain.
Both of you played the same game—
You both wore masks of righteousness,
While your actions told a different story,
One of exploitation, manipulation, and hypocrisy.

How could you—who fought for the dignity
Of black people, for their rights and respect—
Look up to a man who saw us as inferior,
A man who lived a life of contradictions,
Peddling nonviolence while advocating
For a violent, caste-based, hierarchical society?
Gandhi, a man of brown supremacy,
A man who crushedmy people beneath his feet,
While he was elevated by the world as a hero.
How could you, Martin, inspire us with such a man,
When you knew the truth of his violence,
And his complicity in the oppression of the downtrodden?

We, the black Christians, who live by the message of love,
Cannot accept your hero, Gandhi,
Who turned his back on humanity,
Who supported a system of cruelty,
A system that enslaved untouchables,
A system that condemned my African ancestors
To lives of misery and oppression.
How can we, who follow Christ,
Find anything but disdain for a man
Who worshipped Hindu idols of violence
While calling for a world of peace?

Gandhi is no hero, Martin—
He is a symbol of oppression,
A symbol of lies, of manipulation.
We don't need his inspiration,

We don't need his solidarity.
We need true freedom—
The freedom of self-respect,
The dignity of life,
The moral values of love, peace, and truth.
We need to break free from these false idols
And build a world where no one is enslaved
By the past, by lies, by caste, or by color.

138. The Western Educated Indian Gold-Diggers

She drapes her form in a veil of gold,
A lustrous garment, the story untold.
Glimmering jewels catch her eyes' embrace,
Yet her heart, a prisoner, locked in place.

With every roll of silk upon her skin,
She seeks not love, but the shine within.
For what is gold but a fleeting flame,
That swallows her soul, but forgets her name?

Her education, a polished art,
Can't shield her from the emptiness in her heart.
Degrees from Yale, from lands afar,
Yet they don't heal the wounds beneath the star.

She pleads for diamonds, not for truth,
A chain of desire binds her youth.
And though the world may call her wise,
Her worth is lost in the web of lies.

Yet there are voices that rise, unbroken,
Women who seek a life unspoken.
Jewish, Dalit, Western too—
Fighting for what is theirs by right, not view.

For no one should be a thing to trade,
No heart should be for gold's charade.
Her spirit, untouched by the jewels' weight,
Is destined for a different fate.

139. The 1948 Refugee Convention: Globally Accepted Antisemitic Law

In the year of 1948, a pact was made,
A law, wrapped in the guise of aid,
The Refugee Convention, a welcomed hand,
Yet, for the Jewish soul, it built a land
Of fear, of darkness, of unspoken dread—
Where safety vanished, and hope bled.

Three hundred million Islamic voices surged,
Their presence in Western lands emerged,
But behind their cries and desperate calls,
The Jew, behind thick walls,
Compelled to live with shaking hands,
And the cost of refuge was not as they had planned.

A world-wide gesture to appease the strife,
Yet the Jew was hounded to his life—
Threatened by whispers, agents unknown,
In cities once so peaceful overthrown;
Where safety is, death dogs the night,
A dying light in the shadows of fear.

Let the IDF, our shield and might,
Guard against the rising blight,
Against hate that festers so deep inside,
And the terror unceasing, which does chide.
Their courage bold, their duty so true,
For innocent lives, they see this through.

In the land of Palestine, they are fighting for something more
Than borders, more than mere land-more than the stories of yore.
Standing watch, like sentinels at bay,
To shield all living from those in hiding array,
Who seek to choke the desperate cry,
Of the innocent, who meet their death.

But in this fight, not only men,
But animals too, must find their pen.
For the killers and eaters, the hands of fate,
Show no mercy, and decimate.
Thus, may God bless them, the guardians of life,
In the face of terror, they rise above strife.

140. Indian Drama

In the shadowed halls of Indian lore,
Where saints preach and hypocrites soar,
The drama unfolds, its act unkind—
Bedding with buds, and raping the mind.

It tells the story, day and night,
Words of saints that no one believes,
For under a garb of righteous light
Lies the cruelty of an endless night.

It rapes the tender, just-born blooms,
Talking rights within hollow rooms.
A world of flowers, tender and pure,
Snipped away by unsure hands.

They sing of ethics, of moral might,
While raping buds out of sight.
They preach of justice, singing songs,
Yet killing roses, righting wrongs.

Feminism wears a mask of grace,
Voice of gender rights, disgraced.
Fortune chases and wealth,
Sell the truth for hollow health.

The drama has one more act,
Where the voices of morals crack.
Justice and freedom, peace they say,
And in darkness, these traits slay.

Indian drama, pride-wrapp'd round,
Nobel's leading star touted around,
Shining bright, but lo, below,
Caste and racism-the wounds that grow.

UNO and the West, they hold the stage,
Puppets in the hands of a bygone age.
Age-old ideologies in golden light,
Pushing falsehoods, suppressing right.

The world beholds a stage show play,
Heroes of truth, in broad array.
Yet in the wings, where dark falls,
Lie secrets that break the highest walls.

They claim to heal, to save, to teach,
While drowning truth within their reach.
A theatre of false ideals,
Where only pain and silence heals.

Indian drama, a tragic tale,
A system built upon dust and stale.
Caste, race, and lies of untouchability,
Veiled by a mask of nobility..

141. Hindu Swaraj (Hindu Self-Rule) Atrocities

When India was under colonial rule,
India's crime was zero,
A land untouched by the hands of lawless men,
A place where peace, though imposed,
Hushed the cries of the oppressed.

But when India fell to its own rule,
When the chains of colonial masters fell away,
India's crime rose—
By 1100%,
An earth birthed the caste-based genocide
And untouchability-based genocide against the untouchable.
A land marred by corruption, oppression,
A place where the promise of freedom
Turned to dust beneath the feet of the downtrodden.

This is called Hindu self-rule.
This is called Hindu Swaraj.
The vision of Gandhi, the father of the nation,
The dream of every nationalist,
Yet it is a dream painted with blood.

Under the guise of freedom,
A new caste tyranny was born,
The unbroken chains of caste,
The same oppressions dressed in new robes.
A so-called independent land,
But in truth, it was only an illusion.

Gandhi's ideal, a self-rule built on purity and impurity,
A system where the untouchables remained outcasts,
Where the dark-skinned were relegated to shadows,
Where millions were made to serve the whims of the few.

Nationalism, a banner of false glory,
Hiding the stains of caste-based violence,
It was not the freedom of all,
But the enslavement of many in the name of unity.

The colonial master is gone,
The spirit of oppression never died,
But was reincarnated into the heart of the new rulers.
All this is the reality of Hindu Swaraj:
A country still in chains with fetters forged by itself,

A nation still haunted by the ghosts it has brought into being.
All that was desired was this much,
And this is the desire of every nationalist;
A separated nation,
A land of wails and lamentation of the suppressed.
Echo louder than the voices of the free.

142. Western Educated Hindu Mother: Partner in Crime Against my Skin

Mother, I never saw you enlightened,
Even though you are a Cambridge scholar,
Your degrees and accolades line your walls,
But your heart remains bound by ignorance.
You speak of justice, but your actions are shackled,
A mind trained in knowledge, but a soul unfree.

Mother, I never saw you enlightened,
Even though you are a NASA scientist,
With knowledge that could touch the stars,
Yet your spirit is grounded in the dirt of caste.
You reached for the universe,
But never once extended a hand to the oppressed.

Mother, I never saw you enlightened,
Even though you are a UNO leader,
A voice for human rights on the world stage,
Yet your own people suffer beneath your gaze.
You call for peace, but you practice division,
You fight for freedom, but deny it to the most voiceless.

Mother, I never saw you enlightened,
Even though you are a Western lawmaker,
With power to shape laws, to grant equality,
Yet you upheld the system that condemned the lowest.
You passed laws in favor of justice,
But still looked away from the untouchables' plight.

Mother, I never saw you enlightened,
Even though you are a Colombian professor,
Teaching the world about humanity's grace,
But never once questioned the cruelty in your own house.
You trained minds to think critically,
But never applied it to your own hypocrisy.

Mother, I never saw you enlightened,
Even though you are a poet here,
Writing about love, about freedom, about light,
Yet your own heart remains darkened by caste.
You wrote with passion for equality,
But lived in silence while your own kin suffered.

Mother, I have seen you as oppressive,
Even though you are a global human rights scholar,
You speak of justice but practice caste,
You use your power to control, to suppress,
To keep the lowly in their place,
While you rise on the backs of the oppressed.

Mother, I have seen you as casteist,
Even though you are a global human rights voice,
You raised me to believe in equality,
Yet never once applied it to your own life.
How could you teach me to love the world
When you couldn't love the ones closest to you?

143. An Untouchable Anthem Against The Indian Ideology

From the ashes of millennia,
India rises not in glory,
But in shadows forged by caste,
By untouchable blood spilled on sacred soil,
By brutal hierarchies carved into the marrow of its existence.

This land of so-called ancient wisdom,
Its scriptures a doctrine of division,
Where birth seals fate with chains unbroken,
Where a Brahmin's whisper outweighs an untouchable's scream.
A nation birthed and buried in barbarism.

What civilization grows from the roots of oppression?
What humanity flourishes when life itself is a sin for some?
In the ghettoes of caste, love withers,
And in its temples, hatred is sanctified.
From the womb to the pyre,
The untouchable walks in chains,
Their dignity crushed beneath feet of privilege,
Their worth measured by distance from purity's shadow.

Untouchable hands feed the nation,
Untouchable backs bear its weight,
But their voices are never loud,
Their lives whispers drowned in the cacophony of ritual.
This is the Indian ideology:
A prison of beliefs passed as culture,
A weapon of morality turned on its own.

How much reason has survived in this land?
Where the breath of the cow is holy,
And the human breath a pollutant, provided it comes from "lower" lungs.
Where the shadow falling on the "pure"
Is a sin punished with fire and blood.
India, a country that claims light,
Yet worships darkness in its actions,
A paradox carved into its soul.

Civilization wants progress,
But India clings to the chains of old,
Her way of life a theatre of cruelty,
Her ideology a hymn to hate.
Day after day, caste kills,
Untouchability maims,
The worth of the human soul
Is weighed against the weight of shame inherited.

O India, land of sages and slaughter,
Thy ideology is a graveyard of hope.
Nothing stirs in thy depths to evolution,
Only the repetition of crimes wrapped in tradition.
You are an anesthetic to progress,
A poison to peace,
A betrayer of humanity's promise.

Let the winds of truth blow through your borders,
Let your walls of prejudice crumble.
But until then, the cries of the oppressed will echo,
A testament to your unyielding cruelty.

144. The Journey of an Untouchable

I was born in shadows, unnamed and unseen,
In the Hindu spaces where caste cuts deep and clean.
My mother, a warrior of fields, worked under the sun's fire,
Fifteen hours for two rupees, exploited by greed's desire.

My father, a rickshaw puller, hid in the night,
Pulling the weight of shame, avoiding the light.
My sister's dignity guarded, my mother stood tall,
Yet vultures circled, waiting for her to fall.

From the ghetto of Madiga, I sought to be free,
But chains of caste followed wherever I'd be.
Brazil, Australia, Ethiopia—I roamed far and wide,
Yet casteism and racism always walked by my side.

Mamidi Richa, a Kapu by caste, stole my virginity's thread,
But her family's honor left my first child dead.
A Hindu wife's promise turned into ash and despair,
In the name of purity, love was stripped bare.

I found love again in Ethiopian lands,
But war tore us apart with its brutal hands.
We fled to the Czech Republic, a supposed sanctuary,
Only to meet racism's raw, dehumanizing cruelty.

Rooms with cockroaches, utensils stained with grime,
A black cross judged by their hatred and crime.
Social workers who should mend and care,
Instead stripped us of humanity, left us bare.

My son Stanford, bright as the sun's light,
Lost to a German gynecologist's plight.
Saviour, my youngest, faces stares and disdain,
In lands where truth and justice are slain.

India called me crow, buffalo, pig,
Europe echoes those slurs, just under a new rig.
No matter where I wander, no matter where I go,
Caste and race whisper, casting the same shadow.

I search for a homeland, a sanctuary, a place,
Free of untouchability, free of race.
Like Jews who found their land of hope,
I dream of a refuge where I can cope.

But until that day, I carry my pain,
In every land, under every name.
An untouchable, unheard, but still alive,
Through the grief, I persist, I strive.

145. Against the Madness of Cremation

They claim that the flames are for purification.
That the body is just a mere musk,
A place that the soul inhabits for some time in the life of an individual.
Soon to be scattered,
Ashes in the wind,
Returning to the earth, polluting rivers
Eternal to the process of reincarnation.

But I hear the screams of the trees,
They felled the trees for the funeral pyre,
The crackled of life was reduced to ashes,
A land blackened by such old cruel rituals.
What happens to the smoke?
Does it rise up to the sky?
Or hang, luxurious, over our heads?
A reminder of the lives that were sensely sacrificed
The earth scorched,
For the sake of culture.
They say that the flames purify,
But where is this greatness or dignity in the act of cremation? A body brutally consumed by flames.
Succumbing later to be in ashes only to sprinkle.

Is this final act one of love, respect or basic humanity?
Where is the respect for the life that was led?
The heartbeat that once marked breathing, lovers, desire?
And in Christian way, we bury our relations.
A humans gentle, enduring, beneath the earth.
Wrapped in the pairings of family.
The grab that embraced or grabbed them closely.

An act of passing on love, respect, and other basic courtesies back and forth.
A parting that acknowledges joy and love for life and the revered soul.

What remains of knowledge, after the cruel ritual?
Ideas burn, leaving behind only hollow vessels.
Where fire's cruel hiss resides, we stifle wisdom.
Turning intellect to ashes,
To conceal truth in smoke and lies.

Should we burn it and call for the new day?
Claiming to be honor to the departed,
Can there be no humane or rationale or softer or civilized way?
There is no gentle way to free the soul.
Without provoking an explosion in the world?
Must the air be laden with the stench of suffering?
The rivers filled with the remains of the desecrated?

I am on the edge of the flame.
And I wonder,
If we are not burning more than bodies,
If we are not sacrificing more than just bodies.

146. Against the Madness of Hindu Culture

Fire starts to climb up, nearly touching the heavens.
The sound of crackling wood sounded like a death wail.
But what of the air that chokes and sighs?
When another body starts to turn to ashes and flies?

Smoke is present, and it is as black as only hopelessness is.
Possessing sorrow, yet polluting the weather.
Rivers that were once clear are now tainted.
There are memories of burnt ashes; there are memories of grief.

Would this be the way their memories can be honored?
Thus, feeding the flame, fueling dread?
By casting their ashes and polluting the streams,
Is it possible to actually transform sacred waters into the dreams of death?

It hears tradition and its lore, but does it ever look?
The forests cut down, the dying trees?
The breath of life, now heavy and gray
When have funeral pyres been burning day after day?

For sake of peace, we started burning the earth.
But what and to what? Other names, other people, and the future—what is worth it?
When the environment we live in, the air we breathe
Is turned into poison by the very rites that we contemplate and hold sacred?

Believe that people leave us to go to a better place,
But at the same time, let the living be happy?
Cornered both make a way for both to survive.

For in death that falls and in the coals that burn.
They are the constructs beneath which lies a truth we all must know.

Earth is not ours to burn and to betray.
To honor the dead, there must be a new way.
Let there be some cool-off period where passions cool down and flames die out.
And all the smoke clears.
Hear the dead and the living; let the earth be at rest.

147. Why I Am Not Indian: The Untouchable Rejecting India's Citizenship

I was born in the shadow of temples,
where gods carved from stone turned their backs,
where scriptures wrote my fate in dust,
where my name was an echo—
unheard, unspoken, unwelcome.

I walked the streets of my homeland,
but the soil beneath my feet refused to know me.
To them, I was a ghost, a stain, a shadow,
an untouchable breath in a land
that worships purity, yet bathes in blood.

India is not my mother.
She did not cradle me in her arms,
she did not sing lullabies to my skin,
she did not whisper my name with love.
She carved my back with her sacred laws,
fed me shame, clothed me in silence.

O nation built on graves,
you called me impure, yet you built your empire
upon my father's broken bones,
upon my mother's silent screams,
upon the ashes of my ancestors
who were never given names.

I reject you, India.
Your idols hold no light for me,
your rivers do not cleanse my wounds,

your scriptures do not speak my truth.
I burn your history from my tongue,
strip your citizenship from my skin,
erase your name from my blood.

I am not your child.
I am the voice that rose from your flames,
the rebel who tore your chains,
the exile who will not return.

Let the conch shells wail,
let the cowards tremble,
for I will not kneel
before a nation
that buried my people alive.

I stand against you, India—
against your gods, your caste, your lies.
I do not belong to your genocide.
I belong to the wind,
to the sky that holds no masters,
to a world where my name
is not a crime.

148. A Son's Apology

O my Madiga Christian Father,
you left this world while I was trapped
behind asylum walls,
a prisoner of borders,
a captive of fate.
I never held your hand one last time,
never whispered a final goodbye.
The distance between us—measured not in miles,
but in the silence of regret.

I walked alone through books
that had no teachers,
read words from Oxford, Cambridge, Columbia,
with no Guru to guide me.
From the caste-marked halls of India
to the cold corridors of Sydney,
I stood—an untouchable shadow
in the lands of the free.

And then, I married the storm.
She held my unborn son in her hands,
a threat wrapped in love,
blackmail veiled as devotion.
Saviour, my child, my reason—
I bound myself in chains
to keep him from the abyss.

But, Father, you warned me.
You said, "Do not marry an African."
Not because of skin,

but because of wounds
carved deeper than history.
You knew, as the Bible knew:
"Can the Ethiopian change his skin,
or the leopard its spots?"
Yet I, blind in desperation,
gave my name to a mirage.

She had a husband before me,
and one before him,
and perhaps one after me, too.
A fisherman casting her net,
not for love, but for passage—
a way to the West.

In her world,
no father stays, no mother guides.
Brothers and sisters blur in the night,
husbands and lovers speak the same name.
The home, not a sanctuary,
but a marketplace of bodies,
where promises are shadows,
and love is currency.

I walked into that abyss,
watched morality crumble
into laughter over meat and football.
Saw faith bent and broken,
the cross worn not on the soul,
but as decoration
for hands that hold no truth.

I fled, Father—
not from love, but from the lie.
I ran to the Czech Republic,
seeking a new dawn,
but racism greeted me at the gates,
Europe's hands as cold
as India's caste-bound fists.

I lost you in this exile.
I lost my son Stanford to the frost
of a foreign land's indifference.
I lost myself
to the choices I made.

Forgive me, Father.
I write these words, not as confession,
but as repentance.
For me, now, there is only one truth—
I must protect Saviour
from a world built on lies.
And I will.

149. The Fathers of a Nation

O Brahmin, O Bania,
O icons draped in saffron and silk,
tell me, what makes a father of a nation?
What carves his name into stone?
Is it the hand that lifts the oppressed,
or the hand that trembles over a child's skin?

I did not understand
until I read of Gandhi's hands,
trembling not with wisdom,
but with the weight of young flesh,
his nights spent beside naked innocence,
wrapped in silence, cloaked in sainthood.

I did not understand
until I saw Nehru's gaze,
wandering past politics,
past policy, past power,
to the lips of another man's wife,
a legacy written in desire.

And then I knew—
to be a father of a nation,
one must be a devourer,
a saint in daylight, a shadow at dusk,
a hero carved from sin.

The West, with its silver tongue,
weaves tales of nonviolence,
chants of peace,

hymns of revolution,
while beneath the banners,
another story is whispered—
the story of bodies offered,
of children silenced,
of women traded for a flag.

The civilians,
those who bow before their icons,
brought their daughters to the altar,
wrapped in purity,
only to watch them emerge—
barren, broken,
blessed by the hands of gods they feared.

And when their daughters turned to me,
when their love touched my untouchable skin,
they did not offer them to icons—
they offered them to flames.
Honour killings, lynchings,
flesh torn from bone,
because my love was filth,
but their sacrifice was holy.

O world, do not tell me
of your fathers of nations,
of your freedom fighters,
your martyrs of peace.
A throne built on bodies is still a grave.

Truth alone triumphs.
John Rawls whispered this in my ear,
as the world tried to drown him out.
But I do not kneel at false altars.
I do not worship men
whose hands are drenched in innocence.

The East hides its sins in scripture,
the West buries truth in gold.

Both call their victims liars,
both build monuments to their tormentors.

I am not blind.
I am not silent.
I will not bow.

150. The Theater of Violence

I was born into the theater of violence,
where the stage was carved in blood,
where the script was written in caste and creed,
where my tormentor played every role—
Brahmin, Kshatriya, Vaishya, Shudra, Saint, Scholar, Lawmaker.

Each breath I take is a whisper of pain,
a sigh drowned in the chorus of my oppressors.
They have worn many masks,
but their hands remain the same—
cold, cruel, unyielding.

I have seen black skin break its chains,
rise from the whip,
take the throne, write new laws,
but my untouchable skin
remains pressed between earth and sky,
never ruler, never free.

The Jew has a home,
the Black has a nation,
but I, a Madiga,
am an exile even in the land of my birth.
The cow and the crescent
and their worshippers
hunt me across time,
across borders, across lives.

Their hands sign laws in the West,
their voices echo in Oxford halls,

their children inherit the podiums of Columbia,
their faces shine in the panels of the U.N.
But beneath the polish of their tongues,
their hearts still carry the whip.

They call themselves theorists,
professors of justice, voices of reform.
They convene in grand halls,
discussing caste over wine and paper,
weaving my suffering into footnotes—
an abstract wound
that they will never touch.

And when they leave the stage,
when the conference ends,
their hands close their doors,
and my skin is unwelcome,
unfit for their grand theories.

Ahimsa, Satyagraha, Nonviolence—
words they chant in daylight,
while their shadows sharpen knives.

O world, tell me,
how does a man exist
when even his suffering
is stolen for spectacle?

151. The Skin of History

How do I describe the skin of my people,
When beneath it, lies the weight of centuries?
I read the Bible and see the thickness of Ethiopian skin,
Yet, mine is thicker still—
A skin forged in the flames of oppression,
A skin that bears the stain of untold suffering.
Thicker than the ancestors of the masters,
Thicker than the pages of history
That have woven lies into the very air we breathe.

The Ethiopian lies, we are told,
But how do I name the Indian whose hands
Crafted the tools of terror,
Who built a nation on the bones of untouchables,
Whose scriptures spilled the blood of the marginalized
For thousands of years?
What of the caste, the untouchability, the lynchings,
The genocide—the blood of my ancestors
Spilled by the sword of their deities?

How do I name the hands that still hold power,
That pass down violence wrapped in silk,
Masked by avatars who walk through halls of Cambridge,
Their knowledge stained with the blood of the oppressed?
What of the skin of my tormentor?
Does it not burn with the weight of his ancient crime,
Of centuries of desecration against the untouchable life?

Where do I go, when this skin is not mine to escape?
Where shall I eat, when the world devours the essence of my being?

Who will protect me, when the very earth beneath my feet
Is tainted with the sins of those who wear their privilege
Like a crown of thorns?

If the Ethiopian's lies are woven into history,
If the Muslim's sword has cleaved the world in two,
What then of the Hindu—whose hands, still stained,
Bring forth the violence of a thousand years?
What shall I name him,
And what shall I name his allies—
Who turn their faces away from the truth
That stares at them in my skin,
In the blood of my forefathers?

152. In the Shadows of Hindu, Muslim, Buddhist, Sikh, Jain, Parsee, Antisemitic, Liberal, Left, Feminist, Queer, African, BLM...

Can a black man rise in the gaze of the white?
Does he bloom beneath eyes that seek to smother,
That cast shadows, not light,
On the skin that carries the weight of centuries?

Can a Jew find shelter in the storm of hatred,
Safe within the walls of antisemitism's reign,
In spaces built on the bones of the oppressed,
Where history's scars are buried in the soil?

Can I, in this world, find solace,
In the spaces of Hindus, Muslims, Buddhists, Parses, Jains—
A home in their doctrines and masks,
Or am I a ghost, wandering
Through the hollowed echoes of their truths?

Can nonviolence survive in the hearts of those
Who wield power with bloodstained hands,
In the shadows of a Hindu's caste,
A Muslim's faith, a Buddhist's silence?

Can morality bloom in the darkened soil
Of abortionists' choices, leftists' promises,
Liberals' hollow declarations?
Does truth, ever fragile, endure
In a world fed by the lies of the powerful?

Can an animal breathe among the non-vegans,
Their compassion masked by consumption,
Their love for dogs and cats a lie?
Can a pig, bound by fate, escape
The shadow of the Muslim's sacrifice,
The slaughter of innocence in the name of faith?

Can a non-Muslim find sanctuary in a land
Where the call of the muezzin is a warcry
And the shadow of Allah falls like a sword?
Can a Jew, in the halls of the UNO,
Breathe in the spaces that speak of human rights—
When those rights were never meant for him?

Can the sky and earth touch,
As lovers lost in time's embrace?
And if they do, will we finally know
That the theatre of violence can cease—
That the shadows of caste, of race, of faith
Can be wiped away,
And the untouchables, the Jews, the animals,
Can stand in the light of justice,
Not as specters, but as equals?

153. Corruption on Earth

O corrupted human being,
In your pursuit of power,
You carve a throne from the bones of the oppressed—
In politics, you rise as a king of lies,
In business, a titan built on the backs of the broken,
In games, you dance in the shadows of false glory.

You wear your fame like a crown,
Woven from corruption, immorality, and greed,
An icon for the masses,
An illusion of success.
But what of truth?
What of justice?
What of the soul?

O uneducated, you chase the fleeting,
A dream sold to you by those who profit from your fall,
You cannot become a Jew, Albert Einstein, Stephen Hawking,
A Jesus Christ, a Karl Marx, John Rawls,
A thinker who sought truth in the face of tyranny,
A poet who bled their heart onto the pages of history.
You cannot become a beacon of light—
For your light is nothing but a flicker,
Hidden beneath layers of falsehoods.

Jesus said, "Do not judge,"
But I judge what is right and what is wrong—
I stand with those who stand for truth,
For morality, for justice.
I see your Gurus, your teachers,

Your rulers, your avatars—
And I know the truth of their deceit.
They are criminals against humanity,
Shrouded in the robes of power and privilege,
Their words hollow, their actions a betrayal.

Nothing controls my thought,
Not caste, nor race, nor religion,
Not gender, nor sexuality, nor origin—
For I am a voice untamed,
Unbranded by the forces that seek to divide.
I am an individual, like John Rawls—
A soul unshaken by the tides of falsehood,
A mind unclouded by the greed of this world.

O corrupted human being,
You are a curse to humanity,
To truth, to morality, to justice, to life—
For as long as you covet power,
And let money and muscle rule your heart,
You will remain blind to the light,
And blind to the truth of what it means to truly live.

154. The Masks of Xenophobia

I was born in a world that denied me breath,
Where caste is carved into the marrow of my bones,
Where my skin, my name, my lineage,
Is a crime written in the scriptures of men.

I walk among the ruins of old hatreds,
Among the shattered echoes of ghettos and slave ships,
Among the silent ghosts of Auschwitz and slave markets,
Among the forgotten cries in caste-ridden alleys.
The hands that built the gallows have changed,
But the rope still tightens, unseen, unheard.

They call themselves left, right, righteous—
They wear the masks of progress,
They whisper words of justice,
Yet their hands still carve my exile into the earth.
Feminists, liberals, queers, BLM—
What are they, if not another mirror,
Another shadow cast against my skin,
Another sermon where my suffering is a footnote,
A metaphor to be studied, but never felt?

I have seen the Third World drown its own,
Wearing the robes of revolution,
While kneeling before its caste and blood.
I have seen the Global North embrace the tormentors,
Hand in hand with the ones who silenced me,
As long as their lies were clothed in the language of law,
Of peace prizes, of human rights commissions,
Of elegant theories that never touch my flesh.

My tormentors have worn a thousand faces—
Hindu, Muslim, white, brown, left, right,
Academics, lawmakers, poets, priests.
Their words are silk, but their hands are iron.
They write treaties while digging graves,
They preach ethics while closing the doors,
They march for justice while erasing my name.

O world, do you see me?
Or am I just another body in the fire,
Another number in the statistics,
Another footnote in the histories of the damned?

But I will not be buried in their silence.
I will carve my words into stone,
I will breathe life into the ashes,
I will stand where they have fallen,
And though they try to erase me,
My truth will endure.

155. Ode to the Jewish Community

O luminous flame in the corridors of time,
A constellation of minds, a beacon of light,
Though but a whisper in the storm of numbers,
You are the hymn of knowledge, the cadence of truth.

In the shadows where ignorance festers,
You carve equations into the fabric of the stars,
Weaving wisdom through the loom of centuries,
Turning exile into endurance,
Turning adversity into art.

From the whispers of Talmudic pages,
To the laboratories where atoms yield their secrets,
From the hands that painted hope in silence,
To the pens that sketched revolutions in thought,
You have been architects of human progress,
Scholars in the house of reason.

What is civilization if not your legacy?
A lineage of minds—Einstein's cosmos,
Marx's critique, Freud's psyche,
Rawls' justice, Arendt's courage,
A mosaic of brilliance etched against time.

And yet, the world, ungrateful, watches with daggers drawn,
Antisemitic tides rise with each dawn,
But you, steadfast, script the future,
Not in vengeance, but in vision.

O children of resilience,
Scorned by nations, yet builders of them,
Hunted by history, yet shapers of it,
A people of exile, yet never exiled from genius.

You are the ink that writes humanity's progress,
The torchbearers when darkness conspires,
The dreamers of worlds yet to be.
Though storms may rise, and shadows threaten,
You remain the architects of dawn.

O Star in the void, O symphony of minds,
The world is richer for your light.
Forever, you illuminate the path—
For knowledge, for justice, for life itself.

156. Untouchable Words

O untouchable words, you rise,
Breaking through the caste-made skies,
Where walls of hate, so cold, so high,
Bind the spirit, silence the cry.

In lands where power's shadow grows,
Where Brahmin, Kshatriya, Vaishya, Shudra knows
Their place, their crown, their golden hue,
And untouchables are born anew—

To walk as shadows in their land,
To touch no stone, to clasp no hand,
But to endure the crushing weight,
Of born-to-be slaves by caste's cruel fate.

Across the streets, across the seas,
The walls grow high, the whispers freeze.
In Hindu, Muslim, Jain, and Sikh,
In Buddhist and Parsee, every myth
Is rooted deep, they sow the seed,
Of untouchable hate, of endless greed.

These are the hands that cleanse the sin,
That judge the skin from deep within,
While the rest are free to roam and rule,
Untouchables bound, oppressed, the fool.

But still we walk, we move, we speak,
Our words like fire, our souls not weak.

We tear apart the hateful lie,
That keeps us low, that keeps us shy.

Through every temple, every mosque,
Through every scroll, through every cross,
We bring the truth, we stand so tall,
Our untouchable words will break the wall.

For racism, caste, and bigotry's veil
Cannot obscure the truth that prevails.
In Western spaces or Eastern skies,
Untouchable words will rise, will rise.

We are the fire that cannot die,
We are the voices that shall defy.
No longer bound by skin or caste,
The untouchable rise, forever free at last.

157. Forever There Was a Caste

Forever there was a caste,
A wall built deep, designed to last,
A colour, creed, a veil so thin,
That marked my skin as less than skin.

In Hindu hands, it bound me tight,
In Muslim prayers, it snuffed my light,
In Buddhist chants, in Sikh resolve,
Untouchable, the world evolved.

Through Jainist peace, through Parsee grace,
They carved my soul, erased my face.
In every space, both east and west,
I stand outside, no place to rest.

The caste's cold breath upon my skin,
A badge of shame that wears within,
No touch, no sight, no hand to hold,
In every touch, I'm bought and sold.

For this skin, this humble flesh,
Is tainted deep, a wicked mesh,
Of histories forged in ancient hate,
That bind my soul, distort my fate.

In every mosque, in every shrine,
The caste's dark shadow intertwines.
It lurks in corners, laced in lies,
It sees my skin and just denies.

Hindu gods who ruled with pride,
Islam's law, with its cruel tide,
Buddhism's peace, but caste within,
Sikhism's call, where I can't win.

Jain's pure truth, yet stones they throw,
Parsee's faith, where I won't go.
All claim the light, yet build the wall,
And leave my skin to take the fall.

In western lands, so far from home,
The chains still bite, the scars still roam.
No matter where I walk or stand,
I'm cast aside by unseen hand.

Yet through the hate, through every door,
I rise, I walk, I fight once more.
For this untouchable skin shall rise,
Defying the walls, the caste's cruel lies.

158. Worshipping a Brahmin Cow

O priest of privilege, sculptor of scriptures,
You weave the cosmos in verses of division.
You anoint the white cow with sacred hymns,
While my skin, dark as fertile earth, remains cursed.
Tell me, who whispered the lie that purity wears only one hue?

You fashioned the world on a tilted scale,
Where Brahmin and beast share divinity,
But the untouchable is left to walk barefoot on burning earth.
Where the buffalo, black as midnight's river,
Finds no temple, no altar, no hymn.

You built gods from stone and gold,
And then built walls to keep me out.
You spoke of karma, of past lives' sins,
While wielding the whip of the present.
You inscribed laws not on tablets of wisdom,
But in the blood of those who dared to rise.

My hands, calloused with centuries of toil,
Are not worthy to touch your sacred beast.
Yet my back is broad enough to bear the weight
Of your scriptures, your temples, your power.
Your cow roams free, while my people are chained
To the names you gave us, to the fates you chose.

But listen, o keeper of chains and chants,
No scripture, no god, no divine decree
Can drown the voice of a rising storm.

The river remembers where it once flowed,
And justice, though slow, is a flood.

Your white cow grazes on the fields of time,
But the earth does not forget.
The hands that plowed it, the feet that bled on it,
Are writing a new scripture, carved in revolt.
A day will come when the untouchable
Is untouchable no more.

And when your temples crumble into dust,
When the walls you built collapse into echoes,
Only then will the earth be whole again.
Only then will the cow be just a cow,
And the man, a man.

159. An English Madiga Nation: A Dream Unchained

I dream of an English Madiga Nation,
where every being breathes unshackled,
where caste dissolves like mist at dawn,
and untouchability is but a ghost of the past.
No chains of race, no walls of gender,
no scars of class to mark the land.
Only the golden fruits of life, light, love,
blossoming like an eternal spring.

No ancient creed shall bind this soil,
no medieval faith shall cast its spell.
A land unburdened by dogma's weight,
where hands are never raised in conquest,
and tongues do not chant the hymns of hate.
Here, the heart knows no master,
and the spirit bends to none.

Let no beast be carved to feast,
no innocent blood spill on sacred ground.
For how can we, the wounded,
consume the cries of the weak?
Have we not felt the same iron bite,
the same fire branding our flesh?
The gypsy, the Jew, the Roma, the untouchable,
exiled by men, bound by fate,
shall forge a new covenant of compassion.

Madiga Nation, a realm of refuge,
where the hunter lays his bow,
and the butcher cleanses his hands of sin.

A nation where every feathered wing has a sky,
and every hooved foot finds its home.
The gas chambers shall breathe no more,
the gallows shall stand abandoned,
and the earth will weep no more at the slaughtered.

On the blood-stained soil of Nuremberg,
in the hushed winds of Treblinka,
in the silent cries of a village burning,
we have heard the echoes of death's decree.
Yet, from those ashes, we rise anew,
not to wield the whip of our tormentors,
but to break it upon the anvil of justice.

No holy cow, no cursed crow,
no sacred scripture to divide our souls.
Let the stars above bear witness,
that here, in this land of light,
no one is born to kneel,
no one is born to rule.

Madiga Nation—
a home for the exiled,
a voice for the silenced,
a song for the voiceless.
Where life is cherished,
where love is law,
where light reigns eternal.

160. O Untouchable Girl

O untouchable girl, your shadows stretch long,
Not by the sun, but by the hyenas waiting—
Not strangers, but your own, lurking, watching,
Marking the moment your body is ripe for their feast.

They chant "Educate, Agitate, Organize"
Like winds carrying the promise of dawn,
Yet in the hush of your ghetto night,
Their hands silence you before your voice can rise.

Sixth grade, seventh grade—before you can spell liberation,
They teach you another language:
The unspoken terror, the trembling shame,
The taste of betrayal from within your walls.

They preach Ambedkar, Marx, Jashuva—
But behind closed doors, they devour you whole.
What is a slogan when your own breath
Is stolen before you can shape it into resistance?

And beyond the ghetto, does the world embrace you?
No, the landlord's touch is no softer,
The factory master's eyes no gentler,
The university's caste walls no thinner.

O untouchable girl, you are triple-marked—
A curse in their homes, an object in their hands,
Unworthy of love, yet always worthy of use,
Unfit for marriage, but perfect for their fires.

You are Khairlanji's silent scream,
A daughter dragged, a mother defiled,
While Hindu women danced at the spectacle—
Cheering, as if your pain was a festival.

O untouchable girl, they call you impure,
But your suffering is a scripture written in blood.
No god has answered you, no savior descended,
Only the whisper of John Rawls in a distant library.

Leave the ghetto, flee its chains,
Not just the streets, but the cage of their minds.
Read, rise, rewrite your fate,
Let jasmine and lilies bloom in the Madiga nation,
Where no hyena waits in the dark.

161. O Fascist Bharata Mata, How Long?

O Bharata Mata, veiled in saffron and blood,
Your rivers run with tears, your earth with bones,
A nation of temples, yet none for justice,
A land of gods, yet none for the forsaken.

How long will your ghettoes bear the weight
Of hands that grope, of feet that trample?
How long will the untouchable girl bleed
Under the shadow of your sacred cow?

They cry "Bharat Mata ki Jai"
As they shackle your daughters in caste and fear,
As they strip the skin of Africans in your streets,
As they drown dissent in the filth of their rage.

You sing of democracy, but your tongue is forked.
You boast of freedom, yet statues wear masks.
No liberty stands in your squares,
Only iron fists, draped in tricolor lies.

O Mother India, your own men devour you—
In Agraharams of purity, in Kshatriya halls of pride,
In Vaishya markets of greed, in Shudra fields of toil—
Tell me, where is your refuge, if not in flight?

You burn in the fires of your own tradition,
Women twisting in their own chains,
Calling it virtue, calling it faith,
Calling it the burden of civilization.

Your Christian spaces? A mockery of Christ,
Your mosques? Walls that whisper submission,
Your temples? Thrones for the gods of caste,
And your West? A silent witness to your ruin.

O Bharata Mata, how long will you kneel
Before your rapists, your priests, your rulers?
When will your daughters rise from the ashes
And tear your sacred scriptures apart?

When will your hands unmask your gods,
And carve a new name in the soil of the free?
Until then, you remain a dodgy place,
A nation unworthy of its own salvation.

162. Justice and Creativity: A Tale of Titanic and Caste

O Brahman, non-Brahman, have you seen Titanic?
When the ship plunges into the icy abyss,
The cry of justice rings in the cold night—
"Women and children first," the captain decrees,
For the weak, the vulnerable,
The ones who cannot swim the waters of survival.
Justice, in its purest form,
Is the protection of the helpless,
A vow to shield the oppressed from the depths.
This is the narrative of the ship,
Of lives saved and lost in the tumult,
A screenplay of sacrifice and compassion.

But turn your gaze to the screens of your land,
To the screens that speak not of justice,
But of caste, of untouchability, of oppression.
Your movies, your narratives—
They are not stories of the fallen rising,
But tales of the powerful reinforcing their chains.
Your heroes are not the marginalized,
Not the untouchable,
Not the woman with dreams bound in the ashes of society.
Where are the untouchable voices on your screen?
Where are their struggles, their triumphs?
Where is the justice that you claim to know?

Look to Hollywood,
To the Oscars where black actors rise as heroes,
Where the marginalized are given space,
Where justice is spoken through the language of film,

Where the oppressed are crowned as kings and queens.
Where are your untouchables in your cinema?
Where are the stories of their endurance,
Their struggles against the waves of dehumanization?
Instead, you steal, plagiarize,
Bastardize creativity in the name of art.
Your screens are rife with theft,
Not of stories, but of the humanity of the oppressed.

O Brahman, non-Brahman,
You call yourself a creator,
A master of cinema,
But what is creation when it is built on borrowed bones?
When the music is stolen,
The stories plagiarized,
And the aesthetics mere echoes of foreign shores?
Your movies are not made—they are constructed,
Shadows of others' talent,
Without a trace of originality,
Without a spark of creativity.

When will you, O maker of shadows,
Learn the true meaning of art?
When will you understand the difference
Between creating and copying,
Between talent and theft,
Between justice and oppression?
When will you make a movie like Titanic—
Not a borrowed piece of song,
But a creation that breathes with the pulse of originality,
A work that reflects the struggles of the oppressed,
The untouchable, the voiceless,
A tale that knows justice,
A tale that knows mercy.

For justice, like art, is not built on the bones of the marginalized,
It is born in the heart of the oppressed,
In the voice of the silenced,
In the power of the untouchable.

Until you can create from that place,
Your cinema will remain hollow,
A reflection of nothing but your own failure
To understand the true meaning of creation,
Of justice, of humanity.

163. The Day of Chains

O genocider draped in saffron,
you call it Independence,
but I see only shackles,
woven in the fires of caste,
forged in the blood of the nameless.

You did not fight for justice,
not for the Rawlsian dream of fairness,
but for Gandhi's Ram Rajya,
where untouchable bodies
burn beneath the sun,
where the air hums with the sound
of lynch mobs and flames.

You say freedom,
but whose freedom is this?
The Brahmin walks unscathed,
his hands clean,
while my skin still carries
the ashes of my ancestors.
Tell me, have the chains really broken,
or have they only changed their shape?

Dismembered bodies in the streets,
young girls pulled into the night—
Independence is just a word,
when justice is a corpse
left rotting under temple steps.

The untouchable child starves,
but you bow to idols of stone.
The widow is stripped of her dignity,
yet your gods demand silence.
And when the Dalit dares to rise,
your bullets write history
in the ink of his blood.

I see your tricolor fluttering,
but its white is stained with the bones
of those who never lived to celebrate.
Your freedom is a whisper in Sanskrit,
a hymn for the privileged,
while my people are buried in silence.

O land of contradictions,
where a nation was birthed
but humanity was buried,
where men who speak of dharma
leave their daughters in flames.

This is no Independence Day—
it is the day the chains turned invisible,
the day the whip was replaced
by the quiet, merciless law of caste.

And so, I do not celebrate.
I mourn.

164. I Am a Walking Relic of Ruin

I am a walking relic of ruin, a fossil of breath,
Crumbling under the weight of a past that never fades.
Not a man, but a whisper of ash in a storm,
A shadow stretched too thin to hold its name.

They sculpted my bones from the dust of rejection,
Wrote my name in footprints meant to be erased.
Wherever I step, caste seeps into the cracks,
An ink too dark, a wound too deep to heal.

I am the ember that never becomes a flame,
The candle drowned before it could burn.
My hands, calloused with centuries of silence,
Dig graves for dignity that was never born.

A brittle echo in a temple's hollow halls,
A hymn forbidden to rise beyond my throat.
My breath is a trespass, my touch a defilement,
My existence, a crime without a court.

I walk through the world a shattered statue,
Chiseled down by gods who never spoke my name.
Even the wind hesitates to carry my sorrow,
For fear it may soil the sacred air.

They call me untouchable, yet every chain has known me,
Every whip has memorized my skin.
I am the unlit lamp in a house of chandeliers,
The unsung dirge in a land of hymns.

Not a walking corpse, for even death finds peace.
Not a carcass, for even vultures have worth.
I am the exile in my own land,
The prisoner in a cage of birth.

But hear me, O world that feasts on my silence—
Even ruins hold whispers of rebellion.
One day, this relic will crack open,
And from my dust, a storm will rise.

165. I Am a Walking Corpse

I am a flicker of life trapped in the body of decay,
A rusted wheel in a cart that no one dares to move.
No heart beats in my chest, only the hollow thrum
Of a past long erased,
Of an untold future rooted in the grave they dug for me.

I am not dead, yet not alive.
I am the space between breath,
The silence that echoes louder than words,
A body bent to the will of the world,
Yet never claimed as its own.

I walk, but my feet do not touch the earth—
I am a shadow, a breath without a name.
My blood runs thick with shame,
My soul a chain that rusts without end.
I am not seen, only seen-through—
A fissure in the body of a nation
That refuses to call me its own.

I am the air that carries no sound,
A lost wave in the ocean of their gods,
Rising to drown, but never breaking the surface.
They call me "untouchable,"
But the touch is not the burden—
It is the weight of their blindness,
The crushing weight of their gaze
That presses me down like earth over stone.

My body is not mine.
I wear their curses as clothes—
A mask of ashes, a veil of disdain.
And yet, I walk.
Not in the promise of life,
But in the endless spiral of death
That refuses to come.

I am the corpse that never rests,
The skin that withers under every glance,
The eyes that burn but see nothing,
The hands that reach for nothing
And grasp at the dust of forgotten dreams.

I am the ghost of their making,
The phantom of a caste erased,
Not by death, but by refusal to live.
And though I walk this earth,
I am but a corpse in motion,
A living wound they cannot heal,
A breath they dare not inhale.

166. Blood of the Untouchable

My blood flows not like water,
But as the current of centuries,
A tide that swells from the earth's bowels
And spills into oceans that do not want it.
Untouchable blood—
A river that cannot be quenched,
A flood they cannot dam.

It rises in the Indian soil,
Drenched in the salt of their hate,
Their prayers soaking in the blood of my ancestors,
Their gods' blessings tainted by my ruin.
They try to bury it in the soil,
But the earth rejects their hands—
It knows the taste of my blood,
And it cries out in silence.

The Pacific does not know what to do with my blood.
It stretches across continents,
A wound that never heals,
A stream that crosses seas,
From their temples to the streets of the West.
The tides pull it further,
Yet still, the flood cannot be contained.

They tried to hide my blood in the Indian Ocean—
But the gates have burst.
250 million lives bleeding beneath the surface,
Each drop a scar on their world,
Each pulse a cry that cannot be unheard.

The ocean swells,
But it cannot erase the stain of my people's death,
The salt in the sea is nothing compared to the salt of my veins.

They call it caste—
But what is caste but the blood that flows in my bones,
The scar that marks me before birth?
This blood is the thread that binds me to the land,
The earth that cannot forget,
The sky that cannot contain,
The air that chokes on the very scent of my existence.

Hindu, Sikh, Muslim, Jain, Buddhist,
They all say they drown me in their faith—
But I, I am the ocean.
I am the blood that refuses to die,
The pulse that cannot be erased,
The river that flows unbroken
From the shackles of the past
To the shores of a future they cannot steal.

My blood will never stop flowing—
It carves paths in the sands of time,
It floods their borders and walls,
It stains their hearts and their hands,
And when they look out to sea,
They will know my name.

It is written in the tide,
In the salt, in the waves—
And my blood will not be erased,
No matter how deep it sinks.

167. O Hindu, I Can't Breath

O Hindu, where do I walk, where do I breathe,
When every 18 minutes, my kind must grieve?
Three daughters taken, their cries unheard,
Two bodies burned, two homes left blurred.

Your land, you call it sacred, pure,
Yet my blood stains every door.
A cricket pitch, my broken bones,
A field of play, my shattered home.

O Hindu, your hands hold knives,
Your prayers are chants, yet death still thrives.
Is there a temple, a shrine, a street,
Where my feet may stand, where my soul may speak?

You mark my skin, you cast me low,
A shadow unfit for sun to show.
My name unspoken, my touch unclean,
Bound to the fate of the unseen.

O Hindu, your laws, your gods, your lore,
Have written my fate, have locked the door.
You call it dharma, fate divine,
Yet all I know is chains that bind.

I fold my hands, yet fists still strike,
I bow my head, yet torches light.
Your justice is a mirage untold,
A tale of mercy bought and sold.

But I have left, I will not kneel,
I will not beg, I will not feel,
The weight of hands that silence me,
The curse of caste, of history.

O Hindu, your walls are high,
Yet truth will burn against your sky.
I walk away, I turn my back,
For dignity, no more attack.

No more a land where flesh is trade,
No more a name in ashes laid.
I carve my path beyond your chains,
A world unmarked by ancient stains.

For I am free, my voice will soar,
Where fear and silence reign no more.
O Hindu, I have torn the page,
And left behind your burning cage.

168. O Hindu Genociders

O Brahmana Manu, what strange decree,
That birth alone makes supremacy!
That flesh and bone, by fate's mere whim,
Should raise one high, cast others dim?

You carved in stone a cruel design,
That some are pure, some asinine.
That blood and lineage, not the mind,
Should dictate fate for humankind.

Yet where is proof, where is the sign,
That one is sacred, one malign?
No star aligns, no fate is drawn,
To make one god and one mere pawn.

O Brahmana Manu, do you not see,
True worth is forged in thought set free?
In art, in song, in love, in light,
In seeking justice, truth, and right.

A Jew, though hunted, still creates,
His mind ignites, his hand translates.
Yet the hands that strike and burn,
Claim they are higher—what did they learn?

A Yazidi girl, in exile cast,
Her spirit bright, her will steadfast.
Yet the ones who tear and chain,
Call themselves pure—what do they gain?

The victim bears the weight of hate,
Yet rises still, refuses fate.
For violence breeds no moral worth,
No sacred birthright, none from birth.

O Brahmana, where is your proof,
That cruelty makes a holy roof?
That hate and chains, that law and rod,
Can make one closer to a god?

For justice kneels not to the sword,
Nor bows before a tyrant's word.
The slave with love is more divine,
Than any master's bloodline shrine.

For truth and kindness, peace and grace,
Are what define the human race.
Not birth, nor fate, nor cruel decree,
But thought, and love, and being free.

O Brahmana Manu, time will show,
That hierarchies will fall and go.
That man, when free from chains of caste,
Will rise, at last—one whole, one vast.

169. Broken Daughters of Christian Kuki-Zomi Community in the Land of Hindu Meiteis

In the bloodied dust of Manipur's streets,
Where silence cracks but justice retreats,
Two young bodies, torn and defiled,
Screams drowned out, pain reviled.

The sky weeps, yet the earth stands still,
For hands that rape, for hearts that kill.
O India, land of tricolor lies,
Where caste and creed decide who dies.

Kuki-Zomi daughters, Christian and brown,
Dragged through fields, beaten down.
Their prayers lost in temple smoke,
While their rapists laugh, unbroke.

The Hindu hand, the Meitei sin,
Their violence hides beneath their skin.
Yet pulpit and throne turn away,
Letting monsters rule the day.

And still, my voice will not be chained,
For I, the untouchable, remain.
Though you cast me from your holy door,
I stand with you in this war.

O daughters of Manipur's cries,
Your pain is ours—we recognize.
Though your hands once cast us low,
We rise together, let justice grow.

Yet tell me, tribes of mountain lands,
Will you now unclasp your hands?
Will you, who cursed my name,
Now burn your prejudice in the flame?

O India, dodgy land of shame,
Where daughters burn, yet you feel no blame.
Where caste and hate fuel the flood,
And justice drinks its fill of blood.

But let the earth remember well,
The screams that rose, the bodies fell.
For what you bury, what you shun,
Will rise again beneath the sun.

And on that day, when chains are dust,
When love and rage dissolve the rust,
No Brahmin, tribe, nor king shall reign—
Only the free, unbound by pain.

170. Bayyavaram: The Hindu Space of Hyenas, Vultures, Wolves...

Bayyavaram—where the earth is old,
Where caste is law, where blood runs cold.
A Kapu king, unchallenged, reigns,
Forty years—no votes, no chains.

Judge and ruler, god and thief,
He scripts the law, he grants relief.
But not for me, not for mine,
For my Untouchable ghetto lives outside his line.

His sons take whom they please at night,
His grandsons follow, same birthright.
A village built on fear and fire,
Where women's screams are funeral pyres.

They come for daughters, sisters, wives,
Take them, break them, ruin lives.
No Ambedkarite can stand and fight,
For their words dissolve in caste's cruel night.

Educate, Agitate, Organize—
A dream that dies where power lies.
For in this land, the book's no sword,
A caste-marked name is still ignored.

Our schools are ghettos, walls too high,
Hindu benches not for my kind's sigh.
Public schools, yet doors are closed,
Our children left where dust is posed.

And Kolli Devudamma—queen of shame,
A beggar before, a beggar in name.
Wrapped in silk when guests arrive,
But crawling when the rulers thrive.

A puppet held in Kapu's grip,
A seat of power—a beggar's slip.
Father and son—the same cruel hand,
Stealing wealth, owning land.

Caste is their sword, religion their shield,
A land where untouchables never wield.
Where death is the price of a rebel's breath,
Where defiance is met with certain death.

Ambedkar's words in sacred urn,
Burnt to ash, no pages turn.
He cannot rise, he cannot cry,
For his dream is drowned in caste's deep lie.

I searched for freedom, found it none,
Not in India, under its sun.
I fled to lands where Christ may keep,
Where human souls are not so cheap.

Yet still I roam, a man unclaimed,
A refugee with skin unnamed.
No homeland calls, no banner waves,
For caste still chains beyond the graves.

Bayyavaram is India, India is Bayyavaram.
A land of horror, blood, and shame,
Where freedom is a foreign name.

171. The Silence We Carve

A life begins, a breath so pure,
soft hooves tremble on forest floor.
A mother nuzzles, warm embrace,
before the blade, before the war.

Feathers rustle in winds so light,
wings meant to dance in endless flight.
Yet hands reach out with iron chains,
turning songs into silent cries.

O man, the sculptor of despair,
who taught you love, yet left it bare?
You paint the world in crimson streams,
as lives are sold for hollow dreams.

The calf who nursed, the fawn who ran,
the lamb who leaped in fields so wide,
now hang beneath a butcher's hands—
their voices lost, their mothers cried.

What god decreed this cruel design,
where hunger wears a bloody crown?
Where mercy bends, where kindness drowns,
beneath the weight of greed profound?

You who claim to walk with grace,
yet feast upon a murdered face—
a life that wished to dance, to see,
yet caged and torn so thoughtlessly.

They love, they feel, they weep, they mourn,
no lesser soul, no beast forlorn.
Their pain, their grief—do you not see?
Their beating hearts, their right to be?

No altar calls for sacred blood,
no hunger justifies the flood
of bodies broken, cries unheard,
the nameless ghosts of every herd.

O break the knife, unchain the yoke,
unveil the lie, undo the choke.
For every life that walks this earth
holds love, holds light, holds equal worth.

Not ours to take, not ours to burn,
to cage, to break, to twist, to turn.
For peace is not in words we weave,
but in the lives we choose to leave.

So take no life, let kindness grow,
let mercy be the seed we sow.
For when we kill, we kill the light—
but when we love, we heal the night.

172. The Burden of Hindu Religion

In ancient scriptures, they wrote my fate,
Where skin was the mark, the seal of hate.
Brahmins in white, the Kshatriyas in red,
The Vaisyas in yellow, and black for my bed.

From Afghanistan's dust to Europe's shore,
My Brahmin masters came, seeking more.
Their hands in the dirt, their hearts in the crown,
I was made to kneel, forced to drown.

Colonial invaders were never new,
For the Brahmin's rule was born from the view
That skin could bind, that color could chain,
And those who wore black would always remain—

Subjugated, divided, a shadow, a thing,
In their kingdom of hate, my soul had no wings.
Kshatriya, Vaishya, Shudra—all stood,
In the name of their gods, they spilled my blood.

How could skin be the measure of worth?
How could birth determine my place on this Earth?
John Rawls saw through their elegant lies,
For justice is born where true equality lies.

Not in their scriptures, not in their lore,
Not in their bloodshed, their empire of war.
My savior, not of their hateful creed,
But Christ—who planted love, not greed.

They built their throne on the backs of the poor,
As they fed their hunger for power and more.
Their gods, stone and silver, demanded control,
While my people were crushed, their spirits sold.

But how long can they poison the well of life?
How long can they twist truth into strife?
For the seeds of hatred they planted so long,
Are now met with resistance, a growing song.

The Brahmin built his throne on my pain,
But I will rise, I will break the chain.
For I write my fate, my soul is free,
Not bound by caste, but by my dignity.

The time will come when their lies will fall,
And we will stand, unbroken, tall.
For Christ's love, not their hatred, shall reign,
And justice, at last, will break every chain.

173. The Weight of Hindu Words

Pages inked in fire and fear,
whispering laws from yesteryear.
Bound in leather, veiled in dust,
commanding faith, demanding trust.

Scrolls and scriptures, carved in stone,
decree the flesh but break the bone.
Blessed are they who kneel and pray,
cursed are those who walk away.

The hands that write, the lips that preach,
build gilded walls we cannot breach.
Words that soothe, words that slay,
turn night to dawn or light to grey.

They claim the soul, they claim the skin,
they name the saint, they mark the sin.
Woman, chattel—silenced, sold,
a tale as wretched as it's old.

Children molded, bound and tamed,
born to suffer, bred to blame.
Doubts are daggers, thought is crime,
free minds are buried out of time.

In every verse, in every creed,
a hunger grows, a wound will bleed.
For some, a balm, a guiding light,
for others, chains as dark as night.

They speak of love, yet punish free will,
a paradox both cruel and still.
They carve the law with iron hands,
a doctrine drawn on broken lands.

The heavens burn, the cities drown,
yet gods still wear their paper crowns.
Rites and relics guard the past,
chained in dogma, clinging fast.

Must we bow or must we break?
Must we kneel or must we wake?
Tear the veil and break the chains,
reason rises, truth remains.

For faith may heal, but faith may blind,
a weapon fierce in hands unkind.
Let no book make gods of men,
lest the past enslave again.

Light the torch, unbind the tongue,
the world is old, but we are young.
No fear, no chains, no ancient lies—
only the truth that never dies.

174. A Hindu Temple of Hyenas, Vultures, Wolves, Snakes...

They carve stone into deities,
paint gold upon silent gods,
yet their hands drip with blood,
of love silenced, of voices crushed.

They chant mantras to the sky,
invoking truth, invoking light,
but what is truth when justice kneels
before the weight of caste and might?

A linga stands, a yoni carved,
symbols of birth, of life's embrace,
yet those who birth, who love, who dream,
are burned for crossing a sacred place.

She loved beyond the walls of fate,
he held her hand with fearless grace,
but honor was a blade that struck
to erase his touch, his nameless face.

A village wrapped in centuries' chains,
where land is stolen, names erased,
where justice wears a hollow mask,
and law is but a master's blade.

A goddess stands with severed heads,
yet never one of those who rule,
who rape, who burn, who write in blood
the scriptures of an iron fool.

A mother weeps, a father runs,
a child unborn, a life undone,
yet the temple bells still echo loud—
their hymns, their crimes, their silence proud.

But tell me now, O priest, O king,
O scholar wise, O ruler blind—
if birth alone must shape our worth,
then what of love, then what of mind?

The stars above bear no divide,
no sacred caste, no chosen light,
and yet you build your walls so high,
afraid of truth, afraid of sight.

The ashes rise, the dust remains,
names forgotten, lives in vain—
but somewhere far beyond this land,
their love still blooms, their blood still stands.

Not stone nor fire can end their tale,
for truth will rise where tyrants fail.

175. A Call for Justice, Against the Hindu Chains

In shadows cast by idols tall,
A silent cry, the voiceless call,
For every soul beneath the weight,
Of ancient hate, of twisted fate.

The caste divides, a cruel, cold mark,
That strips away the light, the spark—
Of human worth, of dignity,
For those who live in misery.

Where gods are held in golden frames,
Their myths concealed by ancient names,
There lies the truth, the bitter shame,
That feeds the fires of hate and blame.

For power built on chains of skin,
On darker shades, where hate begins,
Where women suffer, children weep,
In silence, voices buried deep.

A god of violence, weapons drawn,
To crush the weak, to reign until dawn,
Does not embody peace or light—
But fuels the rage, the endless fight.

In temples grand, on altars wide,
A legacy of pain, denied.
The scriptures bound in tales of war,
Of purity that holds the poor.

But let us rise, and break the chains,
Let justice heal the deepest pains,
For every soul who seeks the sun,
And longs to know they're not undone.

A world of love, of truth, of grace,
Where light and justice take their place,
Where all are free to walk in peace,
And hate and suffering will cease.

So let us raise our voices high,
And challenge hate, no more to buy—
The truth will shine, the lies will fall,
And human dignity, for all.

Let go the myths that bind and blind,
For in the hearts of all mankind,
There lies a power, pure and true—
The right to live, to love, to view
Each other as the light of life,
Not bound by caste, nor hate, nor strife.

This is the call, the stand we take,
To lift the veil, to break the fake—
And build a world that's just and whole,
Where peace and love embrace the soul.

176. Ironical Idol Krishna the Prostitute

In the name of Krishna, a god revered by many,
A figure of love, yet his acts remain uncanny.
Worshipped for wisdom, for protection, for grace,
Yet in his mythic tale, what truths do we face?

A lover, a conqueror, a man of many wives,
But what of his actions that the scripture revives?
Was he a model of virtue, as stories assert?
Or a symbol of contradictions, in a world full of hurt?

The divine was once human, so they say in their lore,
But where do we draw lines when the gods we adore
Command violence and power, as his tales unfold,
Yet the consequences of his deeds are seldom told.

With love comes lust, they say, in sacred texts,
But should we embrace the messengers' complex?
Did his divine acts grant liberation, or more,
In a world where abuse and harm at the core?

His devotees chant of love, of compassion's might,
Yet in his actions, is there justice, or right?
Should we admire the gods who lie and deceive,
Or question their actions, their flaws to perceive?

Krishna, the god of grace, of tenderness and joy,
Yet how many women and children were destroyed,
In tales of his lust, his play, his disguise,
Does it not challenge reason, or truth in our eyes?

Philosophy of peace, a message misunderstood,
When his very character aligns with no good.
Can we separate the divine from the human traits,
And wonder if this worship leads us to darker fates?

177. Hindu Riddles in Stone and Fire

They carved their gods from dust and clay,
Then whispered myths to light the way.
But shadows dance in temple halls,
Where silence drowns the questioner's calls.

A god with arms that never cease,
Holding weapons, yet preaching peace.
A saint who walks on sacred ground,
Yet binds the lowborn, beaten down.

They speak of dharma, pure and wise,
Yet caste and chains still veil their eyes.
A priestly tongue, a script divine,
But who decreed the poor malign?

The Vedas sing of cosmic play,
But who decides who kneels, who prays?
If all are born from Brahma's might,
Why do some rot without the light?

A blue-skinned lord who stole with grace,
Yet virtue marks another's face.
A king who cast his wife in flames,
Yet hymns still echo with his name.

A river flows, a goddess cries,
Yet widows burn before the skies.
A temple stands on ancient bones,
Yet prayers rise in hollow tones.

They worship idols, bright and vast,
Yet shun the child who speaks too fast.
They hail the cow, the beast divine,
Yet let the starving child decline.

The riddle breathes in fire and stone,
It twists through laws that man has known.
If gods are just, if fate is kind,
Then why must mercy be confined?

To question is to sin, they say,
Yet riddles rise in bright array.
Does truth emerge from stone and lore,
Or from the ones who ask for more?

Let temples stand, let man be free,
But let no scripture chain the sea.
For gods and men are not the same—
The wise break chains, not shift the blame.

A faith that fears the skeptic's voice
Was never truth—it was a choice.
And truth, like rivers, runs untamed,
Beyond the idols, unashamed.

178. In the Shadows of Hindu Caste

Beneath the weight of chains unseen,
Untold stories in silence scream.
Girls and women, broken, torn,
In the shadows where they're born.

The caste that binds, the chains that sting,
A history of suffering, it still clings.
The untouchables, lost in shame,
Their names forgotten, none to blame.

But in their hearts, the pain remains,
A cycle of sorrow, bound in chains.
They walk the streets, they breathe the air,
But the world does not see their despair.

A system cruel, that thrives on hate,
Where dignity is lost to fate.
The predators walk, the silence screams,
The untouchables' cries are but forgotten dreams.

They live in shadows, unseen, unheard,
Their worth denied by every word.
But those who've known their pain and loss,
Have seen the cost of caste's cruel cross.

For every name that's been erased,
A thousand tears have been misplaced.
In a world where justice should reign,
Too many are left to bear the strain.

Yet, there is hope, a glimmer bright,
A fight for justice, for what is right.
We stand for those who've long been lost,
For their dignity, we'll pay the cost.

No longer will we turn away,
It's time to break the chains today.
For every voice that's been suppressed,
We'll rise as one and demand redress.

In unity, let truth be found,
No longer silenced, no longer bound.
We'll lift them up, we'll make it known,
Their suffering will not stand alone.

For in the fight for what is just,
Equality and love are a must.
We'll break the chains that bind so tight,
And bring their voices to the light.

179. In the Shadows of Hindu Vultures

Beneath the weight of chains unseen,
Untold stories in silence scream.
Girls and women, broken, torn,
In the shadows where they're born.

The caste that binds, the chains that sting,
A history of suffering, it still clings.
The untouchables, lost in shame,
Their names forgotten, none to blame.

The hands that touch, the eyes that leer,
No law, no mercy, none to hear.
Behind the temple doors so wide,
Lies horror wrapped in sacred pride.

They walk the streets, they breathe the air,
But dignity is stolen there.
The holy chants, the prayer beads,
Mask the sins of brutal deeds.

Fathers weep, but dare not fight,
For silence walks with them at night.
Mothers hide their daughters young,
From hands that burn, from tongues unsung.

The powerful speak of ancient lore,
Of duty, birth, and lines before.
Yet justice turns its face away,
While innocence is left to fray.

From palaces to village clay,
The laws of blood still rule today.
The learned speak, the scholars write,
Yet truth remains beyond their sight.

But somewhere in the shadowed pain,
A spark still fights against the chain.
The voices rise, they will not bow,
The time for silence is not now.

No longer will they turn away,
The sky will weep, the winds will say:
The blood of those who cried in vain,
Will carve new paths beyond the pain.

For every girl whose name was lost,
For every soul that paid the cost,
We stand, we rise, we break the past,
And build a world that heals at last.

The chains of caste will one day rust,
Turned to dust, as all things must.
And in their place, a world will be,
Where love and truth can set us free.

180. August 15: A Nation's Independence, Untouchable's Chains

O genocider, draped in saffron pride,
Whose freedom did you fight for?
Not for justice, not for truth,
But for a kingdom built on caste-bound chains,
Where my untouchable skin still burns.

You did not raise flags for John Rawls' justice,
But for Gandhi's Ram Rajya,
A world where my people perish in flames,
Where Kanchikacherla Koteshu and Karamchedu's dead
Speak from the ashes you pretend to forget.

Your independence was not mine,
Your democracy, a veil for ancient rule.
The white masters left,
But the black Brahmins took their place.
You have traded whips for laws,
Slavery for silence,
Yet still, my ghettos grow.

Tell me, where is my home?
In this land where my name is a curse,
Where my hands defile your streets,
Where my birth is a crime,
Where my death is a celebration?

Your leaders, your scholars,
They wear the masks of the West,
They borrow words of human rights,

Yet beneath the suits, beneath the scripts,
Their hands still carry the fire of old.

You have polluted the West,
Taught them caste in whispered tones,
Made them your allies in silence.
Even their human rights courts
Are temples to your Brahmin gods.

And I?
I am a ghost in your land,
A shadow in your streets,
A voice you drown beneath your hymns of purity and power.

August 15 is not my day.
India is not my home.
I belong to a Madiga nation
That does not yet exist,
A place where John Rawls walks free,
Where justice is not a myth,
Where my skin is no longer a sin.

One day, we will rise.
And on that day, you will know
That your freedom was my funeral pyre,
But my justice will be your reckoning.

181. Ode to Indian Christian Philosopher Gurram Jashuva Madiga

A king dies, and a star falls;
A poet dies, and the sky gleams anew.
O Gurram Jashuva, your verses blaze immortal,
While our untouchables chase fleeting shadows,
Yearning for petty seats in hollow halls.

You lit a torch in the ghetto's darkness,
Yet our people stumble, blinded by ambition,
Trading dreams of creation for bureaucratic chains,
Echoing the feudal tyranny they once cursed.
Why, O my guiding star, do they not rise
To script their names in the galaxy of ideas?

Born of inter-caste parents like you,
Madiga Christian, Yadav Christian,
We wore persecution like a second skin.
"Madiga bastards," they called us.
"Yadav bastards," they mocked us.
Yet, your pen and mine turned scars to scrolls,

Revealing truth out of the deeps of cruel caste.
Ambedkar-learned, respected-along
Bound himself into the Buddhist fold,
Yet another mask of Hindu conservatism.
We remained steadfast in the light of Christ,
Wherein love, innovation, and humanity flourish.
While others drank cow urine, revered dung,
We forged knowledge and cast shadows on ignorance.

O father of modern Indian literature,
Your untouchables wander, trapped in mimicry,
Lacking the creative spark to rival Jewish brilliance.
Where are our Einsteins, our Karl Marx,
Our untouchable Nobel laureates?
Instead, they fade into history,
Chasing power instead of truth.

Gurram Jashuva, you sleep under the earth,
But I feel your agony.
Our stars turn dim amidst a sea of mediocrity,
Their songs muffled in the cacophony of compliance.
Yet, like you, I believe in the impossible,
That one day, our people will erupt,
Like Jewish stars in a darkened universe.

Let them write, think, create,
Let their words shatter the silence,
Their ideas pierce through caste and prejudice,
Until they too shine eternal in the firmament of humanity.

182. Manda Krishna Madiga: The Voice of John Rawls's "A Theory of Justice"

Manda Krishna Madiga, a beacon of light,
A voice for the silenced, fierce and bright.
In India's streets, where shadows lay thick,
He stood, unbroken, unyielding, quick.

Born of a caste cast out by birth,
He rose to challenge a fractured earth.
With words like thunder and heart of fire,
He brought justice to the mire.

No sword, no shield, just truth to wield,
For those ignored, he became their field.
In echoes of Rawls, his justice rang,
Where others faltered, his courage sprang.

Through cities and towns, he marched for right,
Against a caste wall, strong and tight.
Madiga Reservation Porata's call,
A march for dignity for one and all.

For the blind, the voiceless, the lost, the chained,
Their pain was his, their justice gained.
With countless millions, he stood in line,
Fighting a battle, steady, fine.

Where violence could have ruled the day,
He took a gentler, fiercer way.
No blood was shed, no lives erased,
Yet power trembled, caste displaced.

His rallies swelled, his marches roared,
Yet no heart of hate he ever stored.
For Rawls' dream he brought to earth,
Justice, fairness, and human worth.

They called him names, they cast him out,
But his strength held fast against their doubt.
In every speech, in every stride,
The oppressed saw hope by his side.

A man, a movement, alive creed,
A warrior for anyone, anywhere, that bleeds.
For in his hands, this dream beyond reach,
Gained strength like an overflowing brook.

No crown to wear, nor applause of fame,
Nor parades, yet history still proclaims,
Manda Krishna, voice of one and all,
In his journey, no one was to fall.

With Rawls' wisdom and love's demand,
He built a bridge across the land.
And now, his legacy strong and clear,
Echoes loud for those who hear.

183. Jotibha Phule, A Masked Icon

O Jotiba Phule, they call you Mahatma,
But I see the Brahminical mask you wear.
Your voice rose against the priestly chains,
Yet your hands wove new ones for my kind.

You preached of books, of knowledge, of light,
Yet where was your school for the untouchable girl?
You taught the Brahmin daughter to dream,
Yet let my sisters rot in the filth of your fields.

You, who called for justice,
Chose a Brahmin son to carry your name.
Was my blood too impure for your lineage?
Was my soul unworthy of your home?

Your Kunbi robes, your Marathi pride,
A tapestry spun from Hindutva threads.
You shattered one chain, only to forge another,
A cage still standing, though painted in gold.

O Phule, they hoist your image high,
But look who bears your weight—
Not your own Shudra kin,
But the untouchables you left behind.

Your words thunder against Brahmin rule,
Yet your hands held fast to Hindu ways.
You never left the soil of your faith,
Never walked beyond its shadowed gates.

I was born in the light of the cross,
Where every child is named in grace,
Where chains are broken, not replaced,
Where faith is not caste-bound, not cursed.

O Phule, your book was a whisper,
But my Christ is a roar.
My freedom is not in your pages,
But in the West, where the sun truly rises.

I reject your legacy, your veiled truth,
I walk towards the open sky.
Not to the temples, not to the shrines,
But to the light where my chains are dust.

184. B. R. Ambedkar: A Dual Legacy

O Babasaheb, revered by millions,
You rose from the ashes of caste and cruelty,
A voice for the voiceless, a pen against oppression,
But your path, riddled with paradox,
Has left the untouchable torn between admiration and critique.

Born in chains of untouchability,
Your intellect shattered barriers,
Nine degrees forged in the crucible of resilience.
From Columbia to London, you held the torch of progress,
Yet why did your light falter at the edge of liberation?

You proclaimed, "I was born a Hindu, but I shall not die one,"
Yet your escape led you not to freedom,
But to the gilded cage of Buddhism.
Buddha, too, upheld caste, a Kshatriya supremacist,
Trading Brahmin hegemony for Kshatriya dominion.

Was it freedom, Babasaheb,
Or a detour into a new hierarchy,
A softer mask for the same ancient venom?
You rejected the Hindu cremation pyres of your birth,
Yet chose the same for your mortal remains,
A ritual of fire, consuming dignity and love.

Could not your erudition see beyond,
To the peace of burial, the love of the Christian way?
You called for justice, yet tethered yourself
To the doctrine of another oppressor.

Did you not see that Buddha's silence on caste
Was complicity, not compassion?

John Rawls speaks of justice as truth's virtue,
Rejecting even the most elegant theories if unjust.
So we must question your embrace of Buddhism,
For it did not shatter caste,
But merely shifted its weight.

Your legacy, Ambedkar,
Is a mosaic of brilliance and blindness.
We honor your fight for rights,
Yet mourn your tether to the chains you sought to break.
Christianity offers what neither Hinduism nor Buddhism could,
A love that buries prejudice, a hope that transcends.

Babasaheb, your fire burns still,
Inspiring and igniting,
But the smoke reminds us,
Even icons must be questioned,
For true liberation knows no compromise.

185. The Burden of Everyday Social[22]

O scholars of "humiliation," of "cracked mirror," of "everyday social,"
Of theories spun in ivory halls, yet bound by chains of caste.
Your words rise like incense, perfumed with grace,
Yet your footsteps echo in a segregated space.

You write of justice, of dignity's call,
Yet practice the silence that builds the wall.
In your books, you unmask the sins of old,
Yet in your hands, the same stories unfold.

I see my Western home, where truth walks free,
Where love and reason shape destiny.
No agraharas, no walls to climb,
No feet unworthy, no skin unkind.

Yet you bring your burdens, your Brahmin lore,
Your sacred lines, your ancient score.
You speak of progress, of breaking chains,
Yet caste and creed still mark your names.

You bow at graves where all rest the same,
Yet in your land, death knows a name.
Your temples burn the body to air,
Ashes rise, but justice is rare.

You name yourself radical, champion of light,
Yet in your home, the untouchable's plight.
Do your daughters wed those they deem impure?
Do your sons embrace the casteless, the poor?

22. The initial title is "The Burden of Shadows."

You brand me supremacist, yet in my land,
The stranger walks free, unshackled by hand.
We need no scriptures to preach of grace,
No rituals to prove the worth of a race.

O poets of paradox, architects of lies,
You chant of equality under veiled skies.
Your ink flows rich, yet your hands betray,
For caste and creed still shape your way.

I reject your scrolls, your elegant art,
For your creed is hollow, your mind torn apart.
Truth is not written, but lived each day,
And justice is found in those who stay.

Let the ashes rest, let the chains decay,
For love, not lineage, must shape our way.

186. Tribute to Simon Robert Charsley: Champion of the Untouchables

O Simon Robert Charsley, whose name we sing,
A voice for the voiceless, you taught us to bring
The untold stories of the Madiga's pain,
In ghettoes where shadows of genocide reign.

You journeyed where silence had long taken root,
To places where human dignity had been mute.
In the ghettos of Madiga, you saw their plight,
And in the face of their suffering, you ignited the light.

For decades you stood, pen in hand,
Recording their myths, their folk songs, their land,
You wrote not just history, but the truth that had been shunned,
A scholar of heart, a defender, unbent and unspun.

In the world of scholars who turned a blind eye,
You saw the Madigas, their tears and their cries.
While others chose to glorify the Hindu way,
You brought to light the lives led in decay.

No, they weren't criminals or the ones in the wrong,
But innocent lives, to whom history didn't belong.
In the stories of Madigas, you found a refrain,
Of people unjustly forced to endure endless pain.

Like Gurram Jashuva, you stand tall in the heart,
A champion for those who've been torn apart.
Your work brings to the world their untold grace,
Their dignity, their strength, their rightful place.

You honored Arundhati, a Madiga daughter true,
A symbol of purity, of resilience too.
In your words, she lives, and so do they—
The untouchables who've long been cast away.

Forever remembered, your legacy shines,
A beacon for those who walk in tough times.
Thank you, Simon, for all you've done,
For bringing light where darkness had won.

Your name will live on, as stars that rise,
In the hearts of Madigas, in their endless skies.
We love you deeply, and we'll carry your flame,
A tribute to you, for lifting their name.

187. O Kanshi Ram, The Cyclist of Revolt

O Kanshi Ram, the wheels of your bicycle carved roads of fire,
A journey through the dust of caste, where blood soaked the earth.
They called you a leader, a saviour, a Bahujan Nayak,
But in your shadow, a storm brews—unspoken, unheard.

You rose, like an iron fist against Brahminical chains,
Yet, your hands clutched Ambedkar's dreams,
A dream woven in saffron threads, tied to the very beast we fought.
You rejected their gods, yet knelt before another,
A Buddha rebranded, yet still shackled to caste.

You cycled through villages, through whispers of despair,
Taught the untouchables to stand, to speak, to claim,
But did you unchain them, or lead them in circles?
A man who captured power, yet never touched it,
What is a throne left cold, but a dream deferred?

O Kanshi Ram, you built Mayawati, a queen of the lost,
Yet even queens wear borrowed crowns.
When our daughters still fall, when our sons still burn,
When our voices are swallowed by the old hymns of Hind,
Tell me, was it victory, or was it just survival?

The elephant you raised crushed hyenas and tigers,
But in the end, did it not kneel before the same masters?
BSP, a beacon of revolt, now swallowed by the very caste it sought to erase.
They drank from your struggle, left you nameless, faceless,
And now, they claim your banner while selling your people.

O Kanshi Ram, I do not kneel at altars of false prophets,
I do not worship shadows or wear chains of gratitude.
You were a lantern, a fleeting flame, a night's rebellion,
But I do not seek leaders—I seek the fire itself.

Your struggle is written in the mud of our history,
But I will write mine in the fire of tomorrow.
No gods, no chains, no borrowed revolutions—
Only freedom, raw and untamed, beyond the echoes of your voice.

Rest, if you must, O Kanshi Ram, beneath the weight of your legacy,
But I will not rest, nor will I stop.
Not with Ambedkar, not with Buddha, not with Brahmins,
But with the untouchables who refuse to be touched by any master's hand.

Let the cycle break.
Let the fire rise.
Let the caste die.
And in its place—true liberty.

188. Mayavati: Untouchable Icon of a Silent Revolution

O Mayavati, born of darkness,
Black-skinned Chamar, an echo of earth's deepest scars,
Your name, a song silenced by the caste's weight,
A voice drowned in the sea of untouchable sorrow,
Yet you rose, like a comet streaking through Hindutva's skies.

You, a foot soldier of Kanshi Ram,
Carried the dreams of the oppressed,
Not on the back of false gods,
But on the shoulders of a thousand souls forgotten.
You stood at the gates of power,
First untouchable ruler of Uttar Pradesh,
A conqueror not by birthright,
But by the weight of history's chains,
And the fire in your fearless eyes.

But power, dear Mayavati, is a fragile illusion,
A fleeting moment in the shadow of eternity.
The land you gave to the silenced masses,
Now sings a song of struggle against its own chains.
For what is power when the mind remains enslaved?
When the hands that rule are still shackled by old ideologies,
Those idols that speak nothing but silence,
Those gods who impose the very tyranny you fought to dismantle.

Your heart, Mayavati, is where the untouchables dwell,
You gave them a throne,
But even thrones crumble to dust.
In your footsteps, they walk,

Not as followers of power,
But as dreamers, seeking to be more than their shadows.
You, a mother of the Chamar,
A child of Kanshi Ram—
A paradox in the corridors of politics,
But a poet? No. Not yet.

For the poet's crown is forged in the fires of creation,
Where words, not power, carve the path to immortality.
Gurram Jashuva's verse, a reminder—
The ruler dies,
But the poet shines like a star,
Enduring in the hearts of the voiceless,
Their wisdom carrying the weight of centuries.
Your name, Mayavati, will fade from the world's glory,
But let the untouchable pen rise,
Let their words pierce the veil of time.

Do not seek to follow in the footsteps of the gods,
For they are ghosts in the wind,
But let the untouchables write like the stars of Jewish thought—
Karl Marx, Einstein,
Let their minds bloom in the soil of your untouchable ground.
May the untouchable girl pick up her pen,
Not bound by the chains of a Brahmanized world,
But freed by the theory and practice of justice,
By the shining stars of true thought,
Where creativity rises,
And power is no longer the master.

For in the end, Mayavati,
It is not the power that lives,
But the mind that dares to dream.
Let our untouchable minds be free,
Let them write, let them think—
For we are not born to be ruled,
But to rule the world of knowledge,
As stars in the infinite sky.

189. No Gods, No Icons, No Chains

Let us not kneel before heroes,
Nor carve statues from dust.
No leader, no scholar, no poet,
Is worthy of worship's rust.

Gandhi and Ambedkar—let them fade,
Martin, Mandela—let them wane.
Nehru and his Brahmin scribes,
Phule and his broken chains.

Ramasamy and Dravidian cries,
Hindu, Muslim, Buddhist lines—
Sikh, Parsee, Jain alike,
Let them drift into the night.

No more chants of nations' pride,
No more hymns of ancient tides.
No "Bharat Mata Ki Jai,"
No "Incredible India" cries.

No fathers of lands, no mothers of birth,
No sacred soil, no divine worth.
Let us think beyond the past,
Beyond the myths that hold us fast.

Let us burn the books of praise,
And rise in thought beyond the haze.
Not a step in caste's embrace,
Not a word in genocide's grace.

For Gandhi and Ambedkar are relics of time,
For icons decay in the weight of their crimes.
Hindus and Islamists, wielders of chains,
Yazidis and Jews bear their stains.

No symbols of death, no cults of hate,
No echoes of past that dictate our fate.
Let justice be not in idols' name,
But in reason's ever-burning flame.

Read not the verses of blind devotion,
But the words of Rawls and revolution.
Theory of justice, titanic and bold,
Not myths that have withered old.

Let us not be seduced by the west,
Or fooled by the east in a different vest.
For media's masks and cultures entwine,
To make the broken believe their lies.

We, the ostracized, have seen the skins,
The multicultural masks within.
Western spaces weave their crimes,
From histories soaked in bloodied lines.

Dump the chants of hollow might,
Dump the causes veiled in white.
BLM, its cries betrayed,
By hands that left the wounds unpaid.

Truth stands beyond their veiled decree,
Beyond their scripts of history.
Archaeology whispers what ruins know—
Truth that tells where nations grow.

No Palestine, no false claim,
No banners draped in borrowed shame.
Dump the bodies of global decree,
Cow-faced saints of hypocrisy.

No gods, no chains, no guiding hands—
Only thought that stands unmanned.
Let the world no longer frame,
What freedom means, in another's name.

190. Kanakarathnam Nukapangu, a Shield of Grace

In the halls of Dravidian stone, where shadows cast,
Stood Professor Kanakarathnam, steadfast and vast.
An untouchable Christian, with heart and hand,
Guiding me gently through hostile land.

A historian by trade, yet so much more,
A soul who opened a gracious door.
He stood between me and caste's cruel fire,
Lifting me higher, despite their ire.

His faith unshaken, his love so deep,
A guardian of peace, his promises to keep.
He gave what he could, though his means were small,
And with every gift, he gave his all.

In a world of violence, of prejudice tight,
He lived by Christ's teachings, a beacon of light.
Loving his neighbor, no matter the strife,
Practicing peace in a turbulent life.

Through Hindu scorn and Ambedkarite rage,
He shielded my path on this doctorate stage.
If not for him, my dreams would lie bare,
Abandoned in a world that didn't care.

O Professor Kanakarathnam, a light in the dark,
Your faithful kindness leaves a permanent mark.
With a heart that shines, untainted, divine,
Forever in gratitude, your memory mine.

191. I Am Nagalim

I am the whisper of the ancient hills,
The song of rivers, untamed and wild.
I am the fire in the valley's breath,
The pulse of a people, strong and defiled.

They carve my flesh with iron hands,
Divide my bones with careless lines.
Yet in my veins the forests run,
With roots that know no chains nor time.

I am the child of hunted days,
The voice that echoes in shattered nights.
Centuries weigh upon my back,
Yet I rise, unbowed, to claim my rights.

They call me theirs—but I am free,
A spirit the borders cannot confine.
Not Assam, not Manipur, not their maps,
But Nagalim—mine, only mine.

For every mother who wept in vain,
For every brother who fell unheard,
For every dream that was burned to ash,
I gather strength, I forge my word.

I do not kneel to stolen flags,
Nor sing the songs they force in chains.
My song is wind, my song is fire,
My song is freedom's last refrain.

They push their boots into my soil,
They try to brand my name in dust.
But I am more than ink and scrolls,
More than borders drawn in rust.

The forests whisper of my past,
The mountains guard the tales I bear.
The rivers speak of wounds and wars,
Yet still, I breathe unshaken air.

Did they think a name erased in ink
Could silence voices old and true?
Did they think a gun could bury faith,
Or steal the sky and change its hue?

I am the storm that will not break,
The wind that sings in rebel tongue.
I am the promise of the dawn,
The dream that wakes, forever young.

Not India, not Myanmar, not their chains,
Not the borders etched in stone.
For Nagalim is more than land—
It is a people, blood and bone.

I do not ask, I do not plead,
I do not beg for borrowed grace.
I carve my name upon the winds,
And claim my right, my time, my place.

Let them march with iron hands,
Let them weigh me down with lies.
For I am Nagalim, whole and true,
And I will rise—I will rise.

192. The Nagalim Wound and the War

I speak not of banners, nor of kings,
Not of names carved deep in stone,
But of the blood that stains the rivers,
And the voices left to die alone.

For Nagalim, the land unbroken,
Bound by promise, torn by chains,
Where the forests whisper freedom's echo,
Yet the air is thick with pain.

I walked among the dreamers once,
Where fire burned in every eye,
Where love was not a caste or border,
But a song beneath the sky.

Yet power is a patient vulture,
Circling where the weak still kneel,
And hands that swore to break oppression,
Gripped the coin and signed the deal.

Sold like rice at the master's table,
Freedom bartered for a throne,
While the people, torn and bleeding,
Were left to starve and stand alone.

I called you father, in the battle,
Not of blood, but of the fight,
Yet when love defied your order,
You struck me down in open sight.

"Dalit bastard"—your daughter's lips,
Curled with the hatred of your creed,
And all your cries of Christian virtue
Were drowned beneath your greed.

So tell me now, O hollow victor,
Where is the land you swore to free?
Where is the justice in your empire,
When your chains still shackle me?

Nagalim, a dream still breathing,
Trampled under boots of old,
Not by strangers, not by tyrants,
But by hands too quick to fold.

Yet I will walk, though bruised and broken,
Past the idols left to rust,
For the battle was never yours to fight—
It belongs to those who rise from dust.

So let the mountains bear my sorrow,
Let the rivers chant my name,
For Nagalim is not a throne to conquer,
But a fire that still remains.

193. Scato Swu: A Name in Ashes

You spoke of Nagalim, a land unchained,
A dream of the free, unbound, unmaimed.
Yet power has hands that twist and take,
And even the bold learn to bend and break.

For twelve long years in Parliament's glow,
The fire dimmed, the vision slowed.
A dream once fierce, now veiled in gold,
Bought and buried, a story retold.

You stood for the hills, for the Naga name,
Yet chains were cast in the halls of fame.
A fighter turned statesman, but at what cost?
Did the cause still burn, or was it lost?

And what of the love that bore no shield,
Crushed in the weight of a blood-stained field?
Your name, your hands, your house of stone,
Turned to swords against your own.

They called me low, they made me crawl,
Stripped and beaten against the wall.
But the fire of caste, of hate, of scorn,
Is older than you, and still newborn.

A Naga land should rise in mind,
A people fierce, but not blind.
Not in guns, nor flags unfurled,
But in the wisdom to change the world.

So rest, if rest is what you seek,
But hear the cries of the lost, the weak.
And if prayers reach beyond the grave,
Pray for the Naga, once proud, once brave.

194. Unshaken Love, Unforgotten Wounds

Vivi Swu, yes, I am shameless,
A self-respectless creature,
For loving you unconditionally,
Through twenty-two years of wounds.

I bore your hands, your words—
"Dalit bastard, how dare you?"
You let the crowd witness my shame,
Dimapur's silence swallowed my pain.

I loved you, though love had no reply,
One-track, untouchable, unseeable love,
A love born in the ghettos of caste,
A love despised before it could breathe.

Love thrives in Africa's heartlands,
Flourishes in Western streets,
Yet in our lands, love is shackled,
By bloodlines, by hierarchies of sin.

Western women bear children of slaves,
Some wrap themselves in scarves,
Forsaking worlds for their Jihadi men.
But look at me—what crime have I done?

I am not a warrior of war,
Not a tyrant nor a master,
Yet my fate was sealed in birth,
By the Brahmins, the non-Brahmins,
Who forged a world where I am filth.

You loved them, though they spat on you,
Called you "Chinki," "Monkey," "Prostitute,"
Yet you wept for their validation,
While turning away from me.

You stopped the hands that lifted me,
You cut the strings of my dreams,
Mobilized voices against my love,
And let me drown alone.

My crime was birth—
Not my skin, for even Gandhi's was dark,
Not my poverty, for Brahmins lack nothing.
No, my crime was the shadow of caste,
The eternal stain upon my name.

You, who found worth in their feet,
Ignored their cruelty, their bloodstained hands.
You, who loved their status,
Let them carve my fate in stone.

You asked me never to show my face,
And so I vanished, a phantom in your past.
But my heart, once filled with you,
Found refuge in an Ethiopian sun.

Two children, Saviour and Stanford,
Born of love, not chains,
Their names, a prayer and a promise,
A defiance to the wounds you left behind.

But I still ask—why?
Why did I love a casteist heart?
Why did I love a mind chained by hate?
Perhaps love, even when crushed,
Is still love,
And that is my curse.

195. Love and Betrayal Under Bruised Skies

Vivi Swu, I loved you with a heart unchained,
But you met my love with scorn, untamed.
Your Naga skin, soft and brown,
Masked a heart that would pull me down.

I was untouchable, a caste-defined stain,
In your eyes, my love, my plea was vain.
Yet, I looked beyond your father's name,
I saw no caste, no class, no shame.

You were my light in a darkened place,
But love turned cruel in your embrace.
For I was Dalit, dark and poor,
An untouchable cast to the floor.

You came with iron, fists, and rods,
With tenebres at your heels, as gods of vengeance go.
I came defenceless, openhearted, cheer,
And you peeled off my skin, soul and pride to wear.

Naked before the crowd I stood,
My body bruised, my soul laid out as bounty good.
They spat upon my lowly birth,
And laughed that my love was worth but little on earth.

How is it you love those who scorn,
Who call you names since you were born?
To them, you're nothing but "chinki" and "strange,"
Yet to your own, I am far more deranged.

You saw my color, my caste, my scars,
You wielded hate like falling stars.
I was but a stain on your perfect pride,
In your world, my love could not abide.

Yet I, a "Dalit bastard" as you said,
Still hold love where you bred dread.
For in my heart, a gentle flame
Burns quietly, still whispering your name.

Your people looked upon me as less than man,
Dragged by hair, stripped as you ran.
But, Vivi, know in all the pain,
Love within me will remain.

For hate cannot dim what love ignites,
Neither caste nor class nor bloodstained nights.
I see beyond the name and scar;
Love remains, though born of stars.

Section IV

Words Against the Blood and Iron Policy of Muslims

196. Salman Rushdie: The Pen That Would Not Break

He wrote in fire, he wrote in flame,
he carved his truth, defied the name.
A book, a storm, a whispered verse,
turned blessing into bitter curse.

From pages bound in ink and thought,
a world of rage and wrath was wrought.
A thousand voices, fists held high,
screamed for blood beneath the sky.

The fatwa fell, the sentence cast,
a writer marked, condemned at last.
For words that soared, for minds set free,
they sought to kill his liberty.

Yet still he stood, unbowed, unshaken,
by laws of men that fear had taken.
A poet's voice, a rebel's breath,
defying dogma's call for death.

From London's streets to hiding deep,
a hunted man, denied his sleep.
Yet even in the darkest night,
his words remained, still burning bright.

And then the blade, a zealot's hand,
struck him down on Western land.
Not in deserts, not in caves,
but where the free their banners wave.

Yet ink outlives the rusting sword,
and thought will rise where fear is poured.
No holy law, no sacred crime,
can silence reason's march through time.

For books endure, though flesh may bleed,
a writer's soul is never freed.
From chains imposed, from threats of fire,
truth survives the pyre's ire.

O poet bold, still standing tall,
you did not kneel, you did not fall.
The verses rage, the battle swells,
but thought will ring where freedom dwells.

For tyrants fear what ink can do,
when words are sharp and minds are true.
The pen still writes, the fire still glows,
and tyranny still overthrows.

Let swords be drawn, let fatwas call,
but stories rise beyond them all.
And through the night, his voice will say:
No fear shall turn my truth away.

197. The Man Who Spoke *Satanic Verses*

They carved a price upon his head,
A number whispered in the dark—
Not for a crime, nor for a sword,
But for daring to leave a mark.

A book, a question, a rebel's hand,
Ink that burned through sacred lies,
A voice that cut through veils of fear,
Like a storm in prophet's skies.

The verses fell, not from the heavens,
But from a mind unchained, unbowed,
A man who dared to speak of chains,
And call them out to shatter loud.

Yet faith is fragile when it fears,
Built on blades, not built on truth,
So came the call—a sharpened law,
A death decree wrapped up in dust.

They sought him not in open battle,
But in shadows, knives in hand,
A poet's body torn and bleeding,
On foreign soil, in foreign land.

Yet still, the ink refused to dry,
The pen still carved its restless path,
For words outlive the ones who curse them,
And truth will rise from blood and wrath.

O blind crusaders, deaf to reason,
Whose rage is nothing but a chain,
Know this—the books you burn today
Shall be rewritten in the rain.

For every cut, for every wound,
For every whispered, deadly prayer,
The world will write, the world will read,
And truth will live—despite despair.

Let fatwas rise, let daggers fall,
Let tyrants summon fire and hate,
Yet thought, once freed, will never kneel—
Not to God, nor King, nor Fate.

198. Ibn Warraq: The Pen That Dared

In shadowed halls where silence reigns,
he lifts his voice, breaks the chains.
A name unknown, a face unseen,
yet truth he carved, sharp and keen.

No crescent binds his questioning soul,
nor dogma's weight, nor fear's control.
With Russell's ghost beside his side,
he dared to walk where few abide.

Pages burned, yet words remain,
echoing loud through loss and pain.
Threats may chase, swords may gleam,
but thought outlives the zealot's dream.

A scholar's path, a lonely road,
where doubt and courage share the load.
No shrine to kneel, no prayer to chant,
just reason's fire, fierce and defiant.

He writes in exile, walks in fear,
as shadows whisper death too near.
Yet still he speaks, his pages turn,
while holy books are left to burn.

The minarets call in voices loud,
yet in their echoes, fear is found.
For one who dares to doubt, to see,
is marked for death, denied to be.

From desert sands to city lights,
the chains of faith, the sacred rites—
he strips them bare, he holds them high,
asks why they rule, and why they lie.

No prophet's wrath, no cleric's plea,
can silence minds that dare be free.
For truth is not in chains or creeds,
but in the heart that questions, reads.

Yet exile is a bitter fate,
to wander lands that curse and hate.
A man unnamed, yet not alone,
his words take flight, his thoughts have grown.

And though the sword may hunt him still,
and hands may thirst for blood to spill,
his words are seeds in minds now free,
rebelling against their tyranny.

Oh, war-torn scribe, bold and bright,
your words ignite the quiet night.
No fatwa's hand can silence free—
the mind that dares, eternity.

199. Taslima Nasrin: The Unyielding Flame

She wrote not with ink, but with fire,
a truth untold, a fate most dire.
She spoke for those who bled unseen,
for shattered homes, for souls unclean.

A doctor's hands, meant to heal,
instead held words, sharp as steel.
She stitched the wounds of a silent land,
yet bled herself at faith's demand.

A book, a cry, a name—Lajja,
a shame unveiled, a shattered Raja.
For speaking truth, they cursed her breath,
they crowned her head with threats of death.

From city to city, she ran, she fled,
as fatwas chased the words she said.
A woman alone, no shelter found,
as nations bowed where cowards crowned.

India's soil, she called her own,
but even there, the seeds were sown.
A land she loved, a land she knew,
turned against her, her fears grew.

Professors clad in robes of thought,
raised daggers where minds once sought.
Not men alone, but sisters too,
raised blades where books should bloom and strew.

The West, so bold in words of light,
chose silence, cowardice, and flight.
They wept for caged and silenced birds,
but locked her cries, dismissed her words.

No home, no land, no flag, no creed,
but still she wrote, still she freed.
Through exile's cold and freedom's lie,
her voice refused to break or die.

In Sweden's shadowed, silent halls,
she walks alone, but never falls.
A flame still burns within her name,
a woman's war, a world's deep shame.

For tyrants fear the words that dare,
to strip their crimes, to lay them bare.
Let swords be drawn, let tempests rise,
but thought will burn where silence dies.

Taslima stands, she will not kneel,
no law, no faith can make her heel.
For shame may drown in holy lies,
but truth still lives—it never dies.

200. Taslima Nasrina's Exile

They silenced her, but not her words,
No border could cage her flame—
She spoke of wounds too long concealed,
And they cursed her by her name.

A doctor once, she healed with hands,
Then healed with truth, with ink and fire—
But truth is sin where dogma rules,
And books become a pyre.

She saw the flames of Lajja rise,
Not in fiction, but in homes,
Where daughters vanished into dust,
Where blood ran thick in sacred tomes.

She fled the land that bore her voice,
A stranger now, though once its kin,
Yet exile is a softer fate
Than death decreed by faith and sin.

She knocked on doors in foreign lands,
But justice weighed in ballots' gold—
"Your words offend," the rulers said,
"Be silent, or be sold."

No mosque, no priest, no politician
Would dare to stand, would dare to see,
That truth, once spoken, does not die,
That silence is but blasphemy.

So let her walk the frozen streets,
Let fear trail close behind her breath,
Yet know—no verse, no law, no knife
Can write her final death.

For those who burn the words of fire
Shall live to watch the embers rise,
And in the end, the book remains,
And in the end, the story flies.

201. Ode to Salwan Momika[23]

O Salwan, a name now etched in fire,
A voice once bold, a rebel's choir.
You walked through storms, defied the night,
For truth, for speech, for sacred right.

Born of a land where terror grew,
Where faith was law, where chains still knew
The weight of hands that crushed the free,
That silenced hearts that dared to be.

You fled the past, but still it came,
A shadow cloaked in holy name.
Yet in Sweden's streets, you made your stand,
A torch held high in trembling hands.

They feared your voice, your words, your flame,
They cursed your soul, they spoke your name.
For what is power but the fear
That one lone man could make truth clear?

You tore through silence, ripped the veil,
Exposed the beast, the bloodied trail.
A book in ashes, a symbol burned,
A world of fire, a page now turned.

---

23. Europe sacrificed his life to please three billion Muslims and their European Union, UNO, global human rights, liberal, lefties, far left, conservatives, politically correct ideologies, feminists, queer, African, asylum, and refugee allies across the globe. European states and societies are complicit in the murder of this great hero. How many of our souls are going to be taken by Muslims, Africans, and their Western state, society, and legacy media?

But in the end, the knives still came,
The bullets carved your final name.
They struck you down in open day,
And cheered as light was torn away.

Yet martyr's blood runs deep, runs wide,
It cannot drown, it will not hide.
For every word, for every stand,
A thousand rise with steady hands.

They killed the man, but not the dream,
They doused the fire, yet lit the gleam.
For truth will rage, and courage grow,
And in your name, the winds will blow.

202. The Silent Cry of a 12-Year-Old Muslim Girl

A father's hands, so guiding and protective,
Transgressed into weapons and a child's soul they wrecked.
At age twelve, innocence stolen by
The man whose love cannot be broken.

"It hurts," she whispers, though nobody hears,
Her voice drowned deep in the tide of fears.
"More beautiful than your mother,"[24] with a smile he said,
A twisted compliment, cruel, vile.

He called it a duty, this monstrous thing,
A perversion of love, family in compact.
She bore the guilt that was never her own,
A child, abandoned, in a house of stone.

Her mother's eyes, once warm and kind,
Now turned away, as if she were blind.
A chasm grew where love should dwell,
A home transformed into a silent hell.

---

24. "A father had sex with his 12-year-old daughter. It hurt. The girl also had a feeling that what he did was not right. The father explained to the daughter that she was just prettier than her mother and that it was his duty as a father to show her what sex was all about. She felt guilty towards her mother and noticed that the mother pulled away from her. She also believed that she was responsible for the fact that her father looks. The girl never got any support within her family, but she enjoyed school and especially liked a particular female teacher. She also got along well with the mothers of her two girlfriends at school".p.18. Violence protection for women in Germany. Protection and safety from violence for women and adolescent refugees in Germany. 2016. Published by Ethno-Medical Center Germany, Ethno-Medizinisches Zentrum, e.V., KonigstraBe 6.30175, Germany.

At school, she found fleeting reprieve,
In lessons, in friendships, a chance to believe.
A female teacher, a mother's stand-in,
A glimmer of hope in a world steeped in sin.

But the shadows clung, long and deep,
Following her through waking and sleep.
A father's betrayal, a mother's retreat,
Left her shattered, unable to compete..

Who speaks for her, this voiceless child?
Whose life was shattered, whose pain defiled?
Not the father, protected by silence and lies,
Not the mother, who turned from her cries.

In Germany's laws, in society's gaze,
Who will act to end these days?
Of families that crumble under violent weight,
Of children trapped in an unthinkable fate.

The girl deserves more than fleeting relief,
She deserves justice, acknowledgment of grief.
For every silent cry, there must be a voice,
For every broken soul, there must be a choice.

203. The Agony of Silenced Innocence of a 12-Year-Old Muslim Girl

In the quiet corners of a home,
Where shadows stretch and secrets roam,
A father whispers of love's cruel guise,
Masking darkness in his daughter's eyes.

"You're my treasure, my sacred jewel,
Let me teach you," he claims, "life's cruel rule."
Touching tender innocence with hands profane,
Inflicting scars that words cannot explain.

Grandma[25] comes, her smile a mask,
Demanding kisses, an unwelcome task.
"Hold still," they say, "this is our way,
In silence, our family must stay."

The father speaks of a distant land,
Where such horrors are deemed grand.
"Your mother's weary, her love is cold,
Now it's your turn, as you've been told."

He binds her voice with threats of blame,
"Speak a word, and I'll bear no shame.

---

25. Ibid.p.8. *"A father asserts that he loves his 12-year-old, female child more than anything. He explains to the child that this is the reason why he cuddles it. He wants to touch every part of its body. Grandmother comes to visit every Sunday. She wants a kiss from the 12-year-old. Both Dad and Grandma cite 'good reasons' for touching or kissing the child. "That's what we do in our family, that's why you have to hold still and why you mustn't talk about it. "Her father explains that in his country of origin, all fathers have sex with their daughters and now it is her turn because, after four children, Mum is no longer sexually active. But the father also says that she is not allowed to talk about it. Otherwise, it will be her fault if her Dad goes to prison".*

Your silence keeps me safe and free;
Your silence, child, protects me."

Her world grows smaller, her trust decayed,
Innocence lost, but guilt displayed.
At school, she clings to fleeting light,
A teacher's kindness, a moment's respite.

Yet the chains of home draw her back,
To a life lived under attack.
A culture's shadow, an ancient creed,
Nurtures violence and plants its seed.

How many daughters must bear this weight?
How many homes will close the gate?
In the name of love, they justify,
The monstrous acts that make children cry.

Raise your voices, shatter the night,
Expose the wrongs, demand the right.
Let no child endure this fate,
Break the cycle; it's not too late.

204. The Agony of a Four-Year-Old Muslim Girl Child Forgotten

A girl, tender, only four[26],
Innocence stolen, trust no more.
Her world, a home, a fractured space,
Became the stage for vile disgrace.

A mother's heart, bound by fear,
Could not shield the one held dear.
She chose her silence, her desperate plea,
Afraid of the solitude abandonment would decree.

A man came with a shadowed plan,
Not seeking love, but a darker span.
He sought a child, not a home,
Preying where innocence was left alone.

Through cunning words and calculated charm,
He gained their trust, causing harm.
Access granted, doors swung wide,
No one to hear the silent cries inside.

The mother stood, paralyzed and frail,
Her voice a ghost, her strength would fail.
Fear of being left alone
Let evil root within her home.

---

26. Ibid.p.17."*Girl, four years of age. All perpetrators in this case were partners or friends of the mother. One had purposely chosen the mother. He had looked for her using a personal advertisement and then noticed that she had a young daughter. This partner was looking for sex with children and quickly gained 'access' to the little girl as they were all living in the same household. The mother did nothing to stop the violence. She was afraid of being abandoned.*"

What justice speaks for a girl so small?
Who answers when the voiceless call?
Her pain, a wound, a scar unseen,
A life forever torn between.

Let us weep for this stolen youth,
For lives destroyed by twisted truth.
Where love should guard, and care defend,
Let no such agony descend.

Raise the banners, sound the cry,
Protect the child, let no one deny.
Fear's silence must not be her fate,
Break the cycle before it's too late.

205. The Lost Four-Year-Old Muslim Girl Childhood

A child of four[27], in shadows raised,
Where darkness thrived and evil grazed.
Her world was twisted, a cruel façade,
Where innocence was sold, and trust outlawed.

Her mother, bound by ignorance and fear,
Did not see the cries so near.
Unaware, unarmed, she stood aside,
As her daughter's spirit was crushed, denied.

The child grew in this fractured realm,
Her body a ship without a helm.
Taught to seek attention through pain,
Her young soul bore a scarred, dark stain.

Her reflection became her greatest foe,
A loathed visage where shame would grow.
Disgusted with her body's form,
She ceased to care, her spirit worn.

Yet even in despair, she sought the light,
A distorted yearning, born of plight.

---

27. Ibid.p.20. "*A four-year-old girl grew up in an unusual environment where sexual violence was 'normal'. The mother did not want to and could not protect the child; she was unable to ask for assistance because she did not know that her daughter needed help. The daughter lost the sense of her physical self, her self-confidence and was disgusted with her own body. In the end she no longer washed her-self. At the same time, she desired attention: she had learned to get through sex and convinced her school friends to perform sexual acts. This behavior was observed and categorized as sexualized behavior. This was the trigger for involving a professional.*

She mimicked what she had been shown,
Seeking connection, though now alone.

Her acts, misunderstood and grave,
Were cries for help she could not waive.
Her friends became unwitting prey,
Echoes of her world's decay.

At last, her pain could not be masked,
A professional's help was finally asked.
Too long delayed, but a vital chance,
To reclaim her life, a second stance.

O child, your story strikes the heart,
A painful reminder of a world apart.
Where silence shelters evil's creed,
And ignorance neglects the desperate need.

Let this tale ignite a flame,
To fight for those who bear such shame.
To educate, to shield, to stand,
To lend the helpless a guiding hand.

Never again let a child endure,
A life so bleak, a fate so unsure.
Raise the banners, take the vow,
To protect the children, starting now

206. The Weight of the Muslim

"If only I had not come to this place . . ."
A thought that haunts, a lingering trace.
A choice not made, a road not taken,
Now bound by chains, my spirit shaken.

"If only I had agreed to sleep with him,
Perhaps then, my life wouldn't be grim."[28]
The voice within whispers, cold and clear,
As if surrendering could erase the fear.

"I should just accept, he is my spouse,
His will is law, within this house."
The words that drown my sense of right,
That silence screams within the night.

A woman trapped by ancient ties,
Her worth diminished by forced lies.
Her body claimed, her voice withdrawn,
A slave to the idea she must carry on.

But no, the weight of silence steals,
Her dignity, her truth, it feels
As though she's trapped, without escape,
A prisoner in an unseen shape.

If only choices didn't fade,
If only trust didn't come with trade.

---

28. Ibid.p.19."*If only I had not come to this place. . .*" or "*if only I had agreed to sleep with him. I should just accept that he is my husband and has the right to sleep with me.*"

If only she knew that love was kind,
Not driven by a controlling mind.

Let her voice rise and break the chain,
Let her know that she can reclaim.
Her body, her voice, her rightful place,
No longer defined by guilt or grace.

No one should have to question why,
Their worth is rooted in a lie.
To love should not be forced or sold,
It should be given, free and bold.

So let this poem, this truth unfold,
That every woman has a heart of gold.
Her worth is not to be bought or sold,
Her strength is hers, forever bold.

207. Bound by the Muslim Way of Life

For years, he claimed her body as his domain,
A demand cloaked in marital refrain.
"Whenever I please," his words command,
A twisted union, a cruel demand.

She submits, not from love, but fear,
Her heart heavy, her eyes unclear.
Forced to endure, against her will,
A silent victim, her spirit still.

He doesn't strike, but wounds her soul,
Each encounter taking its toll.
"You're my wife; it's my right,"[29] he declares,
A phrase that tightens invisible snares.

Her objections met with scornful blame,
Partners and peers echo the same:
"If only you'd yield, just play along,
His force wouldn't feel so wrong."

A chorus of voices, deaf to her pain,
Justify control in love's cruel name.
Her cries are whispers, lost in the air,
A prisoner trapped in despair's snare.

---

29. Ibid.p.9."*For a period of years, a man has been talking his wife into having sex with him whenever he pleases. This means he also forces her to sleep with him against her will. She is obliged to satisfy him sexually. To get his way, he does not mind hurting her emotionally not physically. Women often submit out of fear of being beaten and because they think the man is acting within his rights. Many partners affirm this view by saying that it is her own fault. If she didn't resist and just played along, he wouldn't have to force her and that, being her husband, he had a right to her after all.*

But she is more than this silent grief,
More than the myths of a husband's belief.
Her body, her own, her voice, her choice,
Let her rise, let her reclaim her voice.

To love is not to conquer or claim,
It's a bond of equals, free of shame.
No duty demands submission or tears,
No marriage thrives on coercion or fears.

Let the silence shatter, let truth ignite,
A woman's worth is her birthright.
No more bound by fear or guilt,
Let her rise, let her rebuild.

For every woman who's been told to yield,
There's a power within, a sword, a shield.
Love is freedom, not chains of despair,
Her body, her choice, her truth laid bare.

208. Islamic Cycles Unbroken

Her childhood was a shadowed place,
A father's violence left no trace—
Except in the scars unseen,
In her heart, where pain had been.

She learned the rules her silence taught:
Love equaled harm; it wasn't fought.
To earn affection, she'd concede,
A life conditioned to others' greed.

Now a mother, her child in tow,
The haunting echoes begin to show.
A man's touch, a dark reprise,
And yet, she doesn't recognize.

The family worker's voice was stern:
"Why didn't you protect in return?"
But her answer, raw and painfully clear:
"It seemed normal—I knew no fear."[30]

For in her world, love bore a cost,
A purity stolen, innocence lost.
Her daughter, twelve, repeats the tale,
Entrapped in a cycle destined to fail.

---

30. Ibid.p.23."*The mother of a four-year-old girl has herself experienced sexual violence from her father when she was a child. As a mother she was unable to protect herself and her daughter. Moreover, she had learned to get into relationships with men through sex. Her daughter has already taken this on at the age of twelve. The family worker asked why the mother had not protected her daughter from the assaults of her partners. The mother answered: "it seemed normal to me—-I had experienced it the same way, after all."*

Generations chained in pain,
Taught that love means loss and strain.
But must this story always repeat?
Must abuse be all they meet?

Somewhere, a spark still tries to glow,
A mother's will to overthrow
The lessons taught by harm and lies,
To rewrite what "normal" belies.

Her daughter's fate need not align,
With hers, with history's cruel design.
There's hope in breaking what came before,
To open, at last, a brighter door.

Let the chains of silence shatter,
Let healing rise where it must matter.
For love is more than scars and pain,
It's safety, freedom—a cherished gain.

The past may whisper, loud and stark,
But the future holds a brighter mark.
Together, they'll reclaim their space,
And build anew on love's embrace.

209. The Scarf of Slavery

When slavery-practicing Muslims migrate to the West,
They bring with them the beheading quest.
Slavery in the West is a shadow of the past,
Yet in Muslim lands, the chains still clasp.

The burqua-wearing master raises her hand,
To kill her black housemaid in Arab sand.
But when the scarf comes seeking refuge in the West,
She is welcomed with open arms, praised as the best.

My former slave-master women raise their glass,
To the scarf, to the veil, letting old crimes pass.
Brown-skinned, white-faced slave-masters unite,
To trample on my black skin, to choke the light.

They call the scarf beautiful, the Islamic grace,
But I see it as a mask, hiding the brutal face.
It's a symbol of cruelty, of ideological hate,
That traps my black Christian maids in a merciless fate.

My labor, my sweat, my very flesh,
Was exploited in their lands, where pain is fresh.
The father and son rape me every day,
The mother and daughter burn me, then turn away.

This is the way of life, the creed,
Of the Arab Muslim community's deed.
My name is "Nigro," their daily taunt,
Even when they come to America, they haunt.

In my land, they exploit with a smiling lie,
While my black skin shivers under the sky.
The scarf that once enslaved my kin,
Now wears the mask of an ally, a grin.

210. The Agony of Homosexual

I did not know until sacred texts spoke,
How love, my essence, was deemed a yoke.
Al-A'raf, al-Hijr, Sahih decreed,
Burn me, stone me, let my spirit bleed.

I should be thrown from the heights of disdain,
My body a spectacle, a symbol of pain.
I should face stones, sharp with hate,
Hurled by hands that script my fate.

I understand the Quran and its voice,
Declaring my being a punishable choice.
They sever my ontology with each sharp blade,
A life of love turned a death parade.

Cast off like trash from lofty heights,
Dismembered in dark corners, bereft of rights.
Stoned into silence that the world will not hear,
Blood tracing patterns on crimsoned shores.

They name it justice; I name it despair,
A war on being, wrapped in the cloak of prayer.
No space to love, no air to breathe free,
A life condemned by dogma's decree.

I know the eyes of those who would condemn,
Their holy books dripping with vengeful spleen.
Beheading the hearts, the erasing of light,

The lynching of dreams by the dark of night.

I am the fire they light to burn,
The stone they cast with no return.
I am the fall from their towering spire,
Their hate, their law, their unholy choir.

And yet I stay, scarred and worn,
Still a spark of defiance born.
For stones can shatter, and fire burn,
But truth will spring, and love return.

Hear me now; let the world deride
Truth is eternal, and love abides.
Not their fire, nor their stones, nor their fall,
Will silence my truth—I will outlast them all.

211. Muslim Immigrant Invaders

Remember,
When they arrive in small numbers,
Their voices soft, their words coated with peace,
"We are a religion of love," they whisper,
Blending into lands not their own.
Their tone humbles, their eyes look down,
But beneath, a simmering storm brews.

Remember,
When their numbers swell,
Their voices grow louder, more demanding,
Special status, they cry, a place above all.
Their tone shifts from humility to command,
Shoulders squared, arms raised high,
As the shadows of intent deepen.

Remember,
When they are the majority,
October 7 becomes your every day.
Land scorched, skies torn apart, seas turned red,
They march with "Islam or else" as their banner,
A history repeated, a warning ignored.
The lessons of time echo in deafened ears.

Remember,
When they outnumber you,
It's no longer coexistence but conquest.
Jewish tears, gypsy fears,
The cries of the Yazidi echo anew.

The gassed, the exiled, the hunted, the erased—
Victims of ideologies cloaked in faith.

Remember,
The ghettoes of fear they build for others,
The ghettos of silence they demand of truth,
The ghettos of violence they defend with scripture.
In the land of refuge, invaders rise,
Transforming sanctuary into battleground.

Remember,
They are not refugees but architects of a scheme,
Not seekers of peace but carriers of conquest.
Their flags of democracy they burn,
Their banners of equality torn down.
What begins as asylum ends as an empire.

Remember,
The cries of freedom drowned beneath their chants,
The rights of many extinguished by the call of the few.
And the gas chambers of hate remain open,
No longer just for Jews but for the truth itself.
History may repeat itself, but the stage differs.

Remember,
Before the tide swallows you too.

212. Shadows of the Crescent

O land of desert winds and veiled truths,
Your sands whisper tales of silenced souls.
In the cradle of civilizations,
Where light once dawned,
Now lingers a shadow of unyielding darkness.

Arab ideology, based on dominance,
A creed turned into a tool to oppress.
Your women, flowers yet to bloom,
Get plucked and locked,
Machines for heirs,
With no dreams, voiceless.

Your laws are chains,
Welded in the heat of patriarchal fervor.
Child brides, their innocence torn,
Must serve men three times their age in years.
Where is your mercy, O Arab land?
Where is your justice, O crescent moon?

Your Yazidis, hunted as game,
Their tears irrigating your holy wars.
Your women, faceless, voiceless,
Enswathed in a coerced modesty,
Their laughter muffled,
Their cries silenced.

You yourselves, pure,
Yet your hands red
With the blood of infidels,

With the lives of apostates,
With the pain of children reduced to ash.

Where is your civilization, O self-proclaimed keepers of faith?
Is it in your mosques that echo with sermons of exclusion?
Is it in your laws that strip humanity
From those who pray differently, love differently?
Is it in your swords raised against truth,
In your lashes against freedom?

The crescent moon watches silently,
As intolerance holds its head high.
Zero tolerance, zero peace,
Zero humanity for those called 'other.'

O. Arabian ideology,
You are but a desert bereft of grace,
An ocean with the cruelty to drown an innocent race.
You enchain your women,
Deify oppression, glorify bloodshed,
Love is a crime in your land,
Freedom forbidden fruit.

Let your veils fall,
Not from faces, but from minds.
Let your swords rest,
Not on necks, but in history.
For the world ruled by your ideology
Is a forsaken world,
A standing testimony to the greatest failure of humanity.

Awake, O Arab world,
From the nightmare that was your own making.
Dare to wear the light
You so fear. Until then, your legacy is but a shadow,
Barren land devoid of life and love.

213. The Shroud of Jamia Milia Islamia

O Jamia, where knowledge was meant to grow,
Do you remember what academia's glow?
Born to foster minds, to challenge the blind,
Yet your halls echo with silence, unrefined.

Where Oxford's books once taught the truth,
You replaced them with pages of medieval ruth.
No scholars, no theories, no light to spread,
Just shadows of scripture, where wisdom is dead.

You spawned not thinkers, but minds enslaved,
Trapped in your lies, the world's hopes depraved.
You burnt the tomes that once gave birth
To freedom, to knowledge, to life on Earth.

O Jihadists, who cloak in your holy disguise,
What do you see when you close your eyes?
Do you not see the damage you've done,
Turning your temple into a place of the gun?

I once loved freely, a Brahmin's embrace,
But you came with chains, defiled my grace.
Like the night on October's bloodied eve,
You stripped us of dignity, made us grieve.

You burn the books, you kill the mind,
You rip apart humanity, one thread at a time.
Like Boko Haram, you trample the light,
Turning knowledge to darkness, extinguishing the fight.

Your pen may flow, but with blood-stained ink,
The wisdom you write is tainted to think.
You send forth your scholars with knives in their hands,
To silence the truth, to smother the lands.

O Jamia, O Satan in academic guise,
You've turned your classrooms into Jihadi Johns.
Your professors wear PhDs as chains,
Teaching violence in scholarly veins.

A Sharia school, disguised in degrees,
A place where peace and learning cease.
You must be stopped, for the world's greater good,
For life, for truth, for all that is good.

214. The Blood of a Gay *Professor Srinivas Ramchandra Siras*

O Aligarh, your halls are stained,
With blood that flows, with hearts in chains.
A professor's life, a bright soul slain,
For loving who his heart ordained.

You killed the man who dared to be,
In a world where love is free.
His words, his poems, his stanzas cry,
Echoes of truth that will never die.

You silenced him with hate and fear,
But his voice, though gone, still draws near.
He lives within the lines he wrote,
Against your crimes, he'll never be remote.

O Aligarh, what have you become?
A place where justice cannot come.
You kill the queer with hateful hands,
And Europe stands with your dark lands.

The West, in its towers, turns away,
While the blood of truth stains the day.
For what is love when hate wears a crown?
For every soul you push to drown.

You think you've erased his story's might,
But his words shine through the endless night.
Against your violence, they stand as proof,
Of love that breaks every brutal roof.

So hear the blood that calls your name,
You cannot hide from your shame.
The fight for love, for truth, for right,
Will carry on, beyond your night.

215. Ode to Mosab Hassan Yousef

Born in the shadow of the green flag's flight,
A son of the crescent, a child of the fight.
Bloodlines woven in a legacy fierce,
Yet truth was a whisper he longed to pierce.

The son of a sheikh, yet he turned from the fold,
Where iron chains of doctrine took hold.
Through the corridors of faith and fire,
He walked the path of doubt's desire.

A torch in the dark, he dared to betray,
Not for vengeance, nor gold, nor sway.
But for the dream of a world unchained,
Where love is honored, and peace remains.

Spy or savior—his name they cursed,
For breaking the cycle, for quenching the thirst.
He fled the walls where martyrs bled,
To speak the words that no man said.

O exile of truth, O brother of light,
The price of knowledge—a hunted flight.
Yet from the ashes of loss and scorn,
A voice was risen, a truth reborn.

He bears no blade, yet battles the lies,
Unraveling dogmas with fearless eyes.
No minaret calls him, no muezzin's song,
Yet his spirit stands, unbroken, strong.

Through betrayals deep and threats untold,
He walks a path both bright and bold.
For he who shatters the chains of the past,
Shall forge a freedom that ever lasts.

O Mosab, wanderer, witness, son,
Your war is fought with words, not guns.
And though the storm may rage anew,
Truth stands unshaken, burning through.

Section V
Words Against the Blood and Iron Policy of Africans

216. Ode to My Great-Grandfather, His Royal Highness Emperor Yohannes IV

Oh, my great-grandfather[31],
Your Royal Highness, Yohannes IV,
Of a heart so wide, a soul so bold,
You opened your arms, embraced the wound,
Came close to the forsaken, their voice to be told.
Five kilometers were shortened to three,
You welcomed the Muslim relatives with dignity,
In front of our palace, they had their request,
A witness of love, a noble embrace it would be.

You gave them shelters, shops to flourish,
In return, however dim the situation,
For their hearts, it seems, were far from alive,
Against you, against the light is what they did.
Whetted swords, armed with destruction,
They burnt churches to stop the praise,
Our Christian preachers, with hate, they did shun,
In a land once holy, now in a fog.

---

31. The poem is narrated by HRH Selamawit Hailu Bezabih and penned by Suryaraju Mattimalla. She is an imperial royal family member of His Royal Highness Emperor Yoahnnes IV and an exiled artist from Ethiopia. She is a great granddaughter of His Royal Highness Emperor Yohanes IV. Yohannes IV was Emperor of Ethiopia from 1871 to his death in 1889 at the Battle of Gallabat and King of Tigray from 1869 to 1871. She is an immediate granddaughter of His Excellency Dejazamtch Negusse Bezabih. H.E. Dejazamtch Negusse Bezabih is a hero of the 1943 Woyane rebellion in Tigray and is considered a father figure of the Ethiopian nation. Her second son, Stanford Suryaraju Mattimalla, was killed by forceful vaccination by a neo-Nazi German gynecologist in Germany. She lives with her six-year-old son Saviour Suryaraju Mattimalla and Indian husband Suryaraju Mattimalla.

Compassion You showed to them was answered back with acid hate,
Wanting to establish their Islamic rule,
Axum and Lalibela are being desecrated,
Our heritage, our sanctity, turned to pain.
The very pillars of our faith laid bare,
By hands that once sought a common ground to share,
The world stands by, blind to our despair,
With UN and UNICEF as allies unbound there.

How You loved and how they destroy,
Your human scents still hanging in the air,
Dreamer king, source of Joy light,
Yet in this new Ethiopia hearts are ill. From peace to violence, a tragic descent,
Under the rule of Abiy, the tides have turned,
Our Tigray community, in anguish, bent,
Their cries of sorrow, a tale that's unlearned.

You fought against the tide of jihad's grasp,
In battles of old, where courage was born,
But they beheaded you, in a wicked clasp,
A history twisted, your legacy scorned.
O great-grandfather, we hold you so dear,
Your vision of justice, your heart's noble plea,
In a world where love seems drowned in fear,
We remember your strength, your spirit, still free.

Though the shadows of hate may rise and entwine,
We cling to your wisdom, your love so profound,
For every life matters, each soul a divine,
In the tapestry of faith where hope can be found.
So let us rise up, as you once did stand,
Against the encroaching dark, we will fight,
With love as our armor, united we'll band,
For the spirit of Yohannes shall guide us to light.

217. Father of Ethiopia, His Excellency Bezabih Negusse Haftu

My grandfather, Dejazmach Bezabih Negusse[32], stood tall, proud, and fair,
His skin, like polished ivory, was beyond compare.
He hated black—black cat, black dog, black hue,
Despising even the shade of his royal view.

He was the Father of the Ethiopian Nation, they say,
But his heart was a labyrinth where darkness lay.
Marrying my mother to his ivory skinned son Hailu was not for love, but her lineage's glow,
For she was royalty, though her skin, like midnight's flow.

When his eyes grew dim with drink, he lost his way.
Felt the warmth from a black-skinned woman, just for one day.
When he awakened the fact of his deed seemed fanciful.
As a ghost, sudden as a chill wind, he deserted her.

He accepted the child, for the skin was his,
But left the mother, as if she did not exist.
She was there, but not there, a shadow in the hall,
A housemaid, unseen, against the royal wall.

   32. The poem is narrated by HRH Selamawit Hailu Bezabih and penned by Suryaraju Mattimalla. She is an imperial royal family member of His Royal Highness Emperor Yoahnnes IV and an exiled artist from Ethiopia. She is a great granddaughter of His Royal Highness Emperor Yohanes IV. Yohannes IV was Emperor of Ethiopia from 1871 to his death in 1889 at the Battle of Gallabat and King of Tigray from 1869 to 1871. She is an immediate granddaughter of His Excellency Dejazamtch Negusse Bezabih. H.E. Dejazamtch Negusse Bezabih is a hero of the 1943 Woyane rebellion in Tigray and is considered a father figure of the Ethiopian nation. Her second son, Stanford Suryaraju Mattimalla, was killed by forceful vaccination by a neo-Nazi German gynecologist in Germany. She lives with her six-year-old son Saviour Suryaraju Mattimalla and Indian husband Suryaraju Mattimalla.

My grandfather's hypocrisy runs deep, like a river of shame,
Though we are Africans, we shun the black name.
He pampered those with fairer skins and shunned the dark,
Drawing his divisions like a hunter's mark.

The hypocrisy of royal blood, the lie of class
Now it's time to break this brass mirror.
For racism, it comes from all sides, all skins.
A wound that deepens, that's always victorious.

218. The 1943 Woyane Rebellion Leader, His Excellency Bezabih Negusse Haftu

Let us extol the name of Dejazmach Bezabeh Negussie Haftu[33]:
King of the jungle, a lion standing tall, undaunted.
In the Highlands of Tigray, where stories are told.
As a result of this conflict, the Woyane Rebellion emerged.
A struggle for life, for freedom.

In 1943, while the empire tightened its grip,
He was leading the fight with courage high enough.
The mountains bellowed with a roar of a fighter,
As Tigray spirit rose ahead.

Not a mere mortal, but a force so strong,
Leading the people in a fight that was right.
Resistance flying in his flag high,
Against those forces which would not yield and lag.

The rebellion spread like wildfire in the grass,
A hope-giving message, none could surpass.
The odds were against them; they did not retreat,
With Negussie in might, they stood, firm and complete.

Battles, however, are shaded by light,
Victory is not just covering flight.
Though brought down, the rebellion did not die in spirit,
A strong, great legacy which was never to be vain.

Bezabih Negussie, thy name doth ring,
Like the sound of mountain winds,

33. Ibid.

Thy bravery, thy spirit, thy unyielding quest,
In hearts that ne'er sleep shall live.

Let's remember your stand, your pride, your way,
Woyane spirit, alive today.

219. Her Royal Highness Mamit Sebhat Weldegebriel[34]

How may I praise your egalitarian grace,
In a world where royal blood often looks the other way?
While other crowns treat their subjects as slaves, untouchables, or things,
You have elevated them, given them wings.

I have seen your humanity, your compassionate touch,
Adopting your subjects, caring for them as much.
You took in the physically challenged, treated them as your own,
They shared our plate, our bed, our home.

With 11 children, yet your heart could still grow,
Embracing the others who had nowhere to go.
You left your palace to live among the poor,
Your Orthodox faith opening every door.

You never treated others as less, as things,
Unlike colonial queens who clipped their wings.
You loved my father, a brown-skinned man,
Even when his own father had a different plan.

---

34. The poem is narrated by HRH Selamawit Hailu Bezabih and penned by Suryaraju Mattimalla. Selamawit Hailu Bezabih is a daughter of Her Royal Highness Mamit Sebhat Weldegebriel. She is an imperial royal family member of His Royal Highness Emperor Yoahnnes IV and an exiled artist from Ethiopia. She is a great granddaughter of His Royal Highness Emperor Yohanes IV. Yohannes IV was Emperor of Ethiopia from 1871 to his death in 1889 at the Battle of Gallabat and King of Tigray from 1869 to 1871. She is an immediate granddaughter of His Excellency Dejazamtch Negusse Bezabih. H.E. Dejazamtch Negusse Bezabih is a hero of the 1943 Woyane rebellion in Tigray and is considered a father figure of the Ethiopian nation. Her second son, Stanford Suryaraju Mattimalla, was killed by forceful vaccination by a neo-Nazi German gynecologist in Germany. She lives with her six-year-old son Saviour Suryaraju Mattimalla and Indian husband Suryaraju Mattimalla.

O mother, you let me marry an untouchable, dark-skinned, poor,
A person discarded by Hindu traditions' door.
When the colonial queens enforced their chains,
You stood tall, banishing their claims.

You've shown us that humanity knows no class,
While others still walk in their colonial past.
Thank you, my Highness, for your unending light,
For treating housemaids as equals, giving them their right.

I am proud to call you mother, my beacon, my guide,
In a world where others hide behind their pride.

220. Her Royal Decree[35]

When you see a poor Ethiopian, you hand them a cross of wood, rough and plain,
But when my Royal Family enters, you bring forth rich crosses, adorned, ordained.
Why this discrimination, this class divide,
In a faith where God's love should abide?

We are all born equal, in His divine light,
Even though I am a Royal, and many struggle in the night.
God's love is not a crown, it's not a throne,
It does not favor, it is unwavering, wholly known.

I know your hearts don't carry hate, but still I see,
A hierarchy, a division, a broken decree.
Treat everyone with the same holy cross, the same love,
Unlike the white churches where my black skin they shove.

I have seen it, in Czech Republic and Germany's air,
A look of disgust, as if my presence pollutes their prayer.
There, they love a Muslim, but turn from my black cross,
As if my faith were a burden, a cost.

We are not like the Brahmin, Untouchable divide,
Or those who seek genocide when differences collide.
We do not dehumanize the ostracized, like those who claim,
Pure hate in Hindutva, Islam, or Western liberal fame.

In my Ethiopian Empire, we are humane, fair,
We don't turn love into hate, we don't compare.

35. Selamawit Hailu Bezabih

We can't be what the world has made of itself,
No millionaires, billionaires, no material wealth.

For we are African, without the greed's art,
We carry only hospitality, love, and a pure heart.
Love our slaves as you would my kin,
Unlike the Western and Asian masters, where true love grows thin.

221. The Madness of African-American Leaders Adoring Gandhi

O Martin Luther King,
Now I see why you praised a man
Who called himself a champion of peace—
But what peace did Gandhi preach?
What nonviolence did he truly believe in,
When his soul was stained with caste, with racism,
And with a dark, twisted notion of purity?

How can you call him an inspiration,
A man who saw African lives as inferior?
A man who saw my black skin as dirt,
Who denied us our humanity,
While preaching about freedom and justice?
Did you not see his true face,
The face of a man who used his power
To oppress, to dehumanize, to silence?

You, Martin, spoke of freedom and love,
But did you not hear the echoes of Gandhi's hate?
Did you not see the lies he built his empire on,
The false doctrines of purity and supremacy
That he preached,
While my people starved in his shadow?
How could you admire such a man?
How could you, a champion for the oppressed,
Lift up a man who wanted to eliminate
Not just Africans, but untouchables too?

He used the poor masses of India,
Their struggles, their hopes,
As a backdrop for his self-serving revolution.
Just as you used the slums of black America
For your political and professional gain.
Both of you played the same game—
You both wore masks of righteousness,
While your actions told a different story,
One of exploitation, manipulation, and hypocrisy.

How could you—who fought for the dignity
Of black people, for their rights and respect—
Look up to a man who saw us as inferior,
A man who lived a life of contradictions,
Peddling nonviolence while advocating
For a violent, caste-based, hierarchical society?
Gandhi, a man of brown supremacy,
A man who crushed my people beneath his feet,
While he was elevated by the world as a hero.
How could you, Martin, inspire us with such a man,
When you knew the truth of his violence,
And his complicity in the oppression of the downtrodden?

We, the black Christians, who live by the message of love,
Cannot accept your hero, Gandhi,
Who turned his back on humanity,
Who supported a system of cruelty,
A system that enslaved untouchables,
A system that condemned my African ancestors
To lives of misery and oppression.
How can we, who follow Christ,
Find anything but disdain for a man
Who worshipped Hindu idols of violence
While calling for a world of peace?

Gandhi is no hero, Martin—
He is a symbol of oppression,
A symbol of lies, of manipulation.
We don't need his inspiration,

We don't need his solidarity.
We need true freedom—
The freedom of self-respect,
The dignity of life,
The moral values of love, peace, and truth.
We need to break free from these false idols
And build a world where no one is enslaved
By the past, by lies, by caste, or by color.

222. O Barak Obama, Where Is Your Western Knowledge?

O Barak Obama,
Where is your intellectual rigor?
Why don't you possess the analytical skills
Of our African-American leaders,
Of those who truly understand
The venomous legacy of Gandhi?
Why, when the world sees him for what he is—
A racist, a casteist, a man who dreamed
Of eliminating our black skin,
Our untouchable skin—
Do you still wish to dine with this thug?

Is it your dream, Obama,
To break bread with a man
Who saw you as nothing more than a criminal,
A thief, a monkey, a chimpanzee?
A prostitute, a fakir, a barbarian,
Unworthy of his so-called 'pure' society?
Is this who you choose to honor,
To celebrate, while turning a blind eye
To his vision of a 'pure' Hindu state,
Where people like us—black, untouchable—
Are to be eradicated?

You, Obama,
Are no intellectual.
You may have walked the halls
Of Western universities,
But your mind remains shackled

By the same chains of ignorance
That hold many in your community—
The same ones that keep you from seeing
The true face of Gandhi,
The true face of your own complicity.

You claim Gandhi as your inspiration,
But what knowledge have you gleaned
From your books, from your supposed studies,
That could blind you to the truth?
Have you even read the work of
The University of Ghana?
The same institution that rose up
And removed the statue of this racist thug
From its campus?

No, Obama, you are not my representative.
You are another leader of empty gestures,
A corrupt figure in a line of African leaders
Who have carried the weight of racist ideals
On their shoulders.
Like Martin Luther King,
Like Nelson Mandela,
You too have aligned with the wrong side.
You have embraced the wrong man.
Gandhi, a man who hated our black skin,
Who condemned our untouchable skin—
You, Obama, have chosen to glorify him.

Gandhi is rolling in his ashes now,
Laughing at your foolishness,
Laughing at your dream
Of having dinner with him.
How can you sit at his table,
When he will come for you,
Not with peace, but with poison,
With venom from his brown skin,
And the venom of his followers

That has poisoned our bodies and souls
For generations?

Ask the University of Ghana,
The one that fought against Gandhi's racism,
The one that stood up for the dignity of my people,
And ask them what they know
About the venom of Gandhi's words,
And what they did to remove it
From their campus.
You, Obama, are no better than those
Who helped keep his poisonous legacy alive.

So while you dream of dining with Gandhi,
Know that he would not welcome you
With open arms—
Not when your black skin
Is the one he tried to crush,
Not when your untouchable soul
Is the one he tried to erase.

223. O African Mother, Teach Me

O Ethiopian mother, why did you shape me so
To chase after gold, to wander, to go?
Why did you not teach me right from the start,
That love is a promise, not a game of the heart?

You were born without a name to call,
No father to claim, no lineage at all.
And now your children bear the same fate,
Seeking fathers lost in the hands of fate.

We are shadows that slip through the night,
Traded for coins, forgotten by light.
No vows to honor, no truths to keep,
Only fleeting desires that run so deep.

At ten, I learned the ways of the street,
Not from books, but from hands that greet.
Not from wisdom, not from care,
But from whispers of lust that filled the air.

O mother, our men are taught to prey,
Our daughters barter, then walk away.
We count lovers, not years, in our lives,
We carry children, yet never be wives.

We pray, yet faith is a hollow sound,
A mask we wear when others are around.
Our hands lift high, yet our feet still stray,
From the paths of truth, we turn away.

O mother, our hearts are stained with lies,
Dressed in deceit, cloaked in disguise.
We name love, but know it not,
We chase pleasure, and truth is forgot.

We are winds that never stay,
We love, we leave, we drift away.
O mother, I wish I knew what's right,
But darkness blinds where there is no light.

One man, one woman, is it a dream?
A life of love, so far it seems.
Teach me, mother, before I fade,
Before my soul is lost, betrayed.

Can the river change its course?
Can the leopard lose its spots?
O mother, tell me, is there hope?
Or are we bound to this endless knot?

Teach us more than wandering desire,
Teach us more than fleeting fire.
O mother, be the guide we lack,
Lead us to the road we never track.

224. Chicken Tenderloin

The tenderloin, a delicate piece, a symbol of power's line,
The head of the family, the father dines first—this is a sign.
The mother waits, her hands clasped, her eyes down,
For the male must feast, wearing his carnal crown.

Tenderloin—soft, yet a hard truth it tells,
Of male chauvinism, in which the belief dwells.
The blind beliefs, the superstitions that bind,
That a man is pure, and a woman must stay behind.

Tender meat, tender lies, they say,
That a woman's worth is to serve, obey.
But in the African way, there's no pure hate,
No untouchable caste, no unapproachable gate.

Our women contest, they fight back, they speak,
They are not made to be meek, they are not weak.
Unlike the Hindu, where caste crushes dreams,
Or the Muslim, where the veil silences screams.

In my African home, there's no pure divide,
No racial caste, no brutal tide.
Slaves in Africa were not untouchable ghosts,
They had no chains of hate, no shadowed hosts.

But see, black Muslims have pure hate, they say,
Like the Hindu, the Arab, who would cast me away.
Europe, too, wears its mask with pride,
The liberal, feminist, queer, BLM, where truth hides.

Tenderloin—the cut of power, a muscle of pride,
But it's the African spirit that cuts, that divides.
We don't need your titles, your chains, your sin,
We'll love without hate, let light in.

For there's hypocrisy in how you dine,
How you decide who must wait in line.
But not in my Africa, where women rise,
Where we see truth beyond the tenderloin lies.

225. We the Pathological Liars

We are the Africans, civilized, more than any master who came,
Colonial, Hindu, Islamic, they all brought their shame.
We have no untouchables, though our wars may flare,
We see humans as humans; our compassion laid bare.

We don't objectify women, like Muslim or Hindu,
Though violence still scars, we fight for what's true.
Our women are not chained nor sexual slaves,
They are warriors, and for their rights, they dig graves.

We aren't that woman of the West, a liberal so fine,
Sharing a bed with those who hate, and spread Jihad or caste and lies in their shrine.
Hospitality exudes, freedom rings, love abounds,
A race never colonized by traditions from above grounds.

We are the most egalitarian race on this earth,
From birth itself, struggling for freedom of birth.
No burqua, no saree, no chains of culture to bind,
Liberty we wear in our heart and mind.

While the Western masters lynched, raped and enslaved,
We fought within the spaces they paved,
Things they view us as, yet we stand tall,
Spirit not broken, it will never fall.

226. African Drama

We are the Africans, the sun-baked, the strong,
More civilized than any master who came along.
Colonial, Hindu, Islamic, each carved their claim,
But we never bowed, never bore their shame.

We walked these lands before they knew our name,
Before their ships, their scriptures, their violent game.
They called us savage, yet we stood tall,
While they built empires that would crumble and fall.

We have no untouchables, no caste in our veins,
No divine decree that shackles in chains.
Our wars have flared, our struggles are vast,
Yet human to human, we stand steadfast.

We don't objectify women, don't veil them in fear,
No locked doors, no whispers, no silencing here.
Though wounds may linger, and scars still burn,
For their rights, our women rise, their battles return.

Not shackled in burqas, nor draped to appease,
Not hidden away, nor forced to please.
No marketplace trade, no bodies sold,
Our women walk fierce, their stories bold.

We aren't that woman of the West, so fine,
Who lies with men who draw the caste line.
They preach of rights, of justice they say,
Yet bow to systems that cast us away.

Our hospitality flows, our freedom rings,
Our love is vast, it shatters kings.
A race uncolonized in soul and mind,
Though shackled once, we left chains behind.

We are the most egalitarian race to stand,
No gods to separate, no cruel demand.
From birth itself, we claim our right,
Not by scriptures, but by the fight.

No burqa, no saree, no culture to bind,
Liberty lives in heart and mind.
No forced purdah, no sacred rule,
No man declares what makes us whole.

While Western masters lynched, raped, enslaved,
We carved our path within spaces they paved.
They see us still through a broken frame,
Yet we walk unbowed, untouched by shame.

We are the Africans, the world should know,
Our spirit unchained, we rise, we grow.
Though they call us lost, though they call us small,
We stand as giants—they fear we stand tall.

227. River of Lost Hyenas

They fled their homes, hope as their guide,
Seeking refuge where shadows reside.
Tigrayans, souls worn from flight,
Crossed lands of sorrow, searching for light.

But the Fano, with eyes cold and gray,
Stood like vultures in the dying day.
No mercy given, no questions asked,
Their terror concealed by shadows masked.

Slain innocents, left to dead,
Their silent screams of blood turned red.
Each life stolen, each heart torn,
Into the river their bodies were borne.

Clear water now it runs dark and deep,
Silent witness of secrets that keep.
In the murmuring deep, their spirits drift,
Bound by currents, adrift their tales.

Irony dances on the skin of the river,
A lifeline now turned into a grave herein.
Those who crossed with a glimpse of hope in sight,
Were in darkness, lost from light.

The river hisses out their names in futility,
Each wave a tale of wrappings in pain to tell.
The banks speak testimonies of obscenity,
A canvas dripping in human screams.

Once so clear, like the song of life that flows,
Now tainted, crimes dragged along its nose,
Memories of souls un-free,
Ghostly traces of tragedy.

But in silence, voices die,
And injustice is left to rot and lie.
Bodies drift, spirits cry,
In waters where innocence came to die.

Oh, river, take their tales upstream,
To echo in every haunted dream,
For while the peace may die, truth will survive,
Bound to their lost and stolen lives.

It carves the truth into silent stone.
For in each wave and mournful bend,
The river holds what none defend.

228. Hyenas of Mai Kadra

In Mai Kadra's fields, red as dusk,
A silence grows where lives were hushed.
The air, once sweet with harvest's yield,
Now thick with sorrow, unhealed, unsealed.

They fell like the dark of night,
Cloaked in the dark, nurtured in spite.
The voices of Amhara were choked in pain,
As earth was stained with blood just like the summer's rain.

Irony cries when justice failed,
Where truth was buried beneath false tales.
Death's cruel hand was carried by the politics,
Then Mai Kadra became haunted..

Distant between fathers and sons or mothers,
Ripped by hatred's blade, worn sharp.
Their cry rises to fall unheard,
Whispers lost, wings unclipped, deterred.

The soil still remembers every silent plea,
Every broken bond, every tree broken.
Not a stone unturned, nor a life unscarred,
In the valley where humanity marred.

Through tears, the Amhara mourn,
For loved ones lost, for lives forlorn.
Yet in their grief, a strength remains,
Bound not by vengeance, nor by chains.

But unto the fields of Mai Kadra, with the darkest hue dyed,
Seeds of hope for rise anew.
They stand and fight against nights,
Against wrongs in the light of memory.

O World, bear witness to this pain,
Into lives lost not in vain.
For though their voices fell in a silence so deep,
Yet murmurs their legacy to keep.

Let Mai Kadra's scars bear truth's embrace,
For justice to find its rightful place.
In each new dawn, a promise stays,
That no more lives should end this way.

229. Ashes of the Hyenas

In the dark of a ruthless night,
Where fires rose to steal the light,
Tigrayan voices, once strong and proud,
Were silenced beneath a blazing shroud.

Amhara hands that held torches high,
Kept ablaze with the fires of hate to burn and pierce.
Men were reduced to ashes, flesh to dust,
As trust was cast aside for savage lust.

Their dying cries hung heavy in the air,
And gross untruths about humanity were shared.
There, in the light flicker of those so bright flames,
A world collapsed, without mercy or place to hide.

Each crackling spark, each blistering flame,
Carried the weight of a brutal name.
For in their hearts, no compassion grew,
Only anger, fierce and cruel.

The irony hangs over the sad song of air,
For the world watched yet moved along.
While lives were taken by such a brutal fire,
Truth in a pyre so wrongfully did acquire.

Oh, silent ashes on haunted ground,
Where only smoke and death are found,
You speak a tale the world must hear,
Of innocent lives held dear.

The spirit of Tigray, charred but intact,
Springs upwards like smoke, a spirit intact.
For they burnt and lives had been taken,
Yet the memory stays, the ache of that burden.

And in the dying glow of every ember,
There stirs resilience, refusing to surrender.
For even in the ashes, life triumphs,
And toughness of Tigray is never broken.

Now let the world behold,
Take this oath to their souls that fell:
Their pain shall never be in vain,
Their tale to be told in fire's refrain.

Let a solemn cry go from its ashes,
Let not justice pass and go.
For every life taken away by burning,
With each new day, a fresh hope is springing.

230. Hyenas of Silence

In Tigray's fields where sorrow grows,
A darkness lingers, a silent throe.
Women's voices, once soft and clear,
Now echo pain, swallowed in fear.

Hands bound by force, spirits betrayed,
Innocence torn, their strength decayed.
They came in droves, with ruthless fire,
Leaving nothing but shame, stifled desire.

One hundred thousand dreams undone,
Under a merciless, blood-red sun.
Ethio-Eritrean State, Amhara, Fano's might,
Casting shadows across the light.

Irony weeps in this land once free,
Where love was life, now agony.
Each woman's scream, a silent plea,
For justice bound in misery.

A mother, a daughter, stripped of pride,
As hope fades in each tear they hide.
Their bodies scarred, yet spirits whole,
Bearing strength in hearts and soul.

How do you break what still must mend,
How can life to death descend?
For in their wombs, stories remain,
Of stolen breath, of silent pain.

And still, these women, though cast aside,
Hold power within, unshaken, wide.
Though hands once bound, they rise anew,
In defiance strong, in courage true.

The world may turn, may choose to flee,
But Tigray's pain demands to see.
For every scar, a tale unfolds,
Of dignity no violence holds.

O world, don't hide, don't close your door—
This cry for justice shakes the core.
For though they suffered, strength remains,
To heal the wounds, to break the chains.

And though their stories, whispered, fade,
In time's embrace, they're unafraid.
For resilience grows in silence's keep,
And memories stir, though buried deep.

Their courage rises like dawn's soft light,
Breaking the power of endless night.
Tigray's daughters, fierce and whole,
Unyielding still, unbroken soul.

231. Can the Ethiopian[36] Change his Skin?

Oh, janus-faced Ethiopian, thy dual mask shows,
Thou speakest of progress, yet thy dark heart doth still grow.
Thou dost inhumanize, exploit, and enslave with ease,
Housemaids who suffer under thy hands-while you are taking your fill of peace.

You leave for the West, searching for dollars, euros, and pounds,
But back home, you arrive to exploit, as nobody's around.
You claim asylum, fleeing a war-torn fate,
Yet, your true nature cannot flee beyond thy gate.

At 70, you chase tender youth's bloom,
Buying several wives, luring them to doom.
A moral human being? You are far from that,
Your bedroom becomes a trap, where young girls are sat.

Let our daughters go to school, not your bed,
Let Ethiopia rise, with morals instead.
No more hawala, human trafficking, or lies,
May God curse the janus-faces who disguise.

---

36. Jeremiah 13:23, *"can an Ethiopian change his skin or a leopard its spots? Neither can you do good who are accustomed to doing evil."*

232. The Myth of White and Black Cloths

White cloth drapes in sunlit grace,
Deemed pure as daylight, life's soft embrace.
They say it's love, peace, truth's attire—
Yet within, darker fires conspire.

White hides secrets, merciless and vast,
Ancient myths clutched tight, unforgiving.
For herein, within its folds, silent truths resound,
A lore where skin was made to cloak and bind.

Still, they would say Black dons the cloak of sorrow worn,
A smudge of night where even shadows mourn.
They say that filth is a detestable color to wear,
And in words and guile, they call black impure

Yet what's the truth beneath these lies?
For who decreed black unwise?
The white-robed saints who penned the lore,
Made purity a color's chore.

Lined with scriptures from holy texts,
They forged a fable that still irks.
White as heaven, black as hell-
Lies in the virtues of woven tales.

That black skin serves as curse and bane,
That only pale is pure inside,
As white robes flow in grand parade,
Black lives bear the darkest shade.

But what lies beneath the clothes we wear?
Hearts that beat, lives laid bare.
In each hue shines love so bright,
In each colour, day and night.

O burn those tales that vilify,
The nursery rhymes which teach us to deny-
The beauty of colours that make complete,
The dignity of each black retreat.

Not black, no stain, but bold,
A strength defined, a heart refined.
And white, no virtue cast,
Nor Heaven won, but a fabric spun.

Then raise the mask from off the lie,
And with unclassed eyes, behold and see
That love respects no hue nor shamed stain,
Nor is one damned by skin or place and name.

O, let us melt the chains of dogma,
Free thy mind and erase these stains,
For every heart deserves the same,
Not bound by cloth, but freed from blame.

233. Paedophilic Africa

Oh, Janus-faced Ethiopia, thy dual mask shows,
Thou speakest of progress, yet thy dark heart still grows.
Thy tongue weaves tales of justice and grace,
Yet behind closed doors, thou leavest no trace.

Thy hands are soft, adorned with gold,
Yet they wield the chains of the old.
In palaces built upon tears and pain,
Thou dost inhumanize, exploit, and maim.

Housemaids suffer beneath thy gaze,
Bound to serve in a silent daze.
They scrub the floors where thy sins reside,
Yet none shall hear their silent cries.

You flee to the West, cloaked in despair,
Claiming oppression, injustice, no air.
You speak of democracy, freedom, and right,
Yet back home, your cruelty ignites.

With dollars, euros, and pounds in hand,
You return, still ruling the land.
Not to uplift, not to heal,
But to tighten the grip, to strike the deal.

At seventy, you chase youth's bloom,
Turning futures into darkened tombs.
Buying several wives, luring them near,
A merchant of bodies, feeding on fear.

What moral man can sink so deep,
Where innocence shudders, and children weep?
Your bedroom, a dungeon, your wealth, a snare,
Yet you preach of virtue—how can you dare?

Let our daughters walk to school, not your bed,
Let Ethiopia rise with dignity instead.
No more hawala, no trafficking, no lies,
No stolen futures, no muffled cries.

Oh, cursed be the hands that buy and trade,
That shatter the dreams young women made.
May the earth spit out your bloodstained gold,
And history remember the stories untold.

No Janus-faced lords shall reign,
For justice shall come to cleanse the stain.
No more disguises, no more disguise—
For Ethiopia must wake and open her eyes.

234. A Dark Glorification

O Ethiopia, what is there to glorify,
When you have made our society the poorest, the darkest sky?
You cling to traditions, old and frail,
While under-aged girls are lost, without a trail.

How can we praise a culture that lets children fall,
Where virginity is stolen behind a classroom wall?
Where are your achievements, like the Jews who shine,
Where is the light that was meant to be divine?

You glorify the dark, at the cost of death,
While your people struggle, out of breath.
Do we have dignity, honor, or peace,
Or just the lies that never cease?

Your hospitality is a Janus face,
Running behind white skin, as if it's a race.
In the name of love, or sympathy you flee,
What kind of pride does that bring to thee?

Do you have any talent, any skill at all?
Or are you content to let your culture stall?
Lazy, dark, from birth to death,
You remain in shadows, without breath.

You say we are all born with equal minds,
But your actions speak louder, leaving hope behind.
Why must you chase Western shores and lies,
To build a life based on cheap alibis?

Why did you teach us to lie at every turn?
Why did our nation fail to learn?
How long will you be a corrupt, deceitful soul,
Raping the land, while pretending to be whole?

The world brands us as liars, dark, thieves,
For we have built our nation on grieves.
Lover of death, a culture so grim,
Lost in shadows, with no swimmer within.

You build no hierarchies as all the rest,
But brutal truth from your actions does shine. But welcome, with some other story darker within,
And girls even today are pale, frail, and full of shame in store.

It is indeed the past glory chaining but not freeing,
Culture leaving ruins without civilization to be seen. Seek civilization, seek scientific routes,
Where children free walk, with the day's leading flares lit.

See the West, with safety impressing
While your lies rob lives.
Read, learn, and thrive, build a better world,
Where no girl must fear, where no child is hurled.

You cannot be civilized with deceit and lies,
You cannot thrive when innocence dies.
Ethiopian girls face rape at every stage,
It's time to turn the page.

From school to university, they are preyed upon,
Their dignity stripped, their hopes long gone.
Stop glorifying what brings death and despair,
And build a new Ethiopia, strong and fair.

235. Impurity of Impurity

How long, O Ethiopia, behind tradition's veil,
Will you hide yourself, dehumanizing, humiliating, ensuring even women fail?
Women barred from the gate of the burial ground,
Kept from their dead, told that this is their lot in life found.

You claim purity, yet with mothers, you show disdain,
That selfsame womb from which you came now is left to bear the pain.
I gave life to you; I am real, the core of the earth,
Yet you appraise my value by rites that you give birth.

You don't even know your father's face,
He vanished into thin air when the womb was carrying me in its embrace.
Yet, you cling to customs-as if they had grace,
While cheating and lying, and defiling the sacred space.

Every Ethiopian man with multiple wives,
Leaving children unknown, living double lives.
You steal, cheat, and scam like stray animals,
But hold on to your rules that enslave and force women to pay.

How these horrible things do not elevate you one iota,
From Hinduism to Islam, so known for their lack of empathy and care.
Their atrocities against untouchables, black Christians, and Yazidis too,
Your customs mirror exactly the same disease.

I want to see an Ethiopia who knows what dignity is worth,
Where respect is given from birth;
A place where human rights may bask in the sun,
Where bribes, lies, and slavery are undone.

I dream of a country like the enlightened West,
Where the throb of humanity is strong in the breast.
No double-faced theory wearies man from man,
No customs foul infect the human brain.

Throw off the cloak of custom's disguise,
And let progress claim its rightful prize.
Cheated no more, deceit no more,
Rise, Ethiopia, rise, dignity restore.

236. Against the Madness of African & Islamic *Female Genital Mutilation*

O Ethiopian mother and father, hear this plea,
It is a cruelty to cut, to take what should be free.
To cut the clitoris of your daughter, in the name of tradition,
Is to strip her of freedom, of choice, of vision.

Let daughters cherish their bodies, their will,
Let them feel love's touch, let them feel the thrill.
For sex is healthy, it's part of life's design,
But you cut her clitoris, to control, to confine.

You do this, claiming culture, faith, and rite,
But it is a sin, a shadow that blots out light.
She is born equal, like any human being,
Yet you reduce her to a thing, unseen.

In our own royal family, my sister was hurt,
Her womanhood mutilated, thrown to the dirt.
It is inhumane to cut what makes her whole,
To rob her of freedom, of body, of soul.

When Muslims cut, you should not follow,
For their path is not one we need to swallow.
They have their ways, from birth to grave,
But we cherish life, we do not enslave.

We are Christians, we honor what's pure,
To mutilate is not a path we should endure.
Our African values must evolve, must grow,
From darkness to light, where freedom can flow.

Let's advance from mutilation to liberty,
Where women exercise their sexuality freely.
Let us not hold on to ways that harm,
But build a society that shelters, not alarms.

Let's discard what is barbaric, let it fall,
From our daily lives, from our cultural call.
Let our girls be equal, let them be strong,
For cutting their bodies is a crime, it's wrong.

Let us treat every living being with dignity,
Unlike those who dehumanize with impunity.
Let African girls breathe, live, and play,
To cherish life, love, and light each day.

Cutting a woman's vagina is barbarity, pure and stark,
There is no civilization in leaving such a mark.
Let us raise our voices, let light be clear,
And build a future where there's no fear.

237. Daughter's of Hyena Lament

I walk the streets with trepidation,
My footsteps haunted by staring eyes,
Lustful, predatory, watching me,
Ethiopian men, you see me as an object,
A shadow, a sub-human created for your desire,
But I am not your possession, not your prize.

Pan-African pain bleeds through my veins,
And then Ethiopia's daughters wear the same chains.
Reduced to bodies, denied our souls,
We are not pure, we are not sacred,
But tools, vessels, objects for control.
You claim culture, you claim tradition,
But what tradition breaks young girls,
At ten, at eleven, before they bloom?
You make brothels of our innocence,
And call it manhood.

Even before the wars, before Tigray's cries,
Our streets were minefields,
Every step a risk, every glance a threat.
You whisper about war and rape,
But we, the daughters of Africa, know:
The violence was always there,
Quietly festering, growing,
Beneath the surface of your holy façade.

Orthodox chants fill the air,
But no sanctuary will open its doors for us.
We are unclean, unworthy, kept away,

While under-aged girls, buds and jasmines,
Are plucked and trampled by your hands.
Your eyes burn with lust, your hands with sin,
But where is your shame, Ethiopian men?

My sisters of Tigray, of Ethiopia,
How long must we endure this?
Your Tigray spaces, like all Ethiopian spaces,
Speak of tradition, of purity, of faith,
But beneath the cloth, the cross, the prayer,
There is only hypocrisy, only pain.

Multiple wives, multiple children,
Their names lost on your tongues,
You speak of family, yet you abandon,
Leave behind the lives you create.
You call it love, but we call it violence,
A lust that strips us of our dignity,
And turns our bodies to battlegrounds.

I am not your thing, your property,
I am not a vessel for your desire.
And I am not alone.
My sisters stand with me,
From Addis Ababa to Tigray,
From every village and every street,
We are rising, we are fighting,
Against the chains of your dominance.

Let us make Ethiopia safe,
Like the Western streets we dream of,
Where men do not leer, do not stalk,
Where women walk with heads held high.
Let our Ethiopian men be civilized,
Not like the colonial masters who came,
But like the world we want to see,
Where dignity is not a dream.

It's time to tear down this culture of rape,
This centuries-old doctrine of control.
Let us break free from these chains,
Let us demand justice, and truth, and change.
We deserve a country where girls grow into women,
Untouched, unscarred, whole.
And we will not stop,
Until our voices are heard.

238. Ode to the Rainbow Community

In Ethiopia, where the sun shines bright,
Yet shadows loom over hearts of vibrant hue,
Our rainbow community lives in silent fright,
In fear of violence, hatred, and cruel view.
I have witnessed the pain, the agony, the strife,
As lives are lost, as souls are torn apart,
The killings of gays, the raping of love's life,
This violence strikes at the very core of our heart.

We are a Christian nation, or so we claim,
Rooted in love, light, and a divine embrace,
Yet where is the love when we play this deadly game?
Where is the respect, the dignity, the grace?
Christ preached to love our neighbors,
To hold each life as sacred and dear,
But how can we call ourselves saviors
When we turn our backs on those we should revere?

Every life matters, each heart has a right,
To thrive in the light, to live without fear,
Let us not kill, let us not blight
The very essence of love that brought us here.
I long to see queers walk free in our land,
Like the Western souls who know no such dread,
To protect every being from violence unplanned,
To shelter each heart, to heal wounds that have bled.

Our society should stand as a beacon of hope,
For LGBTQ souls and those persecuted in pain,
To thrive, to flourish, to love and to cope,

Where the rainbows spread wings and break every chain.
Let us reject ideologies steeped in crime,
For our Lord Jesus preached kindness, not hate,
To cherish life, to uphold what is prime,
To welcome all beings, to open the gate.

Ethiopian queers, stand proud, stand tall,
Let not the world's darkness cast shadows on you,
You deserve a haven, a space to enthrall,
To love who you love without fear or taboo.
We will not succumb to terror's cruel reign,
Nor embrace death in the name of misguided beliefs,
We choose life, choose peace, choose to break the chain,
Standing with Jews, with untouchables, with all who seek relief.

Let our children learn, let them dream, let them soar,
To become scholars, thinkers, icons of light,
No more shadows of fear, no closing of doors,
In our arms, let them find safety and might.
So we gather our voices, united and free,
To reject hatred, to embrace every soul,
Let Ethiopia shine as a land of the free,
A safe haven for all, where love makes us whole.

239. In the Animal Kingdom of Africa

In the shadowy streets of Tigray,
Where the webs of ancient lies were spun,
A girl walks, head down,
The unseen chains weighing heavy on her path.

The men among them, who stare into women with salivating eyes,
More poisonous than storms of chemicals,
Are hiding behind their white crosses,
Their sanctity draped in hypocrisy.

In the Orthodox halls, they kiss the walls,
But within, in their heart, it's dark,
Molesting innocence,
Traumatizing joy,
Every touch a theft, every gaze a malt.

From classrooms to alleys, nobody is safe from them.
Girls caught in the cycle of betrayal,
Brothels born out of ruthless customs.

Promising marriage vows on the altar of deception,
Temporary marriages to foreign hands,
Where asylum stories become horrors,
A vicious circle of exploitation nurtured by lies.

They go to the West for welfare,
But the blot on the souls will remain,
A procession of fraud and inhumanity,
Futures being bonded with the echoes of past committed sins.

At seventy years old, they brag of having young wives,
Never mindful of whose face is left in the spring,
Tons of births out of darkness,
Culture of cruelty-attribute of disintegration.

Women to be used as objects,
Trading love for survival,
Cultural essence laced with moral bankruptcy,
A society devoid of ethics, without direction.

Here is the heart of Tigray,
Mirroring a broken society,
Wherein the echoes of oppression wail,
And the flame of hope towards liberation flickers dimly.

240. The Taboo of Breath

In the ancient land where silence reigns,
A natural truth is cloaked in chains.
Farts are hushed like whispers in the dark,
Each release a spark of shame, a mark.

Children scolded, heads bowed low,
In homes where laughter's denied its flow.
A mother's voice, a warning cry,
"Hold it in, my child, or risk the sky."

How can a breath become a sin?
How can the body's language feel like a spin?
A simple gas, a fleeting breeze,
Yet death looms close when we fail to appease.

Health erodes beneath the weight of shame,
Heartbeats falter, lives lost in the name
Of customs rooted deep in ancient soil,
Where natural acts become the toil.

Let us unchain these burdens of the mind,
Release the gas, let our spirits unwind.
For health thrives in the freedom to be,
In laughter and life's simplicity.

Education calls, a modern dawn,
To cultivate a culture reborn.
Where learning thrives, so shall we grow,
In the light of knowledge, let wisdom flow.

Let us embrace the natural, the true,
Reclaim our breath, let it pass through.
In unity, let us challenge the past,
For a civilized future, let's build to last.

241. In the Forest Culture of Africa

In the ancient land where silence reigns,
A natural truth is cloaked in chains.
Farts are hushed like whispers in the dark,
Each release a spark of shame, a mark.
A simple act of nature, so pure,
But cloaked in whispers, they are unsure.

Children scolded, heads bowed low,
In homes where laughter's denied its flow.
A mother's voice, a warning cry,
"Hold it in, my child, or risk the sky."
A sound so innocent, yet punished with might,
A body's call, muffled in the night.

How can a breath become a sin?
How can the body's language feel like a spin?
A simple gas, a fleeting breeze,
Yet death looms close when we fail to appease.
What harm in the air that moves so free?
Yet fear surrounds it, a ghost to see.

Health erodes beneath the weight of shame,
Heartbeats falter, lives lost in the name
Of customs rooted deep in ancient soil,
Where natural acts become the toil.
The body's truth hidden in dread,
Told to silence what should be said.

How long will we hide in the shadows of the past,
Imprisoned by rules that were never meant to last?

In every laugh, in every sigh,
We are told to bottle up, to stifle, to deny.
The weight of shame is heavy and vast,
Yet nature's breath is free at last.

Let us unchain these burdens of the mind,
Release the gas, let our spirits unwind.
For health thrives in the freedom to be,
In laughter and life's simplicity.
The body speaks a language so true,
A gift of life that we must pursue.

Education calls, a modern dawn,
To cultivate a culture reborn.
Where learning thrives, so shall we grow,
In the light of knowledge, let wisdom flow.
No longer bound by ancient strife,
Let us live fully, embracing life.

Let us embrace the natural, the true,
Reclaim our breath, let it pass through.
In unity, let us challenge the past,
For a civilized future, let's build to last.
For in every breath, there's freedom to find,
A world unchained, where hearts are kind.

242. Blood on Our Hands

O Ethiopia, your sons of seven learn not to read,
But to wield the knife, to see animals bleed.
Cows, goats, chickens lined up in despair,
Their life taken without thought or care.

Seven years old—an age for school,
Yet you teach them to kill, a merciless tool.
They are taught to cheer at the sight of blood,
To revel in the gore, in the pool and the flood.

Where is the mercy, the kindness within?
How can you cheer as life grows thin?
A soul in every feather, a heart in each beast,
Yet they are taught that life is a feast.

They enter churches in robes of white,
But carry a darkness, hidden from sight.
They claim peace but raise a knife,
For cruelty to animals is part of life.

Let our sons touch books, not blades that rend,
Let them learn love, let brutality end.
Raise them not to cheer at death's display,
But to cherish life in every way.

Let them study Rawls, Frere, and Childe,
Turn away from traditions bloody and wild.
For civilization is built on compassion, not fear,
Let Ethiopia rise, let life be revered here.

243. We Love Blood and Immorality

O Ethiopia, your sons of seven learn not to read,
But to wield the knife, to see animals bleed.
Cows, goats, chickens lined up in despair,
Their lives taken without thought or care.
Oh, how swiftly innocence fades away,
As little hands are taught to slay.

Seven years old—an age for school,
Yet you teach them to kill, a merciless tool.
They are taught to cheer at the sight of blood,
To revel in the gore, in the pool and the flood.
Where is the mercy, the kindness within?
How can you cheer as life grows thin?

A soul in every feather, a heart in each beast,
Yet they are taught that life is a feast.
To them, life is fragile, its value dimmed,
As the hands of young ones are stained, grim.
The sparkle of childhood—lost in the dark,
Replaced by blood, where joy once left a mark.

They enter churches in robes of white,
But carry a darkness, hidden from sight.
They claim peace but raise a knife,
For cruelty to animals is part of life.
Oh, how can this be peace, when hearts are torn,
By violence that stains the soul from birth, reborn?

Let our sons touch books, not blades that rend,
Let them learn love, let brutality end.

Raise them not to cheer at death's display,
But to cherish life in every way.
Show them the beauty in the fluttering wings,
Not in the slaughter that bloodlust brings.

Let them study Rawls, Frere, and Childe,
Turn away from traditions bloody and wild.
For civilization is built on compassion, not fear,
Let Ethiopia rise, let life be revered here.
Let hearts be guided by wisdom, not by rage,
Let children learn to turn the page,

Where empathy reigns, and peace is sown,
Where love for life is fully grown.
For if we raise our sons in the bloodied stream,
What will we have left but a broken dream?
May we choose mercy, may we choose light,
For in compassion, true power takes flight.

244. Twelve Wounds of Animal Kingdom

In Ethiopia, twelve scars run deep,
Wounds of superstition, secrets they keep.
They call it tradition, a cultural pact,
Yet lives are broken by each cruel act.

Female genital mutilation cuts away,
A girl's right to pleasure, lost in the fray.
In Gambela, children thrown alive to die,
For "bad teeth" deemed a cursed tie.

Polygamy breeds a hollow love,
With wives like possessions, not given a shove.
Milk teeth extracted, uvula cut away,
Signs of "protection," they falsely say.

Children of Gambela women with foreign men,
Killed at birth, hidden in a den.
Forced marriages, a prison unseen,
Young girls robbed of what could have been.

They ban foods, restrict work, massage in vain,
A mother's body twisted, suffering in pain.
Excessive feasting, scars from a knife,
Each cut a reminder of a stolen life.

Widows inherited like land passed down,
A woman's worth wrapped in a frown.
Twelve wounds inflicted in tradition's name,
Yet none can wash away the shame.

245. Lifeline of African Animal Kingdom

In Ethiopia, twelve scars run deep,
Wounds of superstition, secrets they keep.
They call it tradition, a cultural pact,
Yet lives are broken by each cruel act.
Oh, how these rites have stained the soul,
Twisting hearts, making bodies whole.

Female genital mutilation cuts away,
A girl's right to pleasure, lost in the fray.
Her body becomes a vessel of pain,
A mark of control, a loss that remains.
The cry of innocence, silenced in fear,
As tradition whispers that she must adhere.

In Gambela, children thrown alive to die,
For "bad teeth" deemed a cursed tie.
How could a life be seen as so wrong?
Where is the love, where is the song?
The elders stand, bound by old ways,
Yet their hearts are empty, lost in a haze.

Polygamy breeds a hollow love,
With wives like possessions, not given a shove.
A woman's worth reduced to her role,
Her dreams confined, a silent toll.
Milk teeth extracted, uvula cut away,
Signs of "protection," they falsely say.
Each tear shed becomes a silent plea,
For freedom to be who they long to be.

Children of Gambela women with foreign men,
Killed at birth, hidden in a den.
Their bloodlines tainted, in their eyes despair,
Fate sealed before they even had a prayer.
Forced marriages, a prison unseen,
Young girls robbed of what could have been.
Their laughter muffled, their cries unheard,
Their futures erased without a word.

They ban foods, restrict work, massage in vain,
A mother's body twisted, suffering in pain.
Excessive feasting, scars from a knife,
Each cut a reminder of a stolen life.
A society bound by chains of lies,
Where pain is hidden beneath the skies.

Widows inherited like land passed down,
A woman's worth wrapped in a frown.
Her voice is stifled, her soul laid bare,
She becomes a possession, treated with care.
Twelve wounds inflicted in tradition's name,
Yet none can wash away the shame.

So let us rise, let us heal these scars,
Let love be our guide, no matter how far.
For each wound is a cry for change,
A plea to break from this cruel range.
Tradition must evolve, must learn to see,
The power of humanity, the right to be free.

246. Shadows of the Hyenas War

In Tigray, war has a crueller face,
Where violence is a woman's disgrace.
Not ravaged by bullets nor sword,
Silent cords-caressed hands of men do more.

Women torn, and left with no choice,
Their muffled cries, voiceless in voice.
This is a weapon unseen, a tactic of fear,
A body as the battleground, making it clear.

They came as soldiers but left as thieves,
Stealing innocence, leaving behind only grief in sheaves.
Nothing more remains but shame,
Etching on history each mother's name.

How can peace bloom where violence grew,
When justice remains a distant view?
These scars won't fade, nor the pain abate,
Until truth and healing decide their fate.

247. War of Hyenas, Wolves, Vultures, Mosquitoes

In Ethiopia, war has a crueller face,
Where violence is a woman's disgrace.
Not ravaged by bullets nor sword,
Silent cords-caressed hands of men do more.
The pain, the horror, it never shows,
A wound that deepens where no one knows.

Women torn, and left with no choice,
Their muffled cries, voiceless in voice.
The agony etched in each silent tear,
But no one hears, no one comes near.
This is a weapon unseen, a tactic of fear,
A body as the battleground, making it clear.
Where honor was stolen, dignity lost,
The human cost, an unbearable frost.

They came as soldiers but left as thieves,
Stealing innocence, leaving behind only grief in sheaves.
A life shattered, no future to claim,
Leaving each victim haunted by shame.
Nothing more remains but broken dreams,
The echoes of trauma, a silent scream.
No shelter, no warmth, just the cold embrace
Of a world indifferent to their fate.

How can peace bloom where violence grew,
When justice remains a distant view?
How can the flowers of hope take root
In fields that have borne only retribution's fruit?
The scars won't fade, nor the pain abate,

Until truth and healing decide their fate.
For every woman whose soul was defiled,
Her voice must be heard, her wounds reconciled.

The war is over, but the battle is still fought,
In the silence, in the memories, in the thoughts.
Justice lingers like a far-off star,
Yet still, the darkness feels so bizarre.
These scars, like ink on the skin of the past,
Will not disappear, though we may ask.

Let us rise, let us break these chains,
For peace can only come when justice reigns.
The women of Tigray, their strength untold,
Shall rise again, their voices bold.
For no shadow, no war, no silence of shame,
Can forever stifle the call of their name.

248. Escape from Hyenas Cage to Wolves Cage

We fled from Tigray to Addis, seeking a place to hide,
Escaping the violence that tore our land wide.
I left with a heart heavy, yet brave,
But in Addis, I found no refuge, no save.

I am hunted here, a Tigrayan face,
Labeled, betrayed in this fragile place.
The State and Amhara mark me a threat,
As if survival is something I regret.

For a crime of kindness, we tried to fight,
Supporting the LGBTQ, defending their right.
Our donations stolen, our voices shunned,
As Mekelle University made bribes run.

They turned against us, in the dead of night,
With Tigray police under shadows' sight.
We escaped their grip with bribes to pay,
Our six-month-old in arms, we fled that day.

In Addis, I faced a new fear, raw,
The Amhara's wrath, the State's cruel law.
Each glance, each word, a threat in disguise,
Living in terror, forced to hide.

We crossed lands with our lives in our hands,
Haunted by brutal communities' demands.
Tigray and Amhara, State's iron fist,
We were exiles in our own midst.

In Europe, I seek peace, yet bear the scars,
Of a journey shaped by painful stars.
But I hold our child close, a flame in the night,
Defying the shadows with all my might.

249. In the Shadows of Hyenas, Wolves, Vultures...

We fled from Tigray to Addis, seeking a place to hide,
Escaping the violence that tore our land wide.
I left with a heart heavy, yet brave,
But in Addis, I found no refuge, no save.
We thought we'd find shelter, some respite from fear,
But instead, we were hunted, our cries unheard, unclear.

I am hunted here, a Tigrayan face,
Labeled, betrayed in this fragile place.
The State and Amhara mark me a threat,
As if survival is something I regret.
For a crime of kindness, we tried to fight,
Supporting the LGBTQ, defending their right.
Our donations stolen, our voices shunned,
As Mekelle University made bribes run.

They turned against us, in the dead of night,
With Tigray police under shadows' sight.
We escaped their grip with bribes to pay,
Our six-month-old in arms, we fled that day.
From a homeland shattered, we sought a way out,
But found only betrayal, silence, and doubt.

In Addis, I faced a new fear, raw,
The Amhara's wrath, the State's cruel law.
Each glance, each word, a threat in disguise,
Living in terror, forced to hide.
Their whispers followed, their hate did not cease,
Every corner, a prison, where there was no peace.

We crossed lands with our lives in our hands,
Haunted by brutal communities' demands.
Tigray and Amhara, State's iron fist,
We were exiles in our own midst.
From betrayal's sting to a world that won't care,
We walked in shadows, with only despair.

In Europe, I seek peace, yet bear the scars,
Of a journey shaped by painful stars.
The cost of survival etched in my bones,
A trail of losses, of all that I've known.
But I hold our child close, a flame in the night,
Defying the shadows with all my might.

For what is survival without a home?
What is living when we are forced to roam?
Yet even in exile, I will not break,
For my child, for hope, for the future we'll make.
In every whisper of betrayal, in every tear we've cried,
I will rise, for the light cannot be denied.

250. Echoes of the Hyenas and Wolves War

I'm the silence that screams through sobs,
My soul bleeding under Tigrayan skies.
I witnessed villages being razed to the ground, lives torn asunder,
Haunting shadows of what has happened course through my trembling heart.

They came in darkness, cold faces,
Iron-hearted soldiers, bold and brazen.
They took from us all that we hold dear,
Leaving us with nothing but fear.

Broken homes, dusty fields-all in the tight grip of this war,
None to trust. My family's gone, lost in the fight,
I walk in shadows, renouncing light.

They call it war, or struggle, or fight,
But I'm the victim of inhumane laws.
I bear witness, my voice a flame,
Crying aloud in a shameless world.

www.ingramcontent.com/pod-product-compliance
Lightning Source LLC
Chambersburg PA
CBHW051332230426
43668CB00010B/1239